INTERNATIONAL LAW AND THE WAR WITH ISLAMIC STATE

Armed non-state actors (ANSAs) often have economic aims that international law needs to respond to. This book looks at the aim of Islamic State to create an effective government, with an economically independent regime, which focused on key oilfields in Syria and Iraq. Having addressed Islamic State's quest for energy resources in Iraq and Syria, the book explores the lawfulness of the war with Islamic State from a variety of legal aspects. It attempts to make inroads into the most controversial aspects of contradictions in the application of jus ad bellum and jus in bello, particularly when discussing the use of extraterritorial armed force against ANSAs, and the obligation to protect civilian objects, including the natural environment.

The question is whether the targeting of energy resources should be regarded as a violation of the laws of armed conflict, even though the war with Islamic State was classified as a non-international armed conflict. Ambitious in scope, the study argues that legal theory and state practice are still problematic as to how and under what conditions states can justify resorting to military force in foreign territory, and to what extent they can target natural resources as being part of state property. Furthermore, it goes on to examine the differences between international and non-international armed conflicts to establish whether there is any difference in the targeting of energy resources as part of the war-sustaining capabilities of either party.

Through an examination of the case of Islamic State, the book offers a comprehensive study to close the gaps in jus in bello by contextualising the questions of civilian protection, victimisation and state responsibility, and by evaluating the US's war-sustaining theory as a justification for the destruction of a territorial state's natural resources that are occupied by ANSAs.

Volume 84 in the series Studies in International Law

Studies in International Law

Recent titles in this series

Feminist Engagement with International Criminal Law: Norm Transfer, Complementarity, Rape and Consent
Eithne Dowds

Asylum Control and Access to Protection: Admission, Readmission and Human Rights
Mariagiulia Giuffré

Intertemporal Linguistics in International Law: Beyond Contemporaneous and Evolutionary Treaty Interpretation
Julian Wyatt

The Responsibility to Protect and the Failures of the United Nations Security Council
P M Butchard

The Role of Multilateral Environmental Agreements: A Reconciliatory Approach to Environmental Protection in Armed Conflict
Britta Sjostedt

Prosecutorial Discretion at the International Criminal Court
Anni Pues

Judicial Deference in International Adjudication: A Comparative Analysis
Johannes Hendrik Fahner

Human Rights Commitments of Islamic States: Sharia, Treaties and Consensus
Paul McDonough

Intervention in Civil Wars: Effectiveness, Legitimacy, and Human Rights
Chiara Redaelli

General Principles as a Source of International Law: Art 38(1)(c) of the Statute of the International Court of Justice
Imogen Saunders

The Law of Humanity Project: A Story of International Law Reform and State-making
Ukri Soirila

Extraterritoriality and Climate Change Jurisdiction: Exploring EU Climate Protection under International Law
Natalie L Dobson

For a complete list of titles in this series, see www.bloomsburyprofessional.com/uk/series/studies-in-international-law

International Law and the War with Islamic State

Challenges for Jus ad Bellum *and* Jus in Bello

Saeed Bagheri

•HART•

OXFORD • LONDON • NEW YORK • NEW DELHI • SYDNEY

HART PUBLISHING
Bloomsbury Publishing Plc
Kemp House, Chawley Park, Cumnor Hill, Oxford, OX2 9PH, UK
1385 Broadway, New York, NY 10018, USA
29 Earlsfort Terrace, Dublin 2, Ireland

HART PUBLISHING, the Hart/Stag logo, BLOOMSBURY and the Diana logo are trademarks of Bloomsbury Publishing Plc

First published in Great Britain 2021

A catalogue record for this book is available from the British Library.

Library of Congress Cataloging-in-Publication data

Names: Bagheri, Saeed, author.

Title: International law and the war with Islamic State : challenges for *jus ad bellum* and *jus in bello* / Saeed Bagheri.

Description: Oxford, UK ; New York, NY : Hart Publishing, an imprint of Bloomsbury Publishing, 2021. | Series: Studies in international law ; volume 84 | Includes bibliographical references and index.

Identifiers: LCCN 2021013811 (print) | LCCN 2021013812 (ebook) | ISBN 9781509950515 (hardback) | ISBN 9781509950553 (paperback) | ISBN 9781509950539 (pdf) | ISBN 9781509950522 (Epub)

Subjects: LCSH: Terrorism (International law) | Just war doctrine. | Terrorism—Prevention—Law and legislation. | War (International law) | IS (Organization) | Terrorism—Religious aspects—Islam. | Jihad—Prevention.

Classification: LCC KZ6396 .B339 2021 (print) | LCC KZ6396 (ebook) | DDC 341.609567—dc23

LC record available at https://lccn.loc.gov/2021013811

LC ebook record available at https://lccn.loc.gov/2021013812

ISBN: HB: 978-1-50995-051-5
ePDF: 978-1-50995-053-9
ePub: 978-1-50995-052-2

Typeset by Compuscript Ltd, Shannon

Foreword

THE RISE OF the terrorist organisation known as Islamic State,[1] and the war against it in Iraq and Syria – involving multiple state and ANSAs – raises, as Christakis noted in 2016, 'multiple questions and … several challenges for international law'.[2] In this book, Dr Saeed Bagheri seeks to tackle many of those questions and challenges, head on.

This is no easy task: the war against Islamic State engages various areas of international law, cross-cutting standards found in *jus ad bellum*, *jus in bello*, human rights and environmental law (to offer a list of 'triggered' areas of international law that is far from exhaustive), and it has done so in unique and complex ways. At least at its 'peak', Islamic State was of a size, wealth, power and trans-territorial reach to pose a very particular kind of threat to the international community. This was rooted in the large-scale, voracious 'consumption' of territory, and the consequent ability to exercise certain elements of 'state-like' authority. At the same time, Islamic State is not a state, it is a violent terrorist organisation; the use of the shorthand term 'Islamic State' in this foreword (or – I think it can be safely said without risking misrepresenting its author – this *book*) must in no way be taken to suggest that the group is, or ever was, a state. And, unlike actual states, Islamic State has consistently viewed itself as wholly free from legal standards, beyond, that is, its own warped interpretation of sharia.

A key way that Dr Bagheri approaches the multiple and varied questions of international law that arise from the war against Islamic State is to concentrate on that group's appropriation and exploitation of energy resources as a fulcrum of his analysis. Islamic State's rapid wealth generation, and thus significant power, predominately derived from its exploitation of energy resources in the territories it occupied. This fact has received very little consideration in international legal scholarship; in this book Dr Bagheri makes it his core focus. As he says:

> [T]he overall goal of the book is to offer a realistic account of the relationship between armed conflicts and energy resources to determine whether, and under what conditions, a violent, occupying military group can use the energy resources of the occupied territories, and whether the energy resources controlled by the occupier

[1] Also known as simply 'IS', Islamic State of Iraq and the Levant (ISIL), Islamic State of Iraq and Syria (ISIS), or the Arabic acronym Daesh/Da'ish.

[2] T Christakis, 'Symposium on the Fight against ISIL and International Law – Editor's Introduction' (2016) 29 *Leiden Journal of International Law* 737, 737.

can be targeted as being part of the enemy's war-sustaining capabilities bestowing a definite military advantage.

In the context of international law scholarship, this is an original lens through which to view the war against Islamic State, and it acts as a fundamental through line of this book. Equally, the exploitation of energy resources (and the relationship between such resource-appropriation and armed conflict) is carefully used as a means of sharpening focus, not as a thematic straightjacket. Dr Bagheri does not let it stop him from exploring legal issues that may stray beyond those directly related to energy resource exploitation, where appropriate.

The substantive parts of this book examine, variously but interrelatedly, questions of *jus ad bellum*, and *jus in bello*. With regard to the first of these areas, Dr Bagheri had no choice but to engage with two current 'hot potato' topics: (1) the controversial notion of using force in self-defence against non-state actors where the 'host' state is 'unwilling or unable' to stop the threat posed by that group; and (2) murky questions surrounding the scope of a state's ability to consent to the use of force by another state on its territory. Both have been front and centre in legal debates over the war against Islamic State, and their contours are impressively unpicked and applied here. Of particular note in relation to *ad bellum* issues is that Dr Bagheri also engages meaningfully with possible *treaty-based* consent to Turkey's use of force, something that has been hardly considered at all elsewhere, at least in English-language scholarship.[3]

The book's last chapter is focused on breaches of *jus in bello*, and explores the law applicable both to the appropriation and exploitation of energy resources by Islamic State – and wider legal implications of its occupation of territory – but also the subsequent destruction of those resources, by the US-led coalition, aimed at weakening Islamic State. This chapter is perhaps the book's central pillar, presenting a sustained argument that there have been notable violations of the requirements of international humanitarian law from all parties to the conflict.

Overall, this book offers an important and often unique legal examination of the war against Islamic State. It will make a notable contribution, across various areas of international law, with relevance well beyond the war against Islamic State itself.

James A Green
Professor of Public International Law
University of Reading

[3] Although see C Kreß, 'A Collective Failure to Prevent Turkey's Operation "Peace Spring" and NATO's Silence on International Law', *EJIL: Talk!* (14 October 2019), www.ejiltalk.org/a-collective-failure-to-prevent-turkeys-operation-peace-spring-and-natos-silence-on-international-law/.

Acknowledgements

Writing this book has been a long journey, which has taken me to many different places. The seeds of this book were sown in 2017 when I was serving as a Max Weber Postdoctoral Fellow at the European University Institute in Florence, Italy. I spent a long time visiting a variety of universities and institutions over the past three years and it was with great pleasure that I finalised the book at the Law School of the University of Reading, where I am currently serving my second postdoctoral position. Most of all, it brought me into contact with many people, all of whom contributed to the fruition of this book in their own special ways. I sincerely thank each and every one of them.

This book has benefited from the assistance of numerous individuals, organisations and universities. In addition, participants on the many different programmes and conferences that I attended helped me to refine and clarify my arguments and to augment the evidence used to support them.

Several academic colleagues were always available to comment on the first draft parts and discuss ideas and arguments before they were developed to be put on paper. In these acknowledgements, I would like to thank the following individuals, without whose support this book would not have been written. First, my profound thanks are due to my postdoctoral mentors, Professor James A Green (University of Reading), Professor Martin Scheinin (European University Institute) and Professor Richard Bellamy (University College London), who oversaw the progression of this book and guided me in improving its main structure. They challenged my thoughts and arguments as they developed and encouraged me to look at the subject from different angles. I appreciate their valuable comments and suggestions and I am most grateful for their constant support, encouragement, and their constructive critique. I would like to give additional thanks to Professor Green, who was kind enough to read all parts of the manuscript in detail, and who provided valued suggestions and comments on its content. Warmest thanks are due to him for the time he took to assess the book and to write the foreword.

My thanks also go to Dr Vaios Koutroulis (Université Libre de Bruxelles), who provided valuable critical commentary on the book's structure. I also thank my brilliant colleagues at Global Law at Reading (GLAR), the University of Reading's hub for international law, EU law and human rights law. I am particularly grateful to Professor Chris Hilson, and Dr Stephen Samuel who all contributed in different ways to my thinking on the core issues as I developed my research. Their passion, commitment, and work ethic continue to be an inspiration to me as I go forward through my academic career. My gratitude is also due to

Professor James Devenney, the Head of the Law School of the University of Reading for his support, inspiration, and friendship.

I must also acknowledge the support and inspiration of Professor Nehal Bhuta (University of Edinburgh), Dr Alyson Price, Dr Laurie Anderson and Ognjen Aleksić (European University Institute) during my research as a Max Weber Fellow at the European University Institute. I owe a special debt to my colleagues, Professor Paul J Cardwell (City, University of London), Dr Alison Bisset (University of Reading), Dr Lawrence Hill-Cawthorne (University of Reading), Dr Surabhi Ranganathan (University of Cambridge), Dr Paul McDonough (University of Cardiff), and Dr Alejandro Fuentes (University of Lund) who, at different moments, have provided me with much-valued assistance and friendship during my research.

I am also very grateful to the authorities at the libraries of the University of Reading, the European University Institute, the Grotius Centre for International Legal Studies at the Leiden University School of Law, and the Lauterpacht Centre for International Law at the University of Cambridge for granting me access to these institutions, and for the critical feedback provided by my colleagues there. My gratitude is also due to the wonderful librarians at the EUI Library, British Library, Cambridge University Library, Leiden University Library, and Reading University Library who enabled me to obtain access to various sources and made research there a pleasure.

Outside academia, there are many other people that I should thank but I will mention only a few. My special thanks go to Dr Chiara Steindler, Dr Serkan Yolcu, Dr León Castellanos-Jankiewicz, Gemma J Fenton, Caroline Hobson, Rabia Yolcu, and my brother Amin who has supported me in countless ways during the years it took to complete this project.

In terms of producing the book, my profound thanks go to Hart Publishing for agreeing to publish the book. I am incredibly grateful to Sinead Moloney, in particular, for her enthusiasm on the book as well as anonymous reviewers, and all the other co-workers at Hart Publishing who played a key role in the finalising, printing and publishing of the book. Of course, the arguments and opinions expressed in this book are entirely my own and I take full responsibility for all errors or omissions along with any deficiencies in expression, grammatical misdemeanours, and prejudices.

Last but not least, I am extremely grateful to my parents, without whose spiritual support the mere writing and publication of this book would have been impossible. They were my rock throughout these turbulent years and their unflinching support kept me sane and strong while writing this book. I offer my heartfelt thanks for their seemingly endless levels of optimism.

Saeed Bagheri
University of Reading
June 2021

Contents

Abbreviations and Acronyms

ANSA(s)	armed non-state actor(s)
eg	for example
ENMOD	Environmental Modification Convention
ed/eds	editor/editors
et al	and others
EU	European Union
FARC	Revolutionary Armed Forces of Colombia
HDP	Halkların Demokratik Partisi (People's Democratic Party)
ibid	Ibidem
ICC	International Criminal Court
ICJ	International Court of Justice
ICRC	International Committee of the Red Cross
ICTY	International Criminal Tribunal for the Former Yugoslavia
ILC	International Law Commission
IMT	International Military Tribunal
IOM	International Organization for Migration
KRG	Kurdish Regional Government
NATO	North Atlantic Treaty Organization
OCHA	UN Office for the Coordination of Humanitarian Affairs
OHCHR	Office of the UN High Commissioner for Human Rights
OTP	Office of the Prosecutor of the ICC
PCIJ	Permanent Court of International Justice
PKK	Partiya Karkerên Kurdistanê
PYD	Partiya Yekîtiya Demokrat
SAP	Southeast Anatolia Project

SDF	Syrian Democratic Forces
TAK	Teyrebazen Azadiya Kurdistan
TSG	The Soufan Group
UK	United Kingdom
UN	United Nations
UNEP	United Nations Environment Programme
UNGA	United Nations General Assembly
UNHCR	United Nations High Commissioner for Refugees
UNPFII	United Nations Permanent Forum on Indigenous Issues
UNSC	United Nations Security Council
UNSDN	United Nations Social Development Network
US	United States
vol/vols	volume/volumes
YPG	Yekîneyên Parastina Gel

Table of Cases

Table of International Treaties and Conventions

Introduction

THE WORLD OF the twenty-first century is confronting the emergence of armed non-state actors (ANSAs) around the globe; actors that have different ideologies, and political objectives which threaten international security and stability. Crucially, it will not be possible for these ANSAs to achieve their political objectives without stability and economic strength. The international community faces a new challenge, in that, inevitably, ANSAs will attempt to take control of the energy resources of those countries sitting on the most valuable energy reserves, such as oil and natural gas.[1] The emergence of violent ANSAs such as Islamic State in the Middle East – whose activities include terrorist attacks both inside and outside their host states' borders, and fuel smuggling to reach their political objectives – has created considerable difficulties for the international community.

Ultimately, for the countries sitting on the most valuable oil and gas reserves, the instability created by these armed conflicts, and by the loss of effective control of their territory and local resources, will mean that their governments will be unable to exercise sovereignty over their territory and natural resources. The occupation of the Iraqi and Syrian oil fields by Islamic State in 2014 indicated that access to energy resources was important to this violent group, as a means of reaching its political objectives.

In line with its objectives, Islamic State attempted to create an effective government (the Islamic Caliphate) that would be able to provide an economically independent regime. Achieving such an objective, however, depended on the movement's long-term approaches to finding new revenue sources. In this regard, energy resources inside the territories of Syria and Iraq that were occupied by Islamic State were convenient means by which the group could satisfy its financial requirements. The emergence of Islamic State in Syria and Iraq, and its occupation of critical energy-producing areas in the region, has shown that without energy resources, it would not be able to effectively establish an Islamic Caliphate,[2]

[1] This is subject to the funding of ANSAs that has been placed into the broader research field of the political economy of war. For further discussion, see M Humphreys, 'Natural Resources, Conflict, and Conflict Resolution: Uncovering the Mechanisms' (2005) 49 *Journal of Conflict Resolution* 508; ML Ross, 'How Do Natural Resources Influence Civil War? Evidence from Thirteen Cases' (2004) 58 *International Organization* 35; P Collier, 'Economic Causes of Civil Conflict and Their Implications for Policy', *World Bank* (April 2006), http://citeseerx.ist.psu.edu/viewdoc/download?doi=10.1.1.460.9440&rep=rep1&type=pdf.

[2] See P Le Billon, 'The Political Economy of War: Natural Resources and Armed Conflict' (2001) 20 *Political Geography* 561; ML Ross, 'Oil, Drugs, and Diamonds: The Varying Roles of Natural Resources in Civil War' in K Ballentine and J Sherman, *The Political Economy of Armed Conflict: Beyond Greed and Grievance* (London, Lynne Rienner, 2003) 47–70.

given that the group has been substantially weakened after losing control of key oilfields it once held in Syria and Iraq. The group was in a unique position to achieve its goals by military means after taking control of energy resources in in Iraq and Syria, with an opportunity to generate income to enhance its economic and military capabilities. Given that Islamic State's armed activities were funded by its revenue sources both in the Middle East and around the world, the militaristic reactions of the external powers to Islamic State's presence in Iraq and Syria have brought new challenges for the international laws concerning interstate armed conflicts.[3]

I. BACKGROUND AND SIGNIFICANCE OF THE STUDY

By focusing on the extraterritorial use of force against Islamic State, this book explores the nature of armed conflicts regarding energy resources in Iraq and Syria, and how international law applies to these conflicts. The book's underlying aim is to offer an extensive overview of the applicable laws in a war with Islamic State as an ANSA in the energy-rich countries of Iraq and Syria. Existing literature has not sufficiently observed and evaluated this fundamental interplay between the perception and practices of states. Given the fact that the drafters of the 1977 Additional Protocol I to the Geneva Convention have not included oil installations in 'installations containing dangerous forces' under Article 56, this study has pushed back by showing that targeting the energy resources occupied by Islamic State in Iraq and Syria damaged the natural environment, and more civilians died[4] as a result of violations of the law of armed conflict (*jus in bello*) despite the war with Islamic State being characterised as a non-international armed conflict.

[3] A Van Engeland, 'Statehood, Proto States and International Law: New Challenges, Looking at the Case of ISIS' in J Crawford et al (eds), *The International Legal Order: Current Needs and Possible Responses* (Leiden, Brill Publications, 2007) 75–86; A Lang, 'Legal Basis for UK Military Action in Syria' (2015) 7404 *House of Commons Library, Briefing Paper* 7, 7–11, https://research-briefings.files.parliament.uk/documents/CBP-7404/CBP-7404.pdf; MP Scharf, 'How the War against ISIS Changed International Law' (2016) 48 *Case Western Reserve Journal of International Law* 1; G Kajtar, 'The Use of Force against ISIL in Iraq and Syria – A Legal Battlefield' (2017) 34 *Wisconsin International Law Journal* 535; H Moynihan, 'Assessing the Legal Basis for UK Military Action in Syria', *Chatham House* (26 November 2015), www.chathamhouse.org/expert/comment/assessing-legal-basis-uk-military-action-syria.

[4] See 'Death in the City: High Levels of Civilian Harm in Modern Urban Warfare Resulting from Significant Explosive Weapons Use', *Airwars* (May 2018), https://airwars.org/report/death-in-the-city-high-levels-of-civilian-harm-in-modern-urban-warfare-resulting-from-significant-explosive-weapons-use/; 'US-led Coalition in Iraq and Syria', *Airwars* (November 2019), https://airwars.org/conflict/coalition-in-iraq-and-syria/; 'Annual Report on Civilian Casualties in Connection with United States Military Operations', *US Department of State* (2018), www.fas.org/man/eprint/civcas2018.pdf; 'Civilian Deaths in the Anti-ISIS Bombing Campaigns 2014–2015', *Ceasefire Centre for Civilian Rights and Minority Rights Group International* (November 2015), www.minorityrights.org/wp-content/uploads/2015/11/CEASEFIRE-REPORT-Civilian-deaths-in-the-anti-ISIS-bombing-campaigns-2014-15.pdf.

To better articulate the argument, this book also deals with the relevant oil pollution precedents in the First Gulf War (1990–1991) and the Israel-Hezbollah War in 2006.[5] Furthermore, the book explores the differences between international and non-international armed conflicts to determine whether there is any difference in the targeting of energy resources as part of the war-sustaining capabilities of either party.

This will serve as a basis for the further assessment of attacks on the host states' resources that are under the control of Islamic State. Given the fact that military intervention in a non-international armed conflict may impact the host state's civilians as well as its natural resources occupied by the ANSAs, a fundamental question is whether, and to what extent, the attacks directed against the occupying power and the resources under its direct control could be subject to the same degree of protection from the effects of hostilities as they enjoy under the law applicable to international armed conflicts. In the same way, having looked at the nature of the conflict, the book considers whether external powers' military interventions against Islamic State in Iraq and Syria without invitation can be justified and whether external military intervention in non-international armed conflicts transforms them into international armed conflicts.

Studies of Islamic State have spurred a promising and rapidly growing interdisciplinary debate. Previous research has principally focused on: the emergence of Islamic State and its terrorist activities; Islamic State's inhumane treatment of potential threats; evaluation of armed conflicts with Islamic State from the perspective of conflict classification; and military interventions by invitation against Islamic State in Iraq, Syria and Libya.[6] It is nevertheless clear that in the cases of armed conflicts with Islamic State, important questions and several pertinent research gaps remain regarding various aspects of combat against Islamic State and its relationship with the energy resources in its occupied territories. What are most acutely missing from the literature, however, are empirical accounts that specifically target perspectives on the extent of the military actions of Islamic State inside Iraq and Syria, and the external powers' justifications for violations of *jus in bello* through destroying energy resources in the territories occupied by Islamic State.[7]

[5] UNEP, *Desk Study on the Environment in Iraq* (Nairobi, UNEP Publications, 2003) 65–68; Ø Noreng, *Crude Power: Politics and the Oil Market* (London, IB Tauris, 2002) 187; MG Salameh, 'Oil Wars' (2014) 14-163 *USAEE Working Paper* 7, 7–13, https://papers.ssrn.com/sol3/papers.cfm?abstract_id=2430960; JD Colgan, 'Fuelling the Fire: Pathways from Oil to War' (2013) 38 *International Security* 147, 174; UNGA, Resolution 47/37, UN Doc A/RES/47/37 (25 November 1992).

[6] See C Dyer and C Crismier, *The ISIS Crisis: What You Really Need to Know* (Chicago, Moody Publishers, 2015); M Weiss and H Hassan, *ISIS: Inside the Army of Terror* (New York, Regan Arts, 2015); J Stern and JM Berger, *ISIS: The State of Terror* (New York, Harper Collins, 2015); J Sekulow et al (eds), *The Rise of ISIS: A Threat We Can't Ignore* (Brentwood, Howard Books, 2014); N Zamir, 'The Armed Conflict(s) against the Islamic State' (2015) 18 *Yearbook of International Humanitarian Law* 91; K Bannelier-Christakis, 'Military Interventions against ISIL in Iraq, Syria and Libya, and the Legal Basis of Consent' (2016) 29 *Leiden Journal of International Law* 743.

[7] There is an extensive literature with respect to the use of force against Islamic State which has never addressed the legal justifications for the destruction of energy resources in the territories

Despite the rich empirical insights offered in previous studies, there is still a lack of fine-grained research analysis of laws applicable to the military actions of Islamic State and external actors' intervention in non-international armed conflict in Syria and Iraq, in terms of the destruction of energy resources in hindering the war-sustaining capabilities of the enemy. This study argues that a lack of qualitative analysis diverts the attention of the international community from the more important issue of the extent to which external powers use the threat of Islamic State as a justification for the destruction of the host states' energy resources, which could cause major damage to the surrounding environment. Considering the findings of the International Law Commission (ILC)[8] and the United Nations Environment Programme (UNEP)[9] on the impact of armed conflicts on the environment, this book considers the major conditions recognised by *jus in bello* in which the natural environment might be damaged during armed conflicts.[10]

From a political point of view, energy resources have often been the source of the Middle East's wealth and play an integral role in the evolution of the region.[11] However, since international demand for the Middle East's oil resources is so great, this book focuses mainly on the war with Islamic State in Syria and Iraq in terms of oil resources. Therefore, as this study aims to advance an understanding of the war with Islamic State, and one of the most important causes of the growth of war based on *jus in bello* when referring to the destruction of Islamic State's oilfields, the term 'energy resources' will only mean 'oil resources'.

occupied by Islamic State. See in general, O Corten, 'The 'Unwilling or Unable' Test: Has It Been, and Could It Be, Accepted?' (2016) 29 *Leiden Journal of International Law* 777; L O'Connor, 'Legality of the Use of Force in Syria against Islamic State and the Khorasan Group' (2016) 3 *Journal on the Use of Force and International Law* 70; D Tladi and M Shaqra, 'Assessing the Legality of Coalition Air Strikes Targeting the Islamic State in Iraq and the Levant (ISIS) in Syria under International Law' (2015) *South African Yearbook on International Law* 281; V Koutroulis, 'The Fight against the Islamic State and Jus in Bello' (2016) 29 *Leiden Journal of International Law* 827.

[8] See The Draft Principles on Protection of the Environment in Relation to Armed Conflicts – Report of the ILC (adopted by the Commission on First Reading in seventy-first session), UN Doc A/74/10 (8 July 2019).

[9] UNEP, *From Conflict to Peacebuilding: The Role of Natural Resources and the Environment* (Nairobi, UNEP Publications, 2009); UNEP, *Protecting the Environment During Armed Conflict: An Inventory and Analysis of International Law* (Nairobi, UNEP Publications, 2009).

[10] M Bothe et al, 'International Law Protecting the Environment During Armed Conflict: Gaps and Opportunities' (2010) 92 *International Review of the Red Cross* 569.

[11] Broadly speaking, energy resources have been the principal factors holding up economic development in the Middle East. See MC Aoun, 'Oil and Gas Resources of the Middle East and North Africa: A Curse or a Blessing?' in J-M Chevalier and P Geoffron (eds), *The New Energy Crisis* (London, Palgrave Macmillan, 2013) 133–60. See also generally, KA Chaudhry, *The Price of Wealth: Economies and Institutions in the Middle East* (New York, Cornell University Press, 1997); SH Longrigg, *Oil in the Middle East: Its Discovery and Development* (Oxford, Oxford University Press, 1968).

II. RESEARCH QUESTIONS AND ANALYTICAL FRAMEWORK

The ANSAs' quest for energy resources using military force simply reveals the relationship between energy resources and armed conflict. Having said that, the overall goal of the book is to offer a realistic account of the relationship between armed conflicts and energy resources to determine whether, and under what conditions, a violent, occupying military group can use the energy resources of the occupied territories, and whether the energy resources controlled by the occupier can be targeted as being part of the enemy's war-sustaining capabilities bestowing a definite military advantage. Given the military occupation of Iraqi and Syrian territory by Islamic State, the book first aims to answer the following fundamental questions. Can Islamic State be categorised as an occupier, and if so, under what conditions can Islamic State use the energy resources of the occupied territories as an occupying power?

To answer these questions, the book examines additional cases of relevance, such as the use of Palestinian energy resources (oil and gas) by Israel in Gaza, which it has occupied since 1967. Then the book develops a technical model to explain how external powers, including the coalition forces led by the United States (US), Turkey Iran, and Russia justify military intervention against Islamic State in Iraq and Syria.

The third question the book attempts to answer, when considering the evidence from relevant empirical case studies to determine the legal validity of the coalition states' justifications, is whether the energy resources used by Islamic State in its occupied territories in Syria can be targeted as being part of the war-sustaining capabilities of Islamic State, which bestows a definite military advantage over the US-led coalition in Syria within the context of *jus in bello* and the law of occupation. In other words, is there a legal basis for the destruction of Islamic State's energy resources and installations by the US-led coalition?

The research questions are determined by relying on primary legal sources and materials including relative treaties, the jurisprudence of the International Court of Justice (ICJ) as the principal judicial organ of the United Nations (UN), and secondary sources including books, articles, academic commentaries, reports and soft laws such as resolutions and declarations of UN bodies. This involves the analysis and collation of relevant legislative statutes, international treaties, related case laws, and case studies/applicable laws that elaborate or clarify statutory provisions. The goal is to detect principles or general rules relating to the law on the use of force (*jus ad bellum*), and *jus in bello*. Rules and principles in formal provisions are checked against state practice to determine the form in which, and the extent to which, they are followed and applied by the states involved in a war on ANSAs in practice. In light of this, previous cases and state practices in wars on ANSAs in occupied territories are also evaluated.

To meet all of its specific objectives, this book uses an original legal approach employing doctrinal legal analysis for explaining the legal aspects of the war with Islamic State.

III. PLAN OF THE STUDY

This book is divided into three chapters. As an introductory section of the book, Chapter 1 highlights the correlation between energy resources and armed conflict, the threat of violence resulting from failed resource management, the potential role of energy resources in intensifying a conflict, and the relationship between energy resources and armed conflicts in which different types of entities are stakeholders in the energy resources and where each pursues its own objectives and preferences.[12] To provide a context for understanding the continuing armed conflicts over energy resources in energy-rich countries, Chapter 1 also surveys how Islamic State took control of energy resources in Iraq and Syria. Particular attention is paid to Islamic State's legal status, its actions inside Iraq and Syria, and its cross-border military actions. Chapter 1 also considers the way in which Islamic State constitutes a serious threat to international peace and security. In this regard, the book can be seen to examine the main impacts of Islamic State's military actions, particularly with regard to energy resources.

Chapter 2 addresses the legal justifications for military intervention by foreign states against Islamic State in both Iraq and Syria and looks for the factors that motivated their involvement. Having mentioned the general principle of the prohibition on the use of force in international law as a matter of *jus ad bellum*, Chapter 2 then evaluates the alleged exceptions to this principle contained in Article 2(4) of the UN Charter. Within the context of *jus ad bellum*, this chapter also examines two different forms of international military intervention: intervention based on the 'unwilling or unable theory', which is the US's approach to using force against ANSAs based in foreign territories; and military assistance by request of the occupied state. Having discussed the legality of both concepts, Chapter 2 concludes by evaluating the effectiveness and consequences of the US-led coalition and Turkey's military interventions against Islamic State based on the 'unwilling or unable theory', and Iranian and Russian military intervention by request of the host state.

Chapter 3 discusses the applicability of *jus in bello* to armed attacks on energy resources and *jus in bello* obligations by which the perpetrators are bound. The discussion draws on doctrinal research to analyse the scope and application of the fundamental rules of *jus in bello*. Chapter 3 also establishes the conditions under which *jus in bello* applies to the military actions of the external powers against Islamic State. It also provides a general

[12] P Le Billon, *Fuelling War: Natural Resources and Armed Conflicts* (London, Routledge, 2005) 48; PE Peters, 'Inequality and Social Conflict Over Land in Africa' (2004) 4 *Journal of Agrarian Change* 269; T Craig Jones, 'America, Oil, and War in the Middle East' (2012) 99 *Journal of American History* 208; C-P David and J-F Gagné, 'Natural Resources: A Source of Conflict?' (2007) 62 *International Journal* 5. See also generally, D Dam-de Jong, *International Law and Governance of Natural Resources in Conflict and Post-Conflict Situations* (Cambridge, Cambridge University Press, 2015); M Klare, *Rising Powers, Shrinking Planet: The New Geopolitics of Energy* (Oxford, Oneworld Publications, 2008).

overview of the link between the prohibition of armed attacks on energy resources as installations containing dangerous forces, and the prohibition on unnecessary destruction of the environment during armed conflicts. To contextualise the analysis of the situation of displaced civilians during the war with Islamic State, and the extraterritorial use of military force against it, the final part of this chapter explores the states' obligation to protect the civilian population during self-defence actions under the 1949 Geneva Conventions and its 1977 Additional Protocol II as the basis for *jus in bello*. Rather than automatically viewing the external powers' attitudes towards the terrorist actions of Islamic State both within and outside the Middle East as inappropriate, Chapter 3 seeks to understand how violations of the customary rules of *jus in bello* through environmental destruction as a result of unnecessary and disproportionate military actions against Islamic State are justified by the actors involved through recourse to the right of self-defence.

1

The Rise of Islamic State and Its Military Strength

'The rise of [Islamic State] shows the urgent need to understand what has happened within Arab societies and the international relations of the Middle East'.[1]

I. INTRODUCTION

ALTHOUGH THE OVERRIDING purpose of this book is to consider the lawfulness of the use of force against ANSAs and the destruction of energy resources controlled by them, the first substantive part of the book begins by considering how energy sources have become the focal point for states, ANSAs, and external powers, which have been at constant risk of violence and armed conflicts. Providing a contemporary perspective, this part shows that taking control over and using energy resources has often been one of the leading causes of armed conflicts in oil-rich countries and has invariably threatened regional and international peace and security.

This chapter begins by examining the emergence and strength of Islamic State in Iraq and Syria to see how its quest for energy resources in these countries triggered violence following the national and military intervention in Iraq and Syria. It then proceeds by describing Islamic State's legal status, its actions inside Iraq and Syria, and its cross-border military actions. The ways in which Islamic State constituted an increasing threat to international peace and security will be explored. Chapter 1 then proceeds by analysing what the correlation between energy resources and armed conflict can tell us about the insecurity and the threat of violence as the costs of failed resource management, and the role of energy resources in intensifying Islamic State's advance and its military operations in Iraq and Syria. It demonstrates that failed resource management and ANSAs' quest for energy resources in energy-rich countries have often been the sources of violence and insecurity at the national and international level. A failure to address these issues at the beginning of the book would cast doubt on the validity of this study's main arguments, whose primary purpose draws on the relationship between the quest for energy resources and the extraterritorial use of armed force against Islamic State in Iraq and Syria.

[1] FA Gerges, *ISIS: A History* (Princeton, Princeton University Press, 2016) 7.

II. ISLAMIC STATE AT A GLANCE: GENERAL OBSERVATIONS

A. The Rise and Strength of Islamic State

The emergence of Islamic State in the fragile and generally conflict-affected Middle East has caused significant changes in the political behaviour and position of the Middle Eastern states as well as the regional and international powers. Islamic State, which arose shortly after US forces left Iraq, is one of the most powerful Islamic jihadist groups that has ever existed. Islamic State consolidated its power by occupying major parts of Iraqi and Syrian territory over a very short period and declaring an Islamic Caliphate, and its acts of violence and terrorism focused the international community's attention on the Middle East. The emergence of Islamic State took the international community by surprise, particularly after the group declared a worldwide caliphate. Its success has undoubtedly been undergirded by the radical Islamic beliefs of its members, but more importantly by the failure of the Iraqi central government to ensure peace, stability, economic growth and the reasonable distribution of resources, particularly after the US invasion which provided the grounds for economic inequality and violent competition between a number of parties over Iraq's energy resources.[2]

Part of the story of the rise of Islamic State is tied to the US invasion of Iraq in 2003. Although there are various opinions about the main factors that allowed the rise of Islamic State in Iraq and Syria,[3] it seems that the main factors are the group's radical ideology and its aspirations for an eventual caliphate. Having looked at Islamic State's declarations and statements, it would seem that the group apparently uses Islamic rules to legitimise its violent jihadist campaign across the world.[4] However, other arguments – as originally expounded by the

[2] For more details on the impacts for the failure of States see also R Ehrenreich Brooks, 'Failed States, or the State as Failure?' (2005) 72 *The University of Chicago Law Review* 1159, 1160–61; D Whyte, 'Hire an American! Economic Tyranny and Corruption in Iraq' (2007) 34 *Social Justice* 153, 162–64.

[3] For examples, see B Connable et al, *Beating the Islamic State: Selecting the New Strategy for Iraq and Syria* (California, RAND Publication, 2017) 7–18; S Cottee, 'What ISIS Really Wants Revisited: Religion Matters in Jihadist Violence, But How?' (2017) 40 *Studies in Conflict & Terrorism* 439; M Levitt, *The Rise of ISIL* (Washington, DC, The Washington Institute for Near East Policy, 2015).

[4] N Sandal, 'Apocalypse Soon Revolutionary Revanchism of ISIS' in F al-Istrabadi and S Ganguly (eds), *The Future of ISIS* (Washington, DC, Brookings Institution Press, 2018) 23; Cottee (2017), above n 3 at 440. The group's violence – including the use of weapons of mass destruction, perpetrating genocide, the murder of non-combatants, the taking of sex slaves and hostages, the mutilation of corpses, trade in human organs, beheading, the killing of children along with scorched earth operations and global terrorist attacks – has been justified by Islamic State's leaders' twisted interpretation of Islamic teachings. See B Venard, 'How ISIS Terrorists Neutralise Guilt to Justify Their Atrocities', *The Conversation* (6 October 2016), www.theconversation.com/how-isis-terrorists-neutralise-guilt-to-justify-their-atrocities-66593; M Townsend, 'The Core ISIS Manual That Twisted Islam to Legitimise Barbarity', *The Guardian* (13 May 2018), www.theguardian.com/world/2018/may/12/isis-jihadist-manual-analysed-rebutted-by-islamic-scholar; H Winter and AK Al-Saud, 'The Obscure Theologian Who Shaped ISIS', *The Atlantic* (4 December 2016), www.theatlantic.com/international/archive/2016/12/isis-muhajir-syria/509399/.

Prophet Muhammad – mention that Islam should promote peaceful relations between nations.[5]

Islamic State has been more successful in strengthening and expanding its power in Iraq and Syria than was ever expected, and a sequence of external factors and conditions has undoubtedly facilitated this process. Within this particular context, the invasion of Iraq by the US-led coalition, the failure of the Iraqi central government to provide basic infrastructure for its citizens as a result of weak economic conditions, and the lack of an organised authority or political power to prevent minor conflicts from becoming major ones, has led to political and social troubles, instability and violence.[6] The defeat of the Iraqi army and the establishment of a new government led to violence and an asymmetrical war between the insurgents, the US military and the Iraqi central government.[7] Although the US government was seeking to establish a stable regime in Iraq, the invasion had many adverse consequences. Eventually, instability and insecurity, a humanitarian crisis, the dissolution of the Iraqi army, the inefficiency of the US army in taking control of Iraq in its entirety, the sectarian policies of the Iraqi central government under the leadership of Nuri al-Maliki for the benefit of Iraq's Shi'ite majority and its attempts to weaken the Sunnis,[8] and increasing protests and rebellions within Iraqi society led to a resurgence of Islamic jihadist groups in the country. The marginalisation and exclusion of Sunni leaders from political decision-making in the new government has been the major determinant in the increased uprisings and protests within Iraqi society. Since late 2012, the Sunni protests in Sunni-dominated regions – mainly in Kirkuk, Nineveh, Ramadi, Mosul and Fallujah – against the Shi'ite-dominated central government has led to the deaths of dozens of protestors. As a result of the triggered tensions, the Iraqi central government withdrew its security forces from Ramadi and Fallujah. This presented a golden opportunity for Islamic State, which proceeded to capture Fallujah in 2014.[9] Ultimately, the long-standing disagreements and ethnoreligious conflicts[10] between the Sunni and Shi'ite groups

[5] S Sardar Ali and J Rehman, 'The Concept of Jihad in Islamic International Law' (2005) 10 *Journal of Conflict & Security Law* 321, 331. For more details, see M Khadduri, *War and Peace in the Law of Islam* (New Jersey, Lawbook Exchange Publishers, 2010).

[6] D Carment, 'Assessing State Failure: Implications for Theory and Policy' (2003) 24 *Third World Quarterly* 407, 409–12; A Flibbert, 'The Consequences of Forced State Failure in Iraq' (2013) 128 *Political Science Quarterly* 67, 88.

[7] Y Bassil, 'Iraq War: Operations, Causes and Consequences' (2012) 4 *Journal of Humanities and Social Science* 29, 29.

[8] For more details, see F Haddad, *Sectarianism in Iraq: Antagonistic Vision of Unity* (Oxford, Oxford University Press, 2016) 143–78; International Crisis Group, 'Iraq's Jihadi Jack in the Box' (2014) 38 *Middle East Briefing* 1, https://d2071andvip0wj.cloudfront.net/iraq-s-jihadi-jack-in-the-box.pdf.

[9] S Adnan and A Reese, *Beyond the Islamic State: Iraq's Sunni Insurgency* (Washington, DC, Institute for the Study of War, 2014) 4.

[10] A Wimmer, 'Democracy and Ethno-religious Conflict in Iraq' (2017) 45 *Survival: Global Politics and Strategy* 111; R Visser, 'Historical Myths of a Divided Iraq' (2008) 50 *Survival: Global Politics and Strategy* 95, 100–103.

and the divided Kurdish-Arab ethnic groups have led to insecurity and a loss of confidence in the Iraqi central government.

Failed states have always been a threat to international security. However, because of their weak and fragile dynamics, they are becoming more dangerous, as terrorist groups frequently use them as bases of operation.[11] For this very reason, the failure of the Iraqi central government to perform basic functions such as guaranteeing security, good governance, and a thriving economy has created a power vacuum and has caused instability both in Iraqi society and throughout the Middle East. Due to the inability of weak and failed states to exert central control over their territories,[12] and their inability to take effective anti-terrorism measures, terrorist groups have attempted to take advantage of the power vacuum to further their objectives. Most crucially, terrorist groups often take advantage of regional players. For instance, al-Qaeda expanded its power and influence in the Middle East with the support of Sunni Muslim groups.[13] All in all, weak and failed states provide a more convenient environment in which foreign terrorists can assemble. For instance, as a result of the weakness of the Iraqi and Syrian governments and their inability to fight against terrorism, thousands of foreign fighters from Egypt, Qatar, Saudi Arabia, France, Morocco and Algeria left their countries of origin to join Islamic State.[14]

Following the US-led invasion in 2003, the Iraqi central government lost control over national security, thereby making it possible for terrorist groups to establish themselves. Consequently, the entire world witnessed the presence of thousands of foreign terrorists fighting alongside Islamic State. According to a 2015 report by the Soufan Group (TSG), a US-based security consultancy firm, more than 30,000 foreign fighters from at least 86 countries have travelled to Iraq and Syria to join Islamic State and other violent extremist groups.[15]

[11] As Edward Newman notes, 'weak or failed states should be a primary focus for the prevention of terrorism … Failed states should be seen as a strategic challenge, not only a humanitarian one'. See E Newman, 'Weak States, State Failure, and Terrorism' (2007) 19 *Terrorism and Political Violence* 463, 464.

[12] P Stewart, 'Failed States and Global Security: Empirical Questions and Policy Dilemmas' (2007) 9 *International Studies Review* 644, 652; R Takeyh and N Gvosdev, 'Do Terrorist Networks Need a Home?' (2002) 25 *Washington Quarterly* 97.

[13] Stewart (2007), above n 12 at 652–55.

[14] A Simons and D Tucker, 'The Misleading Problem of Failed States: A Socio-Geography of Terrorism in the Post-9/11 Era' (2007) 28 *Third World Quarterly* 387, 388.

[15] The Soufan Group, *Foreign Fighters: An Updated Assessment of the Flow of Foreign Fighters into Syria and Iraq* (New York, 2015) 4. According to reports, the largest numbers travelled to Iraq and Syria from the Middle East and the Maghreb, with around 8,000 foreign fighters each. Around 5,000 made their way from Europe, with a further 4,700 coming from former Soviet republics. See J Akbar, 'Tentacles of Terror: Chilling Map Shows the 31,000 Mercenary "Gun for Hire" Jihadis from 86 Countries Who Left Their Homes to Join ISIS … and a Third May Return to Carry Out Paris-Style Attacks', *Mail Online* (16 December 2015), www.dailymail.co.uk/news/article-3350779/Tentacles-terror-Chilling-map-shows-31-000-mercenary-guns-hire-jihadis-86-countries-left-homes-join-ISIS-return-carry-Paris-style-attacks.html; A Kirk, 'Iraq and Syria: How Many Foreign Fighters Are Fighting for ISIL?', *The Telegraph* (24 March 2016), www.telegraph.co.uk/news/2016/03/29/iraq-and-syria-how-many-foreign-fighters-are-fighting-for-isil/; A Mohdin, 'ISIL's Foreign Fighters

Similarly, pro-democracy protests against President Bashar al-Assad in Syria, which initially began peacefully in March 2011, led to the killings of several protestors and plunged the country into chaos. This allowed Islamic State to take advantage of the situation and to expand its influence, while Syrian society remained repressive on the eve of the 2011 uprisings. At the onset of the chaos in Syria, Islamic State sent material support and delegates to various anti-government rebel groups.[16] The uprisings and the subsequent civil war developed as a result of President Assad's disruptive statements in which he characterised the opposition as Sunni Islamic extremists in the mould of al-Qaeda, plotting against the Syrian regime. Assad's regime claimed from the outset that the uprising in Syria was the work of criminals, sectarians and terrorists supported by foreigners.[17] This seems to suggest that Sunni sectarianism and ethnic division have been the most crucial factors in the deterioration of the security situation in Iraq and Syria. The Iraqi and Syrian governments' policies and the implementation of strategies in this respect undermined their legitimacy and provided a ground for the resurgence of al-Qaeda and Islamic State in the two countries.[18] The sectarian and ethnic division in Iraq and Syria, which has betrayed people's trust in central government, brought Sunni groups more in line with Islamic State.[19]

B. The Legal Status of Islamic State

Islamic State's leaders call the group a 'state'; however, it should be ascertained whether the conditions required for the formation and creation of a sovereign state in international law exist for Islamic State.

Are Surprisingly Well-Educated, According to the World Bank', *Quartz* (6 October 2016), www.qz.com/802276/the-foreign-fighters-of-isisislamic-state-are-surprisingly-well-educated-according-to-the-world-bank/; A Dworkin, 'Beyond Good and Evil: Why Europe Should Bring ISIS Foreign Fighters Home', *European Council on Foreign Relations* (25 October 2019), www.ecfr.eu/publications/summary/beyond_good_and_evil_why_europe_should_bring_isis_foreign_fighters_home.

[16] S Jayaraman, 'International Terrorism and Statelessness: Revoking the Citizenship of ISIL Foreign Fighters' (2016) 17 *Chicago Journal of International Law* 178, 184.

[17] D Keen, *Syria: Playing into their Hands* (London, Safeworld, 2017) 28; E O'Bagy, *Middle East Security Report: Jihad in Syria. Report No 6* (Washington, DC, Institute for the Study of War, 2012) 9.

[18] H Wimmen, *Syria's Path from Civic Uprising to Civil War* (Washington, DC, Carnegie Endowment for International Peace, 2016) 4; P Sluglett, 'Deadly Implications: The Rise of Sectarianism in Syria' in M Beck et al, *The Levant in Turmoil: Syria, Palestine, and the Transformation of Middle Eastern Politics* (New York, Palgrave Macmillan, 2016) 39–55.

[19] More precisely, sectarianism and the Shia ascendancy that disrupted after the US invasion in 2003, have set the stage for the Sunni backlash of which Islamic State was a part. See H Brands and P Feaver, 'Was the Rise of ISIS Inevitable?' (2017) 59 *Survival: Global Politics and Strategy* 7, 15; A Basir Yosufi, 'The Rise and Consolidation of Islamic State: External Intervention and Sectarian Conflict' (2016) 15 *Connections: The Quarterly Journal* 91; P Cockburn, 'ISIS is Proof of the Failed War on Terror', *Quartz* (24 February 2015), www.qz.com/347398/isis-is-proof-of-the-failed-war-on-terror/; S Hamasaeed and N Garrett, 'Iraq Timeline: Since the 2003 War', *United States Institute of Peace* (9 July 2019), www.usip.org/publications/2019/07/iraq-timeline-2003-war.

There are different views as to what makes a state. Various scholars have defined the concept of a state in different ways. Some analyse the concept from an 'institutional' perspective, while others look at the state from a 'functional' perspective. Michael Mann, a British sociologist, has defined the state from an institutional perspective, as a concept which includes four main elements: (a) a differentiated set of institutions and personnel, embodying (b) centrality in the sense that political relations radiate outwards from a centre to cover (c) a territorially demarcated area, over which it exercises (d) a monopoly of authoritative rule-making, backed up by a monopoly over physical violence.[20] However, from a functional perspective, Max Weber argued that 'a compulsory political association with continuous organisation *(politischer Anstaltsbetrieb)* will be called a "state" if and insofar as its administrative staff successfully upholds a claim to the monopoly of the legitimate use of physical force in the enforcement of its order'.[21]

Despite the institutional and functional definitions of 'state' mentioned above, the most crucial issue is the current absence of an official definition of 'state' under international law. Despite all the difficulties, however, the essential requirements of statehood under international law that have been commonly accepted by the international community are set out in the Montevideo Convention on the Rights and Duties of States (1933).[22] As stated in Article 1 of the Convention, 'the state', as a person of international law, should possess 'a permanent population', 'a defined territory', 'government', and the 'capacity to enter into relations with other states'. In addition to the conditions mentioned by the Montevideo Convention, there is also a widely accepted view, raised customarily by the international community of states and particularly by some legal scholars, that 'independence' and 'legitimacy' are also required conditions for the creation of a state.[23]

At first glance, it could probably be claimed that the jihadist group known as Islamic State has a permanent population, since many of the Sunni tribes in western Iraq, Syria, Libya and Afghanistan pledged allegiance to Abu Bakr al-Baghdadi, the leader of the group, at the creation of the movement. The group entered into armed conflicts in neighbouring Syria under the leadership of Abu Bakr al-Baghdadi. After having extended its control over a substantial area of Syria and Iraq, the group declared an Islamic Caliphate and renamed itself Islamic State.[24] Although the group controlled certain parts of the

[20] M Mann, 'The Autonomous Power of the State: Its Origins, Mechanisms, and Results' (1984) 25 *European Journal of Sociology* 185, 188.

[21] M Weber, *The Theory of Social and Economic Organization* (New York, Free Press, 1964) 154.

[22] Montevideo Convention on the Rights and Duties of States (adopted by the Seventh International Conference of American States, 26 December 1933) (1936) CLXV *League of Nations Treaty Series* 19, 19.

[23] H Lauterpacht, 'Recognition of States in International Law' (1944) 53 *Yale Law Journal* 385, 408; JR Crawford, *The Creation of States in International Law* (Oxford, Oxford University Press, 2006) 37–96; SD Murphy, 'Democratic Legitimacy and the Recognition of States and Governments' (1999) 48 *International and Comparative Law Quarterly* 545.

[24] V Durac, 'The Role of Non-State Actors in Arab Countries after the Arab Uprisings' (2015) *IEMed Mediterranean Yearbook* 37, 39.

territories of Syria and Iraq, its control was neither legal nor legitimate, as it had been achieved as a result of mass violence and the use of force in occupation. Moreover, the establishment of a territory makes no sense for Islamic State since its goal is to rule over the entire Muslim world. On the other hand, although Islamic State built a state of administrative efficiency, it has been politically ineffective. An effective government should adhere to its international obligations if it wishes to become part of the international community.

As confirmed by United Nations Security Council (UNSC) Resolutions 2161 (1999),[25] 2170 (2014),[26] 2178 (2014)[27] and 2199 (2015)[28] concerning 'Threats to International Peace and Security Caused by Terrorist Acts', the occupation of territory in parts of Iraq and Syria by Islamic State, and the grave violations of *jus in bello* and human rights law, particularly in fomenting sectarian tensions in the region, have led to the displacement of millions of people.[29] The Council, once again, has reaffirmed the independence, sovereignty, unity and territorial integrity of the Republic of Iraq and the Syrian Arab Republic by emphasising the purposes and principles of the UN Charter.[30] More importantly, the UNSC's emphasis on sovereignty, unity and the territorial integrity of Iraq and Syria in the preamble of Resolution 2199 (2015) confirms that Islamic State does not legally exist.[31]

As a result, a violent extremist group such as Islamic State, which does not have an effective government, will be practically incapable of having relations with other states. The territory acquired by Islamic State as a result of grave violations of human rights and *jus in bello* could not be described under the conditions required for the creation of a legitimate state. In a sense, recognition of Islamic State as an entity under international law is out of the question.

It should also be noted that many terrorist organisations that have dozens or hundreds of members and routinely target civilians, do not hold territory and cannot combat external armed forces.[32] In contrast, Islamic State acquired territory in both Iraq and Syria and has more than 30,000 fighters. All these characteristic elements make Islamic State and ANSA acting independently from any other state. This suggests that Islamic State is not merely a small-scale terrorist organisation. However, Islamic State fighters have targeted civilians, community leaders and state forces in Iraq and Syria, and have organised dozens

[25] UNSC, Resolution 1261, UN Doc S/RES/1261 (30 August 1999).

[26] UNSC, Resolution 2170, UN Doc S/RES/2170 (15 August 2014).

[27] UNSC, Resolution 2178, UN Doc S/RES/2178 (24 September 2014).

[28] UNSC, Resolution 2199, UN Doc S/RES/2199 (12 February 2015).

[29] UNSC, Resolution 2170, UN Doc S/RES/2170 (15 August 2014).

[30] Ibid.

[31] See C Chinkin, 'The Security Council and Statehood' in C Chinkin and F Baetens (eds), *Sovereignty, Statehood and State Responsibility: Essays in Honour of James Crawford* (Cambridge, Cambridge University Press, 2015) 155–72.

[32] AK Cronin, 'ISIS Is Not a Terrorist Group: Why Counterterrorism Won't Stop the Latest Jihadist Threat' (2015) 94 *Foreign Affairs* 87.

of terrorist attacks on civilian-populated areas.[33] The group has involved itself in armed conflicts in order to achieve its political and ideological objectives, and therefore lacks legal capacity to become a party under relevant international treaties. However, those treaties cannot provide a basis for completely absolving Islamic State fighters of criminal responsibility. Although ANSAs such as Islamic State are not signatories to the 1949 Geneva Conventions and the 1977 Additional Protocols, which contain the core components of *jus in bello*, the majority opinion among legal scholars determines that national jurisdiction is paramount and that ANSAs are therefore bound by the rules of the states on whose territories they operate.

Islamic State is a violent ANSA that presented a unique model, which combines conquering territory and attempting to establish a state with managing a civilian government in the Middle East.[34] However, the group has conducted many violent, terrorist actions in violation of international law, human rights law and *jus in bello*. As a matter of criminal responsibility, the Rome Statute of the International Criminal Court (ICC)[35] imposes obligations upon ANSAs, requiring that, for instance, they forgo the recruitment and use of child soldiers to achieve their political objectives. It seems clear that the international community imposes obligations upon ANSAs without offering such groups any recognised rights or even token legitimacy. At the same time, it is difficult to enforce international law against ANSAs that are already regarded as illegitimate and criminal.[36]

In accordance with Article 8(2)(f) of the Rome Statute:

> Paragraph 2(e) … applies to armed conflicts that take place in the territory of a state when there is a protracted armed conflict between governmental authorities and organised armed groups or between such groups.

Moreover, as stated in Article 8(2) of the Rome Statute, all intentionally directed attacks on the civilian population – or against individual civilians not taking direct part in hostilities – and intentionally directed attacks on buildings, material, medical units and transport, and personnel using the distinctive emblems of the Geneva Conventions in conformity with international law, are defined as

[33] Islamic State has committed brutal crimes which amount to war crimes and crimes against humanity under international law. As reported by the UN Commission of Inquiry, Islamic State committed a series of war crimes during the second half of 2013. See UN Human Rights Council, 'Report of the Independent International Commission of Inquiry on the Syrian Arab Republic', UN Doc A/HRC/25/65 (12 February 2014), www.ohchr.org/EN/HRBodies/HRC/RegularSessions/Session25/Documents/A-HRC-25-65_en.doc. See also S Wheeler, 'UN Panel Reports on ISIS Crimes on Yezidis: "Unimaginable Horrors"', *Human Rights Watch* (26 June 2016), www.hrw.org/news/2016/06/21/un-panel-reports-isis-crimes-yezidis.

[34] C Valensi, 'Non-State Actors: A Theoretical Limitation in a Changing Middle East' (2015) 7 *Military & Strategic Affaires* 59, 72–73.

[35] Rome Statute of ICC, UN Doc A/CONF.138/9 (17 July 1998, entered into force 1 July 2002) (2005) 2187 *United Nations Treaty Series* 90, 90–158.

[36] DM Rosen, *Child Soldiers in the Western Imagination: From Patriots to Victims* (New Jersey, Rutgers University Press, 2015) 139.

war crimes. The following acts are also considered war crimes under Article 8(2) of the Rome Statute: intentionally directing attacks on buildings dedicated to religion, education, art, science or charitable purposes, historic monuments, hospitals and places where the sick and wounded are collected, provided they are not military objectives; pillaging a town or place, even when taken by assault; committing rape, sexual slavery, enforced prostitution, forced pregnancy; and especially conscripting or enlisting children under the age of 15 years into armed forces or groups or using them to participate actively in hostilities.[37]

Ultimately, the identification of Islamic State as an ANSA operating independently of the Iraqi and Syrian governments presents no obstacle to the international community imposing obligations on it. Moreover, as a party to a non-international armed conflict, Islamic State is obliged to apply and adhere to *jus in bello* and, therefore, its leadership and members can be held responsible for any crimes committed in direct violation of Article 8(2) of the Rome Statute.

III. ISLAMIC STATE'S QUEST FOR ENERGY RESOURCES IN IRAQ AND SYRIA

A. The Correlation between Energy Resources and Armed Conflict: A Conceptual Framework

International conflicts are defined as armed border and territorial conflicts between states involved in military hostilities over sovereignty or territory. In other words, most international conflicts have been largely as a result of territorial disputes.[38] Most recent non-international conflicts and civil wars have taken place in energy-rich countries and have revolved around the capture of energy resources by ANSAs or external powers that have intervened in the conflict. Oil has become the world's most important source of energy and a key factor for the victors in any conflict. In a sense, energy sources have become the focal point for states, ANSAs, and external powers that have tried to acquire these resources by force.

Obtaining control of valuable energy resources and then using those resources has often been one of the main causes of armed conflicts in oil-rich

[37] The ICC has ruled that enlisting and conscripting child soldiers under the age of 15 and using them to participate actively in hostilities is a war crime, and has ruled against members of ANSAs in the Democratic Republic of the Congo (DRC) and Uganda. See Investigation in the Democratic Republic of the Congo or the Situation in the Democratic Republic of the Congo, ICC-01/04 (June 2004), www.icc-cpi.int/drc.

[38] See T Pettersson and P Wallensteen, 'Armed Conflicts, 1946–2014' (2015) 52 *Journal of Peace Research* 536; NP Gleditsch et al, 'Armed Conflict 1946–2001: A New Dataset' (2002) 39 *Journal of Peace Research* 615, 619. See also K Eck, 'A Beginner's Guide to Conflict Data: Finding and Using the Right Dataset' (2005) 1 *UCDP Paper* 1, 39–40, www.pcr.uu.se/digitalAssets/667/c_667482-l_1-k_ucdp_paper1.pdf.

countries, particularly those in the Middle East which depend upon oil for their wealth. Having said that, oil-rich countries have been at constant risk of armed conflict and civil wars. The oil-rich and oil-producing states make up a growing fraction of the world's armed conflict-ridden countries that experience frequent civil war. Currently, a third of the world's civil wars have taken place in oil-rich countries, up from a fifth in 1992.[39]

Depending on the circumstances, a correlation between energy resources and armed conflict can be identified based on several economic, political and military factors, the most significant of which are listed below.

i. Dependency on Oil as a Major Source of National Income[40]

The relationship between energy resources and armed conflict comes as a result of the energy-resource dependency of the supplier states, whose national economies are most dependent on their natural resources, including energy resources. However, in many cases, the failure of energy-rich countries to regulate an adequate legal framework for managing their resource revenue can cause public discontent and government mistrust. In such a case, if the energy-rich country includes multiple ethnic, cultural, linguistic and religious minorities, the financial incentive of local minorities to attempt to create a separate country, and thereby the risk of civil war will be increased. This also suggests that an ethnically and religiously divers country faces a higher risk of insurgency when it has a well-organised minority group. In such cases, religious minorities in polarised countries that are dominated by one main religion, or in countries in which political power is divided along ethnic lines, and the ruling ethnic group uses its position to discriminate against other ethnic groups, may feel excluded from the political process and the economic opportunities, leaving them motivated to rebel.[41] In countries with such potential, therefore, plentiful resources will increase the risk of civil war as the opportunity to gain a larger share of a country's resources would give rebel groups an incentive to form a separate state.[42] The point of reference in this regard, therefore, is the fact that oil-producing

[39] See B Smith, 'Oil Wealth and Regime Survival in the Developing World, 1960–1999' (2004) 48 *American Journal of Political Science* 232; P Lujal, 'The Spoils of Nature: Armed Civil Conflict and Rebel Access to Natural Resources' (2012) 47 *Journal of Peace Research* 15; ML Ross, 'Blood Barrels: Why Oil Wealth Fuels Conflict' (2008) 78 *Foreign Affairs* 2, 2. See also P Collier, 'Doing Well Out of War: An Economic Perspective' in DM Malone and M Berdal (eds), *Greed & Grievance: Economic Agendas in Civil Wars* (Boulder, Lynne Rienner Publishers, 2000) 91–111.

[40] M Klare, *Rising Powers, Shrinking Planet: The New Geopolitics of Energy* (Oxford, Oneworld Publications, 2008) 9.

[41] SG Jones, *Waging Insurgent Warfare: Lessons from the Vietcong to the Islamic State* (Oxford, Oxford University Press, 2017) 23; EK Denny and BF Walter, 'Ethnicity and Civil War' (2014) 51 *Journal of Peace Research* 199, 203.

[42] ML Ross, 'How Do Natural Resources Influence Civil War? Evidence from Thirteen Cases' (2004) 58 *International Organization* 35, 41. See also P Collier and A Hoeffler, *The Political Economy of Secession* (Washington, DC, Development Research Group, 2002).

states tend to suffer from an unusually large number of attacks from insurgents and ANSAs, which consist almost entirely of minority groups that have been excluded from economic and political processes.

ii. The General Impression of Scarcity in the International Oil Market

Scarcity of energy and global anxieties about energy prices have often been the cause of violence and conflict.[43] In such situations, scarcity of resources creates grounds for multinational energy companies to establish themselves in energy-rich countries in order to help stabilise global energy security. For example, the US's military campaign in Iraq, which began in 2003, paved the way for the American authorities to reap the long-term benefits of Iraq's oil resources by cancelling and outlawing long-term contractual agreements in Iraq in the aftermath of the denationalisation of its resources.[44] As an outgrowth of several decades of strategic thinking and policymaking regarding Middle Eastern oil, the Iraq War helped the US to fashion a new geopolitical order that provides the political underpinning for the US's preferred economic model, ie one that ensures continuing Western access to Middle Eastern oil.[45] In addition to the more considerable implications of the Iraq War in scale, duration and destruction than previous military misadventures in the Middle East, the war was the culmination of several decades of strategic thinking and policymaking surrounding oil.[46] Accordingly, the scarcity of oil, which is still the world's most important fossil fuel energy source, threatens economic and social earnings and can trigger armed conflicts with oil-rich nations.

iii. The Emergence of Ethnic, Religious and Violent Movements

Threats to global and regional energy security in energy-rich countries, particularly those in the Middle East, have intensified ethnic and religious conflicts due to the emergence of violent ANSAs. These groups compete to take control of energy resources in order to strengthen themselves in all aspects to achieve their objectives. As is the case with ANSAs, energy wealth in energy-rich countries has triggered ethnic and religious conflicts against the respective central governments. More importantly, uneven disruption of energy resources or energy-related incomes in countries that are home to different ethnic-religious

[43] PE Peters, 'Inequality and Social Conflict Over Land in Africa' (2004) 4 *Journal of Agrarian Change* 269; TC Jones, 'America, Oil, and War in the Middle East' (2012) 99 *Journal of American History* 208, 210.

[44] M Kaldor et al, *Oil Wars* (London, Pluto Press, 2007) 17.

[45] Jones (2012), above n 43 at 209; S Bromley, 'The United States and the Control of World Oil' (2005) 40 *Government and Opposition* 225, 254.

[46] K Proninska, 'Energy and Security: Regional and Global Dimensions' in Stockholm International Peace Research Institute (SIPRI), *SIPRI Yearbook 2007: Armaments, Disarmament and International Security* (Oxford, Oxford University Press, 2006) 229; Jones (2012), above n 43 at 209.

minorities has created the grounds for armed conflicts based on ethnicity and religion. If these communities feel marginalised, particularly regarding the distribution of energy resources, then conflict is inevitable. At its core, disputes over resources make it easy for political groups to elicit popular support and can make it difficult to secure compromises, as they provide the lightning rod for regional, ethnic, religious and class tensions.[47] The war being fought against the Shi'ite-led governments of Syria and Iraq by Islamic State is the clearest example of a conflict being fought as a result of political instability, ethnic-religious division, corruption, mismanagement of energy resources and unequal distribution of income and wealth between minority groups. Most crucially, during a civil war within energy-rich countries, ANSAs which are almost defeated will fight to take control of resource-rich territory in order to boost their strength.[48]

Having analysed the major elements regarding the energy resource-wars correlation, it can be argued that 'dependency on oil as a major source of the national economy', notably in Iraq, has given rise to 'the emergence of ethnic and religious movements' in both Iraq and Syria. However, energy resources have always been taken into consideration by external powers. During the last few decades, a number of armed conflicts have broken out around the world, most of which have been fought over the control of energy resources.[49]

Having addressed the relationship between energy resources and armed conflict, we can show that political, ethnic and religious upheavals in the Middle East have invariably threatened both regional and international peace and

[47] J Black, *War and New Disorder in the 21st Century* (London, Continuum, 2004), 35; SHBO Alkaff, 'Evolving Jihadist Landscape in the Middle East' (2019) 11 *Counter Terrorist Trends and Analyses* 1, 76–77.

[48] The evidence indicates that natural resources give the warring parties access to weapons and political support. This has been especially relevant regarding the financing of rebellions since the end of the Cold War, where many rebel leaders who had been dependent on the US or the Soviet Union for financial and military assistance turned to natural resources to fill the gap. For a detailed assessment of this practice, see D Dam-de Jong, *International Law and Governance of Natural Resources in Conflict and Post-Conflict Situations* (Cambridge, Cambridge University Press, 2015) 5; C-P David and J-F Gagné, 'Natural Resources: A Source of Conflict?' (2007) 62 *International Journal* 5, 10.

[49] See AH Cordesman and AR Wagner, *The Lessons of Modern War – Vol 2: The Iran-Iraq War* (Boulder, Westview Press, 1990) 12, 31–33, 95. The most prominent examples of conflicts over energy resources can be listed as follows: the invasion of the Soviet Union by Nazi Germany in 1941; the Attack on Pearl Harbour and the US Entry into World War II in 1941; the Biafran War in 1967; the wars of the Arab-Israeli Conflict, most notably in 1948–1949, 1956, 1967, 1973, and 1982; the Iran-Iraq War from 1980 to 1988; the Iraq-Kuwait War (the First Gulf War) from 1990 to 1991; the War in Iraq from 2003 to 2011 (the Second Gulf War), which led to the invasion of Iraq by the US-led coalition in order to overthrow Saddam Hussein's government; the Sudan Oil War in 2011; the Syrian Civil War, ongoing since 2011; the War in Libya in 2011; and the Russo-Ukrainian War in 2014. Energy production has been negatively affected in all these conflicts as a result of the targeting of energy resources. See P Guha Thakurta, 'Conflicts to Control Oil: Economic Implications of the Wars in Afghanistan and Iraq' (2013) 30 *India International Centre Quarterly* 142; MG Salameh, 'Oil Wars' (2014) 14-163 *USAEE Working Paper* 1, 7–13, https://papers.ssrn.com/sol3/papers.cfm?abstract_id=2430960; See also JD Colgan, 'Fuelling the Fire: Pathways from Oil to War' (2013) 38 *International Security* 147.

security. Considering the recent developments in the aftermath of its violent behaviour and terrorist attacks in both Iraq and Syria, Islamic State then turned to oil production and smuggling in order to fund its campaign. Clearly, ANSAs' access to energy resources may be a motive for initiating or continuing armed conflicts as well as being seen as an opportunity for them to finance their military actions.[50] In other words, they have maintained substantial control over energy resources in the most important oil-rich countries and have used them to buy weaponry on the black market in order to establish their dominance. As Le Billon has pointed out, energy resources serve to shape the armed conflicts taking place, the territorial control objectives and the duration and intensity of the armed conflicts, and can also affect the internal cohesion of the activities of ANSAs.[51] More importantly, ANSAs or rebel groups in energy-rich countries have an incentive to protect energy resources as they are their primary source of finance on the global markets. Evidence indicates that rebel groups have been able to benefit directly from energy resources and have increased their funding due to oil, while governments have sometimes been overthrown due to rebellions.[52] Overall, energy-rich countries have been more prone to conflicts at both the national and international level, which is another indicator of the correlation between energy resources and armed conflict.

B. Insecurity and the Threat of Violence as the Costs of Failed Resource Management

Before turning to the potential role of energy resources in intensifying Islamic State's military operations, this section briefly sets out the extent to which mismanagement of energy resources such as oil and natural gas has been a source of disputes, insecurity, and violence in energy-rich countries. This is particularly true in countries with significant energy resources in which the governance, distribution and management of the resources have been haphazard, leading to insecurity, instability and violent conflict. Evidence indicates that most major armed conflicts in the Middle East arose through disagreements and disputes over access to and the control and distribution of energy resources.[53] For example, following the US invasion of Iraq in 2003, the new Iraqi government

[50] Kaldor et al (2007), above n 44 at 20.

[51] P Le Billon, *Fuelling War: Natural Resources and Armed Conflicts* (London, Routledge, 2005) 48.

[52] CJ Fettweis, 'No Blood for Oil: Why Resource Wars Are Obsolete' in G Luft and A Korin (eds), *Energy Security Challenges for the 21st Century* (California, Greenwood Press, 2009) 71; JD Colgan, 'Oil, Domestic Conflict, and Opportunities for Democratization' (2005) 52 *Journal of Peace Research* 3, 7–10.

[53] JL Kaye, *Renewable Resources and Conflict* (New York, United Nations Interagency Framework Team for Preventive Action, 2012) 8; IO Lesser et al, 'Sources of Conflict in the Greater Middle East' in Z Khalilzad and IO Lesser (eds), *Sources of Conflict in the 21st Century: Regional Futures and US Strategy* (Santa Monica, Rand Publications, 1998) 171–229.

ratified a new constitution in which the Kurdish Regional Government (KRG) was officially recognised under a new federal system; however, the Iraqi central government was not able to resolve disagreements with the Kurds, who have often been at loggerheads with the Iraqi central government over their constitutional rights and right to fair resource allocation.[54]

It is worth noting here that good governance and management of energy resources in energy-rich countries depend on the country's stability. Moreover, instability in energy-rich countries resulting from conflicts would lead to governments losing effective control over their territory and local resources. For these governments, this can mean that they will no longer be able to exercise permanent sovereignty over their natural resources. This can be highlighted with an actual example of Islamic State, which was in a unique position to achieve its goals by taking control of energy resources in Iraq and to use them as an opportunity to generate income to enhance its economic and military capabilities. In one sense, the emergence of divisions and new tensions in Iraqi society after the Iraq War (2003), particularly the rise of Islamic State, also has its roots in the weak governance and mismanagement of energy resources, which are critical elements in ensuring and enhancing equality and political stability in an ethnically diverse society such as the newly federalised Iraq.

Considering the complexity of the political situation in post-war societies and the relationships between the central and regional government and other groups such as ANSAs, it is inevitable that all these groups will have their own political and economic aspirations. Notably, political regimes in post-war societies will undergo significant alterations in order to promote political stability. In such countries, the various complexities, which include political, economic, social and cultural rights violations and disagreements between the central government and other political entities over natural resource governance, may preclude peace and security.[55] Precedent suggests that peace is likely to be lasting only if the security needs of the population are addressed in parallel with the political and socio-economic aspects of post-war reconstruction.

[54] The fair and equitable resource and resource revenues sharing involve questions of distributive justice. In that sense, the fair and equitable sharing of resources is interpreted as an equal overall allocation of access of all members of a society to the resources – either because such a distribution is seen as desirable in its own right (eg a belief that people deserve equal shares of common resources), or because equitability is seen as a prerequisite for effective institutional function to reduce free-riding and maximise compliance. Moreover, the mutual benefits of shared natural resources act as an incentive for sustained peaceful dialogue, which in turn can generate cooperation among states, communities and people. See A Evans, 'Resource Scarcity, Fair Shares and Development' (2011) *A WWF/Oxfam Discussion Paper*, 11–12, https://oi-files-d8-prod.s3.eu-west-2.amazonaws.com/s3fs-public/file_attachments/rr-resource-scarcity-fair-shares-200711-en_3.pdf; UN Secretary General, 'Sharing Benefits of Natural Resources Helps Conflict Prevention, Sustainable Development, Secretary-General Tells Security Council', Press Release, UN Doc SG/SM/19303-SC/13541-ENV/DEV/1896 (16 October 2018), www.un.org/press/en/2018/sgsm19303.doc.htm.

[55] C Bell, 'Peace Settlements and International Law: From Lex Pacificatoria to Jus Post Bellum' in ND White and C Henderson (eds), *Research Handbook on International Conflict and Security Law: Jus ad Bellum, Jus in Bello and Jus Post Bellum* (Cheltenham, Edward Elgar, 2013) 502–503.

It is worth noting here that countries with considerable reserves of high-value natural resources, such as oil, generally face a very complicated situation regarding energy resource governance due to constraints relating to a recurrence of conflict.[56] Ensuring stability and a peaceful environment in these societies necessitates the establishment of effective and dominant governance through the stabilisation of fragile peace arrangements and the strengthening of weak structures of social and constitutional order.[57] In that sense, ensuring the accountability of governments in the effective governance of energy resources through fair and equitable distribution of energy resources revenue, is a primary route to the establishment of a peaceful and stable political environment in such countries.

Given the fact that armed conflicts often weaken the institutional capacities of post-war societies in which there is no governmental authority to control the national economy effectively, an effective governance based on increased transparency, accountability, and fair distribution of revenue (wealth-sharing) among diverse members of a society would prevent the emergence new tensions and conflicts, and instabilities.[58] Improving the effective governance over existing energy resources would allow the government to concentrate on resolving existing conflicts as a pathway to peace, and preventing them from reigniting in the future.[59]

Ultimately, however, unfair and unequal distribution of the revenues from natural resources, as well as the resources themselves, is a reflection of mismanagement and non-accountability in the management of those resources and might well lead to instability, insecurity, and the threat of new conflicts. While these types of conflicts are most prevalent in areas that contain significant energy resources that are poorly governed due to the weak rule of law,[60] transparency and accountability of governments to society in the management and the administration of resource revenues would ensure security and stability in energy-rich

[56] G Brown et al, 'A Typology of Post-Conflict Environments' (2011) 1 *Centre for Research on Peace and Development Working Paper* 1, 3, www.soc.kuleuven.be/crpd/files/working-papers/wp01.pdf.

[57] A Ohanyan, *NGOs, IGOs, and the Network Mechanisms of Post-Conflict Global Governance in Microfinance* (New York, Palgrave Macmillan Press, 2008) 24.

[58] S Rose-Ackerman, 'Corruption and Post-Conflict Peace-Building' (2008) 34 *Ohio Northern University Law Review* 405; C Bruch et al, 'Facilitating Peace or Fuelling Conflict? Lessons in Post-Conflict Governance and Natural Resource Management' in C Bruch et al (eds), *Governance, Natural Resources and Post-Conflict Peacebuilding* (London, Routledge, 2016) 960–95.

[59] D Dam-de Jong, *International Law and Governance of Natural Resources in Conflict and Post-Conflict Situations* (Cambridge, Cambridge University Press, 2015) 426.

[60] See P Le Billon, 'Oil Prices, Scarcity, and Geographies of War' (2009) 99 *Annals of the Association of American Geographers* 836, 839; T Addison and T Brück, 'Economic Agendas in Civil Wars: What We Know, What We Need to Know' in T Addison and T Brück (eds), *Making Peace Work: The Challenges of Social and Economic Reconstruction* (London, Palgrave Macmillan, 2009) 31–50; J Di John, 'Oil Abundance and Violent Political Conflict: A Critical Assessment' (2007) 43 *Journal of Development Studies* 961, 978.

countries. These are also the primary requirements of sustainable development, which have been addressed by the UNSC in various contexts.[61]

C. The Potential Role of Energy Resources in Intensifying Islamic State's Military Operations

Historically, international demand for essential energy resources has been one of the most important strategic assets for any state. Due to increasing international demand for energy resources during the twentieth century, the Middle East's energy reserves, particularly oil resources, have become increasingly important, and oil-rich Middle Eastern countries have always been under threat of military aggression because of their energy resources. In addition, the Middle East's energy resources have ordinarily been considered a strategic and fundamental asset for Western powers due to the scarcity of oil and high levels of energy resource dependency in the West. Oil could also be regarded as the key motivating factor for Western powers attempting to gain influence in the Middle East.[62]

After World War I, the US and major European powers, most notably the UK, which had been worried about their dwindling energy supplies, began a search for foreign energy resources. Since the 1930s, the Middle East has emerged as the most important source of energy in the world.[63] According to a US Geological Survey, two-thirds of the world's oil reserves are in the Middle East, and over 50 per cent of undiscovered reserves are thought to be concentrated in the region,[64] primarily in Saudi Arabia, Iran, Iraq, Kuwait, the United Arab Emirates and Libya.[65]

Since the end of World War II, the economic growth of the industrialised Western countries has increasingly been based on Middle Eastern oil. Western

[61] UNSC, Statement by the President, UN Doc S/PRST/2007/22 (25 June 2007), para 6; UNSC, Resolution 1607, UN Doc S/RES/1607 (21 June 2005), para 4; UNSC, Resolution 1647, UN Doc S/RES/ 1647 (20 December 2005), para 3(a). For a discussion, see D Dam-de Jong, 'Standard-Setting Practices for the Management of Natural Resources in Conflict-Torn States: Constitutive Elements of Jus Post Bellum' in C Stahn et al (eds), *Environmental Protection and Transitions from Conflict to Peace: Clarifying Norms, Principles, and Practices* (Oxford, Oxford University Press, 2017) 169–91.

[62] J Edelman Spero, 'Energy Self-Sufficiency and National Security' (1973) 31 *Proceedings of the Academy of Political Science* 123, 128; PR Odell, 'The Significance of Oil' (1968) 3 *Journal of Contemporary History* 93, 96–97.

[63] AH Taher, 'The Middle East Oil and Gas Policy' (1978) 3 *Journal of Energy and Development* 260, 260–61; RK Ramazani, 'The Changing United States Policy in the Middle East' (1964) 40 *Virginia Quarterly Review* 369, 369; J Darmstadter and HH Lansberg, 'The Economic Background' in R Vernon (ed), *The Oil Crisis: In Perspective* (Massachusetts, MIT Press, 1975) 16.

[64] Considering these attractive features of the Middle East as one of the most important energy pioneers of the world, its oil supplies began to flood the global markets, and feared shortages of oil evaporated after discovering the seemingly limitless reserves in Middle Eastern territory. See Klare (2008), above n 40 at 32–33.

[65] S Stec and B Baraj, *Energy and Environmental Challenges to Security* (Dordrecht, Springer, 2007) 198. For more details on global oil reserves see PR Odell, 'World Oil Resources, Reserves and Production' (1994) 15 *The Energy Journal (Special Issue on the Changing World Petroleum Market)* 89.

countries were often warned that American oil reserves were dwindling rapidly and that the world would become more and more dependent on the Middle East.[66] It is now at the stage that the US is the world's largest oil consumer, while the Middle East is the world's largest producer and exporter. In a sense, the two sides have mutual interests in promoting the stability of the global oil market.[67] Policymakers in the US have considered a national energy policy since the 1930s. Under Franklin D Roosevelt's administration, the US government realised that it could not solve the economic problems facing the country without playing a key role in American oil policies, which were seen as a vital factor in economic recovery. With the US's involvement in World War II, the struggle to formulate a governmental oil policy intensified. Despite the heavy drain on its oil supplies during the war, the US still occupied a strong position with respect to oil resources. In 1950, the US provided 22 per cent of the world's crude oil production, while in 2004 that figure had dropped to approximately 10 per cent. As a result, Middle Eastern oil has been imported into the US in ever-increasing amounts and the notion of 'oil independence' was gradually accepted by many policymakers of the US.[68]

As a result of the growing demand for Middle Eastern oil reserves, the strategic importance of the region has grown over the years.[69] However, territorial disputes in the Middle East, such as those between Iran and the United Arab Emirates, religious-based conflicts, mainly in Iraq and Syria, and the increase in the number of violent ANSAs in the region, etc have created serious threats to the energy-rich and mainly oil-producing countries of the Middle East. More pertinently, these heightened tensions have seriously threatened the security interests of the US and Europe, as they are the biggest consumers of Middle Eastern oil. More specifically, the tensions in the region have critical and significant implications for oil exportation.

Precisely, the Western powers' presence in the region and their intervention in some of the regional conflicts have reflected their energy dependency and their anxieties about destabilised global energy markets. In particular, high oil prices have created great anxiety in Western countries. Higher energy prices as a result of occasional tensions in the oil-producing region of the Middle East would lead to higher living costs, higher rates of inflation, and potential damage to Western economies.[70]

[66] See in general, WJ Levy, 'Issues in International Oil Policy' (1957) 35 *Foreign Affairs* 454; C Issawi, 'Oil and Middle East Politics' (1973) 31 *Proceedings of the Academy of Political Science* 111.

[67] G Bahgat, 'The United States and the Middle East: Interdependence Not Independence' (2006) 30 *OPEC Review* 187, 199.

[68] Ibid.

[69] K Proninska, 'Resource Wars in Contemporary International Relations' (2005) 14 *The Polish Quarterly of International Affairs* 29, 31. For more general information, see Issawi (1973), above n 66 at 111–22.

[70] See L El-Katiri, 'Why Middle East Conflict Is a Bigger Threat to UK Energy Security Than Putin', *The Guardian* (4 September 2014), www.theguardian.com/big-energy-debate/2014/sep/05/conflict-middle-east-energy-security-putin.

However, tensions in the Middle East have not been reduced by the external powers' interventions in the region. The presence of the US and European powers in the Middle East as major energy consumers, especially in Iraq and Syria, has increased the stakes for Middle Eastern oil and has inflamed tensions in the region. In other words, military intervention in Middle Eastern, oil-rich countries has led to a new wave of tensions and violence in the region including the emergence of violent ANSAs with certain ideologies, which have already sparked civil wars in the region. The US invasion of Iraq in 2003 is the most prominent example of militarism in the Middle East which caused insecurity and political unrest throughout the region.[71]

International peace and security are the primary goals of the UN, but human history is fraught with armed conflicts and violence around the world. The international community was shaken by two devastating World Wars in the first half of the twentieth century, meaning that world leaders were pressured to seek a way to reduce and prevent risks and threats and to build global peace and security. The main focus of the world leaders in San Francisco in creating the UN in 1945 was international peace and security. In order to protect the people, they determined in the first paragraph of the UN Charter 'to save succeeding generations from the scourge of war, which twice in our lifetime has brought untold sorrow to mankind'. As mentioned by the UN Secretary-General, 'when [the UN founders] spoke of creating a new system of collective security, they meant it in the traditional military sense: a system in which states join together and pledge that aggression against one is aggression against all, and commit themselves in that event to react collectively'.[72]

The main purpose of the UN, as stated above, is the maintenance of international peace and security. To that end, it needs to take effective collective measures to prevent and remove threats to the peace, to suppress acts of aggression or other breaches of the peace, and bring about by peaceful means, and in conformity with the principles of justice and international law, adjustment or settlement of international disputes or situations which might lead to a breach of the peace. Member states are to seek the settlement of their international disputes by peaceful means under Chapter VI of the UN Charter.[73] The UN considers peace as an international order based on justice. According to the UNSC, the absence of war and military conflict does not in itself ensure

[71] Following the US invasion of Iraq, the international energy companies avoided operations in the Middle East, which paved the way for the US government to award two-thirds of the total contracts without competition in 2003. This process also led to considerably higher energy price increases on the global markets. See G Bahgat, *Energy Security: An Interdisciplinary Approach* (West Sussex, Wiley Publication, 2011) 82; P Le Billon, 'Corruption, Reconstruction and Oil Governance in Iraq' (2005) 26 *Third World Quarterly* 685, 696.

[72] See also UNGA, 'Report of the High-Level Panel on Threats, Challenges and Change on a More Secure World: Our Shared Responsibility', UN Doc A/59/565 (2 December 2004), 11. For more information, see LM Goodrich, 'The Maintenance of International Peace and Security' (1965) 19 *International Organization* 429, 429–31.

[73] UNGA, Resolution 377 [V], Uniting for Peace Resolution, UN Doc A/1456 (3 November 1950).

international peace and security. Now, non-military sources of instability in the economic, social, humanitarian and ecological fields have become threats to peace and security. The [UN] membership as a whole, working through the appropriate bodies, needs to give the highest priority to finding solutions to these problems.[74]

In compliance with the limited concept of international peace, the concept of international security was also only limited to the national security of states in which sovereignty, territorial integrity, political independence and sovereign equality were the main basis of security. The concept of security was mentioned for the first time in the signing of the Peace Treaty of Westphalia in 1648, which gave rise to the idea that the co-existence of territorially separate but equally sovereign states afforded a better chance of peace and security.[75] Nevertheless, the Westphalian concept of international security has evolved since the beginning of globalisation in the 1970s. In this sense, the threats to international peace and security have expanded from simply military threats and now include political, economic, social and environmental threats. For instance, rapid population growth, poverty, climate change and environmental crises, migration and population change, etc are the main factors that threaten international security in its contemporary sense. Viewed from this perspective, the First Gulf War (1990–1991)[76] was one of the most important underlying drivers of insecurity, uncertainty and instability at both the national and international level.

The quest for energy resources is also categorised as a threat to international security and has been the driver of armed conflicts in the twenty-first century. In the new era, inter alia, by expanding the military concept of threats to international peace and security into other areas, including poverty, terrorism, smuggling and organised crimes, migration, human rights abuses, the proliferation of weapons of mass destruction, and territorial disputes, ANSAs could also be considered as major threats to international peace and security due to their economic and political objectives. In this regard, ANSAs' quest for energy resources as a source of revenue within energy-rich countries would lead to armed conflict, given that conflicts have generally been pursued in a calculated attempt by the warring parties to drive their interests, including the economic benefits they can derive from the conflicts.[77] In other words, although violent ANSAs such as Islamic State adopt discourses of economic and political discontent in an attempt to raise their legitimacy, discontent and grievances per se are not the driving forces of armed conflict. The rise of Islamic State, for example,

[74] UNSC, 'Note by the President of the UN Security Council', UN Doc S/23500 (31 January 1992).

[75] D Hassan, 'Rise of the Territorial State and the Treaty of Westphalia' (2006) 9 *Yearbook of New Zealand Jurisprudence* 62, 67; PMR Stirk, 'The Westphalian Model and Sovereign Equality' (2012) 38 *Review of International Studies* 641, 556.

[76] See Ø Noreng, *Crude Power: Politics and the Oil Market* (London, IB Tauris, 2002) 187; MG Salameh (2014), above n 49 at 7–13; Colgan (2013), above n 49 at 174.

[77] See G Frerks et al, 'Conflict and Cooperation on Natural Resources: Justifying the CoCooN Programme' in M Bavinck et al (eds), *Conflicts Over Natural Resources in the Global South – Conceptual Approaches* (London, CRC Press, 2014) 16.

was mostly a result of the political vacuum created by the US invasion of Iraq and its hasty withdrawal from the region after promising the Sunni groups full participation in Iraq's new political system.[78]

In order to achieve their political objectives, ANSAs need a strong economy and financial system. In the absence of a robust economy, they would not be able to launch any military operations. Having been based in an energy-rich country, ANSAs would see a significant opportunity to improve their military capacity by taking control of the host state's resources by force. Middle Eastern countries have been largely recognised as hotbeds of ethnic and religious tensions, which often erupt in violence. The abundance of energy resources in both Iraq and Syria was the primary factor in the rise of Islamic State to become the most powerful Islamic jihadist groups in those countries. Islamic State's military strength, and its wide-ranging operations both in Iraq and Syria, are in fact reflections of a parallel political economy for fuelling wars and conflicts driven by energy resources.[79] As a matter of fact, unlootable energy resources, including oil, natural gas and deep-shaft minerals, have been a source of finance for rebels and violent ANSAs, presenting them with an unceasing flow of extortion opportunities.[80] Islamic State has stolen $425 million[81] of sold or smuggled oil from neighbouring territories as a result of its protracted war in the region, making it the richest jihadist group in the world.

Although Iraqi and Syrian oil resources have not been the only source of revenue for Islamic State, it seems that the group enhanced its military capabilities by exercising different forms of control over oil resources in Iraq and Syria, recognising them as key to its development. According to a report published by the Centre for the Analysis of Terrorism about Islamic State's financing, in 2015, Islamic State controlled 15 oilfields in Syria and ten oilfields in Iraq, even though the group eventually lost the control of them as a result of the US-led coalition's airstrikes.[82] While the group concentrated all of its resources on its military campaign, it did begin to create civil governance mechanisms to establish a local governmental and legal system to protect its economic assets. Iraqi and Syrian oil resources have been used by Islamic State to partially fund military operations, oversee the administration of its occupied territories, and to fund its

[78] See Sandal (2018), above n 4 at 28–32; Frerks et al (2014), above n 77 at 16.

[79] See for more details, P Le Billon, 'The Political Economy of War: Natural Resources and Armed Conflict' (2001) 20 *Political Geography* 561; ML Ross, 'Oil, Drugs, and Diamonds: The Varying Roles of Natural Resources in Civil War' in K Ballentine and J Sherman, *The Political Economy of Armed Conflict: Beyond Greed and Grievance* (London, Lynne Rienner, 2003) 47–70.

[80] Ross, ibid, at 64–65.

[81] See T McCoy, 'ISIS Just Stole $425 Million and Became the World's Richest Terrorist Group', *Washington Post* (12 June 2014), www.washingtonpost.com/news/morning-mix/wp/2014/06/12/isis-just-stole-425-million-and-became-the-worlds-richest-terrorist-group/.

[82] L Bindner and G Poirot, *ISIS Financing in 2015* (Paris, CAT, 2016) 9. For a discussion, see A Basit, 'Foreign Fighters in Iraq and Syria – Why So Many?' (2014) 6 *Counter Terrorist Trends and Analyses* 4, 7.

expansion abroad.[83] In essence, the use of violence to further its political and ideological objectives, most notably the establishment of a caliphate, occurred by virtue of oil smuggling in the region. This made the group more powerful and consistent in using identity-based violence as a political tactic, with the goal of proving its sectarian identity within Shi'ite-dominated Iraq and Syria.

Nevertheless, the threat from Islamic State remains, and losing control of territory and major oilfields in Iraq and Syria does not mean that Islamic State is defeated and is no longer a threat to international peace and security, bearing in mind that 'less territory does not necessarily mean more security'.[84] Indeed, in the wake of the US-led coalition's airstrikes against Islamic State's oil infrastructure in Iraq and Syria, the group has maintained a revenue stream by diversifying into extortion and taxation, robbery, kidnapping for ransom, human trafficking, foreign donations, and the trafficking of Iraqi and Syrian cultural, archaeological, historical and religious properties, as has already been identified in UNSC Resolution 2253 (2015).[85]

IV. CONCLUDING REMARKS

Starting with the rise and strengthening of Islamic State in both Iraq and Syria, Chapter 1 has clarified Islamic State's legal status, demonstrating that it is an ANSA operating independently of any state. This identification of Islamic State's legal status as an actor independent of its host state has been of vital importance. As discussed further in Chapter 2, the legality of the extraterritorial military operations against Islamic State (the use of force against ANSAs) in both Iraq and Syria is directly connected with the group's status in certain respects, including the key issue of whether the operations of ANSAs are attributable to the host state.

Given the occupation of the Iraqi and Syrian oil fields and installations by Islamic State, Chapter 1 has also shown a correlation between energy resources and armed conflict. Often considered a paradigm relevant to the resource war, the link between natural resources and armed conflicts in energy-rich countries has been established in this chapter. Finding a strong overlap between the quest for energy resources and armed conflict, it has been shown that Islamic State's undeniable thirst for Iraqi and Syrian oil has been a catalyst for foreign interventions in both countries. In particular, the central role of energy resources in fuelling the war with Islamic State has been demonstrated. Having identified the vital role of energy resources in intensifying armed conflicts in energy-rich

[83] Valensi (2015), above n 34 at 73; Bindner and Poirot (2016), above n 82 at 4.

[84] UNSC, 'Islamic State/Da'esh Using Social Media, Extortion to Retain Might after Military Setbacks, Territory Loss, Top Counter-Terrorism Official Tells Security Council', UN Doc SC/13202, 8178th meeting (AM) (8 February 2008), www.un.org/press/en/2018/sc13202.doc.htm.

[85] UNSC, Resolution 2253, UN Doc S/RES/2253 (17 December 2015).

countries, this chapter has found that violent ANSAs exercise effective control over the host state's resources to fund their military campaigns. Thus, ANSAs' access to energy resources would motivate them to initiate or continue armed conflicts to achieve their objectives.

Energy resources shape the armed conflicts that take place, both in terms of territorial control objectives and the duration and intensity of the armed conflicts, all of which can affect the internal cohesion of the activities of ANSAs. This chapter has also demonstrated that in situations where a violent ANSA exercises effective control over natural resources in energy-rich countries, governments sometimes lose power as a result. In clarifying how Islamic State gained its strong position in both Iraq and Syria, the chapter has shown that Iraqi and Syrian oil has not been its sole financial source. The group enhanced its military campaign by exercising its control over the Iraqi and Syrian oil fields, which was key to its wide-ranging development in the region. Its economic assets allowed Islamic State to create civil governance mechanisms in order to establish a local governmental and legal system.

The rationale behind this focus on Islamic State's legal status and the role of energy resources in fuelling the war is to establish grounds for the main arguments of this book in terms of using force against Islamic State, and addressing *jus ad bellum* and *jus in bello* requirements in the war. While *jus ad bellum* restricts the choice of military target, the necessity and proportionality of attacks on the Iraqi and Syrian energy resources occupied by Islamic State come into question during the extraterritorial military interventions against Islamic State. Beyond the significance of the targeting requirements during self-defence operations, as subject to *jus ad bellum*, a particular difficulty arises from the idea that the Iraqi and Syrian energy resources occupied by Islamic State are considered to be war-sustaining capabilities. Subject to *jus in bello*, the destruction of energy resources, which are part of both the natural environment and state property during hostilities, as related to the objectives that contribute to the 'war-fighting' or 'war-sustaining capability' of the enemy, needs to be evaluated in the context of applicable law, which will be discussed in Chapter 3.

Having thus demonstrated the overlap between energy resources and armed conflicts, Chapter 3 will attempt to evaluate the legality of the use of force by external powers against Islamic State, and the destruction of energy resources controlled by the group in Iraq and Syria.

2

The War with Islamic State as a Matter of Jus ad Bellum

'… the rhetoric of the "war on terror" has some significance for the law on the use of force in that it has been used to justify a wide right of self-defence against non-state actors …'.[1]

I. INTRODUCTION

The purpose of Chapter 2 is to examine the legal justifications for military intervention by foreign states against Islamic State in both Iraq and Syria. The rationale behind this focus on the war with Islamic State as a matter of *jus ad bellum* is the observation that the legality of the extraterritorial use of armed force against violent ANSAs which are not under the effective control of the host state is still a matter of controversy. This makes it necessary to clarify the main factors that motivated the external powers' military intervention against Islamic State.

This chapter seeks clarification on these issues primarily by examining the general principle of the prohibition on the use of force in international law. It then evaluates the alleged exceptions to this principle in Article 2(4) of the UN Charter. During analysing the legal requirements for the use of force in international law, significant attention is also given in this chapter to two different forms of international military intervention: intervention based on the 'unwilling or unable theory', which is mainly the US's approach to using force against ANSAs based in foreign territories; and military assistance on request, and with the consent of the territorial state to the use of military force.

The purpose of this chapter is to analyse the lawfulness of the use of force against Islamic State, to see whether and to what extent the US-led coalition and Turkey's military interventions against Islamic State based on the 'unwilling or unable theory', and Iranian and Russian military intervention by request of the host state, have been influential in the course of the 'war on terrorism'.

[1] CD Gray, *International Law and the Use of Force* (Oxford, Oxford University Press, 2008) 2.

The examination of these questions plays a significant role in the final chapter of the book, below, by allowing the author to draw well-founded conclusions on the legality of the destruction of energy resources controlled by ANSAs.

II. MILITARY INTERVENTIONS AGAINST ISLAMIC STATE

In this chapter, I have distinguished between two different justifications offered by third countries who have intervened and used force against Islamic State in Iraq and Syria. The first is military intervention at the host state's request/invitation. Both Iran and Russia intervened in the Syrian civil war at the request, and on the side of, the Syrian government, and the US-led coalition's intervention in Iraq was in response to the Iraqi central government's request. The second justification for military intervention is based on the theory of the unwillingness or inability of the host state to fight the aggressor, in this case Islamic State. Examples of this are Turkey's intervention in Iraq and Syria and the US-led coalition's intervention in Syria. The Syrian Civil War, which erupted in 2011, allowed Islamic State to turn the crisis into an opportunity by conquering territories in both Iraq and Syria.

In this particular context, it is necessary to evaluate in a legal sense the external powers' military intervention in both countries under the justifying conditions of military intervention based on the 'unwilling or unable theory' and military assistance on request.

A. Introductory Remarks

The international community witnessed a gradual decline in the number of inter-state armed conflicts around the world after the end of the Cold War. Now, the use of military force by military coalitions such as the North Atlantic Treaty Organization (NATO) against states and ANSAs, such as in Kuwait (1991), Bosnia and Kosovo (1990s), Afghanistan (from 2001), Iraq (from 2003), Libya (2011), and finally the US-led coalition's warfare against Islamic State in Iraq and Syria (from 2014), have put controversies surrounding inter-state armed conflict back on the agenda.

Principally, the legality of the use of force by external powers in self-defence against violent ANSAs inside a third state's boundaries that host such groups is disputed, except in situations where these groups are under the effective control of the host state. Nevertheless, because of the rise of Islamic State in Syria and Iraq, controversies surrounding the legality and acceptability of the use of military force against the group, where the host state is unable or unwilling to deal with the threat, have arisen between states.

Although the 'unwilling or unable theory' has no place in the ICJ's jurisprudence, adoption of Resolution 2249 by the UNSC in 2015, which called on states to use all necessary measures to fight Islamic State in Syria, demonstrated the importance of combatting Islamic State's violent terrorist attacks. However, the ambiguous language of Resolution 2249 (2015) allowed for different interpretations, which have allowed external powers such as Turkey (both in Iraq and Syria) and the US-led military coalition in Syria to use military force without the consent[2] of the host government. According to the US webpage of Operation Inherent Resolve, a total of ten states – the US, Canada, France, Australia, Bahrain, Jordan, Saudi Arabia, Turkey, the United Arab Emirates and the UK – participated in a total 3,350 US-led airstrikes in Syria until 3 February 2016.[3]

Considering the complex problems and consequences of the military intervention in Syria, the case of Islamic State is very significant. Admittedly, justifications for using military force in Syria are among the most important and emotive issues facing the international community, which make it essential to discuss the use of force in the context of contemporary international law. In this regard, the legal basis for exercising the right of self-defence and the legality of the use of military force in self-defence against ANSAs will be evaluated in the context of the UN Charter and other relevant sources of international law.

In order to curtail the freedom of states to use force to settle international disputes, the use of force in international law has been prohibited for the first time by the UN Charter. In accordance with the Charter, in order to maintain international peace and security, all members of the UN shall settle their international disputes peacefully. Hence, the Charter states in Article 2(4) that:

> All Members shall refrain in their international relations from the threat or use of force against the territorial integrity or political independence of any state, or in any other manner inconsistent with the Purposes of the [UN].

This also means that no state can use force for political objectives in international relations. This is an extensive prohibition which has been accepted as one of the primary customary rules of international law. In this respect, the ICJ's judgment on the merits in the case concerning the *Military and Paramilitary Activities in and against Nicaragua* (the *Nicaragua* case) provides further confirmation of its validity. The principle of the prohibition on the use of force, as expressed in Article 2, Paragraph 4 of the Charter of the [UN], may be found in the fact that it is frequently referred to in statements by state representatives as being not only a principle of customary international law but also a fundamental or cardinal principle of such a law.[4]

[2] See K Bannelier-Christakis, 'Military Interventions against ISIL in Iraq, Syria and Libya, and the Legal Basis of Consent' (2016) 29 *Leiden Journal of International Law* 743. See also L O'Connor, 'Legality of the Use of Force in Syria against Islamic State and the Khorasan Group' (2016) 3 *Journal on the Use of Force and International Law* 70.

[3] See 'Operation Inherent Resolve: Targeted Operations against ISIL Terrorists', US Department of Defence (1 January 2017), www.defense.gov/News/Special-Reports/0814_Inherent-Resolve.

[4] *Case Concerning Military and Paramilitary Activities in and against Nicaragua (Nicaragua v United States of America)*, Judgment, ICJ Reports (27 June 1986), para 190. For a more general

Nevertheless, there are some exceptional situations involving lawful use of military force by states in the course of halting or counteracting armed aggression. This approach is clarified by the UN Charter, which states in Article 51 that:

> Nothing in the present Charter shall impair the inherent right of individual or collective self-defence if an armed attack occurs against a Member of the [UN] until the [UNSC] has taken measures necessary to maintain international peace and security. Measures taken by Members in the exercise of this right of self-defence shall be immediately reported to the [UNSC] and shall not in any way affect the authority and responsibility of the [UNSC] under the present Charter to take at any time such action as it deems necessary in order to maintain or restore international peace and security.

Similarly, Resolution 3314 (1974) of the UN General Assembly (UNGA) on the Definition of Aggression states that the UNSC, in accordance with Article 39 of the Charter of the UN, shall determine the existence of any threat to the peace, breach of the peace or act of aggression and shall make recommendations, or decide what measures shall be taken in accordance with Articles 41 and 42, to maintain or restore international peace and security.[5] This is combined with the fact that Article 51 of the UN Charter has foreseen two exceptions to the prohibition of the use of military force in international relations:

(a) the use of military force by a state member only when it has first suffered an armed attack; and
(b) the use of military force, directly or indirectly, by the UN Security Council as the collective security system laid out in Chapter VII of the Charter (Articles 39, 42, 53).

In these contexts, as a response to an armed attack, the right of self-defence is also subject to the customary international legal conditions of 'necessity' and 'proportionality' reaffirmed by the ICJ in its *Advisory Opinion on the Legality of the Threat or Use of Nuclear Weapons* (1996). According to the ICJ, the submission of the exercise of the right of self-defence to the conditions of necessity and proportionality is a rule of customary international law. As the Court stated in the *Nicaragua* case, there is a specific rule whereby self-defence would only permit measures that are proportional to the initial attack and are necessary to respond to it – a rule well established in customary international law. The Court has also pointed out that this dual condition applies equally to Article 51 of the Charter, whatever the means of force employed.[6] This means, therefore,

assessment, see TM Franck, 'On Proportionality of Countermeasures in International Law' (2008) 102 *American Journal of International Law* 715, 729; C Kahgan, 'Jus Cogens and the Inherent Right to Self-Defense' (1997) 3 *ILSA Journal of International & Comparative Law* 767, 780–81.

[5] UNGA, Resolution 3314, Definition of Aggression, UN Doc 3314 (XXIX) (14 December 1974).

[6] *Legality of the Threat or Use of Nuclear Weapons*, Advisory Opinion, ICJ Reports (8 July 1996), para 41.

that both conditions must be met in order to justify armed force used in legitimate self-defence under the UN system.

The necessity principle is rooted in the Webster formula of the *Caroline* case. According to the conditions presented by Daniel Webster regarding the right of self-defence in the *Caroline* incident, self-defence is only justified 'if the necessity of that self-defence is instant, overwhelming, and leaving no choice of means, and no moment for deliberation'.[7] In other words, the victim state can use military force only when there is no reasonable peaceful alternative to preventing armed aggression.

Notably, the victim state can only exercise the right of self-defence under the conditions mentioned above by detecting the source of an illegal armed attack by a state or armed group. In this regard, one of the controversial issues facing the international community is the legality and applicability of the right of self-defence against ANSAs. First of all, it is required to answer the question of whether an attack by an armed group allows a state to exercise its inherent right of self-defence by using military force that would legally be regarded as a violation of Article 2(4) of the UN Charter. The answer will be positive if the armed attack could be imputed to a state. By contrast, the answer would be controversial if the armed attack could not be attributed to a territorial state. This has been challenged by Chatham House Principles, in which it is stated that 'Article 51 is not confined to self-defence in response to attacks by states'.[8] In other words, the wording of Article 51 – 'if an armed attack occurs against a member of the [UN]' – has only designated 'states' as targets of an armed attack and has remained silent on the issue of who conducted the initial attack.

Despite the fact that all states need to defend themselves against armed aggression by other states or ANSAs, they cannot act in a manner contrary to Article 51 of the UN Charter. The ICJ characterised an armed attack in the *Nicaragua* case as follows:

> … it may be considered to be agreed that an armed attack must be understood as including not merely action by regular armed forces across an international border, but also 'the sending by or on behalf of a state of armed bands, groups, irregulars or mercenaries, which carry out acts of armed force against another state of such gravity

[7] Letter from Secretary of State Daniel Webster to British Minister to the United States, Lord Alexander Baring Ashburton (6 August 1842), https://avalon.law.yale.edu/19th_century/br-1842d.asp. See for more discussion, R Jennings, 'The Caroline and McLeod Cases' (1938) 32 *American Journal of International Law* 82; E Collins and MA Rogoff, 'The Caroline Incident of 1837, the McLeod Affair of 1840–1841, and the Development of International Law' (1990) 20 *American Review of Canadian Studies* 81; AC Arend, 'International Law and the Preemptive Use of Military Force' (2003) 26 *The Washington Quarterly* 89; JA Green, 'Docking the Caroline: Understanding the Relevance of the Formula in Contemporary Customary International Law Concerning Self-Defence' (2006) 14 *Cardozo Journal of International and Comparative Law* 429.

[8] E Wilmshurst, 'The Chatham House Principles of International Law on the Use of Force in Self-Defence' (2006) 55 *International and Comparative Law Quarterly* 963, 969.

> as to amount to (inter alia) an actual armed attack conducted by regular forces, or its substantial involvement therein'.[9]

This description, contained in Article 3 paragraph (g) of the Definition of Aggression annexed to UNGA Resolution 3314 (1974), may be taken to reflect customary international law. The Court sees no reason to deny that, in customary international law, the prohibition of armed attacks may apply to the sending by a state of armed forces to the territory of another state, if such an operation, because of its scale and effects, would have been classified as an armed attack rather than as a mere frontier incident had it been carried out by regular armed forces.[10]

In this sense, therefore, an armed attack will give rise to the inherent right of individual or collective self-defence foreseen in Article 51 of the UN Charter only when another state is the aggressor. This means that the ICJ has not recognised the right of self-defence where there is no link between the territorial state and ANSAs. However, as Judge Pieter H Koojmans stated, 'the [ICJ] refrains from taking a position with regard to the question whether the threshold set out in the Nicaragua judgement is still in conformity with contemporary international law'.[11] He believes that although the necessity of launching an armed attack by another state has been the generally accepted interpretation for more than 50 years, such an interpretation no longer seems to be shared by the UNSC since in Resolutions 1368 (2001)[12] and 1373 (2001)[13] the Council recognises the inherent right of individual or collective self-defence without making any reference to an armed attack by a state. In these resolutions, the Council stated that all acts of international terrorism were a threat to international peace and security, regardless of who was responsible.[14] From this perspective, therefore, it seems clear that there is a space for an interpretation accepting that ANSAs can also be the perpetrators of an act permitting the exercise of the right of self-defence against a perpetrator that is not necessarily identified as a state.[15] In summary, if armed attacks are carried out by irregular forces from a state's territory against a neighbouring state, they are still armed attacks even though they cannot be attributed to the territorial state.

[9] *Case Concerning Military and Paramilitary Activities in and against Nicaragua* (27 June 1986), above n 4 at para 195.

[10] Ibid.

[11] *Case Concerning Armed Activities on the Territory of the Congo (Democratic Republic of the Congo v Uganda)*, Judgment, ICJ Reports (19 December 2005), 'Separate Opinion of Judge Koojmans', para 25.

[12] UNSC, Resolution 1368, UN Doc S/RES/1368 (12 September 2001).

[13] UNSC, Resolution 1373, UN Doc S/RES/1373 (28 September 2001).

[14] *Case Concerning Armed Activities on the Territory of the Congo* (19 December 2005), above n 11 at para 28.

[15] D Janse, 'International Terrorism and Self-Defence' (2006) 36 *Israel Yearbook on Human Rights* 149, 166; N Tsagourias, 'Self-Defence against Non-State Actors: The Interaction between Self-Defence as a Primary Rule and Self-Defence as a Secondary Rule' (2016) 29 *Leiden Journal of International Law* 801, 819.

It would be unreasonable to deny the victim state the right of self-defence merely because there is no 'attacker state', and the UN Charter does not so require.[16] Such an approach can be observed in state practice, in which the US used military force against al-Qaeda groups based in Afghanistan,[17] especially after the 11 September 2001 attacks. The day after the attacks, the US informed the UNSC that it had been the victim of an armed attack by al-Qaeda and declared its intent to respond under Article 51 of the UN Charter. In response, the UNSC adopted Resolutions 1368 (2001) and 1373 (2001) in which the Council recognised the inherent right of individual or collective self-defence in accordance with the UN Charter without making any reference to an armed attack by a state.

This action was not a Chapter VII authorisation to use force, but rather a confirmation that the US could invoke its right to respond with force under Article 51 of the UN Charter, despite the fact that al-Qaeda was an ANSA.[18]

Taking the ICJ and the UNSC's practices into account, state practice is currently based on the use of force in self-defence against ANSAs under the interpretation of Article 51 of the UN Charter. It has, however, been a ground for the formation of the 'unwilling or unable theory', which is recognised as a key motivation for 'extraterritorial use of force' against ANSAs based in another state. According to this theory, using extraterritorial force against ANSAs depends on a determination that the relevant ANSAs perpetrated an armed attack against the host state or other states, and the host state is 'unable or unwilling' to suppress the threat. This is, however, quite controversial since it grants permission for the use of force based on that other state's own assessment of the situation. Moreover, an armed attack is still the primary requirement for the use of force in self-defence, and military actions in self-defence against the ANSAs which have perpetrated the armed attack should be compatible with the general rules of *jus in bello*, including the distinction between civilian and military objectives, proportionality and necessity. In that sense, even where self-defence becomes essentially legitimate, operations must be guided by the basic rules of *jus in bello*, which is true of all uses of force, with defensive armed operations being no exception.[19]

[16] *Case Concerning Armed Activities on the Territory of the Congo* (19 December 2005), above n 11 at para 30.

[17] L Moir, *Reappraising the Resort to Force: International Law, Jus ad Bellum and the War on Terror* (Oxford, Hart Publishing, 2010) 151; T Ruys, 'Quo Vadit Jus ad Bellum? A Legal Analysis of Turkey's Military Operations against the PKK in Northern Iraq' (2008) 9 *Melbourne Journal of International Law* 334, 334.

[18] V Lanovoy, 'The Use of Force by Non-State Actors and the Limits of Attribution of Conduct' (2017) 28 *European Journal of International Law* 563, 568; MP Scharf, 'How the War against ISIS Changed International Law' (2016) 48 *Case Western Reserve Journal of International Law* 1, 27–28; ND White, *Democracy Goes to War: British Military Deployments under International Law* (Oxford, Oxford University Press, 2009) 195.

[19] Y Dinstein, *War, Aggression and Self-Defence* (Cambridge, Cambridge University Press, 2012) 195.

Furthermore, it seems that the ICJ has not recognised the legal effectiveness of the 'unwilling or unable theory' and has pointed out that 'there is no rule in customary international law permitting another state to exercise the right of self-defence based on its own assessment of the situation'.[20] The use of force based on the 'unwilling or unable theory' could, thus, be considered as a political consideration that has no basis in customary international law.[21] As is rightly pointed out by Oliver Corten, by conferring every state with the power to unilaterally implement its conception of the necessities of the war against terrorism, the 'unwilling and unable theory' bypasses, if not simply ignores, this core provision along with the entire collective security system established by the UN Charter. This is perhaps why the vast majority of states have not accepted any 'unwilling or unable theory', either in the Syrian case or more generally.[22] More importantly, UNSC Resolution 2249 (2015), which has been interpreted as the main basis for the extraterritorial use of force against Islamic State in Syria, cannot be used as authorisation to prove that the UNSC endorsed 'unwilling or unable' as a justification for the use of force against Islamic State due to the absence of any agreement between coalition members themselves, any endorsement by other UN members, and any acceptance and confirmation by UNSC Resolution 2249 (2015). In essence, the Resolution accepts a very broad reading of the right to use force in self-defence and provides no support for the theory.[23]

When discussing state practice, it is significant to look at the legal basis for the US-led coalition's military intervention and use of force against Islamic State in Syria. Indeed, the military operations of the US-led military coalition on Islamic State have brought new challenges to international law regarding inter-state armed conflicts, taking into consideration the unwillingness and inability of Syria – as a weak state hosting Islamic State – to control and respond to its terrorist actions. This has provided the justification for the use of extraterritorial military force based on collective self-defence in Syria. Far from the importance of the legality and acceptability of the unwillingness or inability of the host state to prevent and suppress terrorist acts in its territory, the external powers' position in the conflict-affected countries will be discussed in Chapter 3 as a controversial and crucial question facing the international community.

The 'unwilling or unable theory' has recently become one of the most controversial issues in international law among scholars of international relations. In fact, the emergence of the theory was a reaction to the increasing threats of ANSAs

[20] *Case Concerning Military and Paramilitary Activities in and against Nicaragua* (27 June 1986), above n 4 at para 195.

[21] See O Corten, 'The 'Unwilling or Unable' Test: Has It Been, and Could It Be, Accepted?' (2016) 29 *Leiden Journal of International Law* 777, 782.

[22] Ibid, at 798.

[23] See K Bannelier-Christakis, 'The Joint Committee's Drones Report: Far-Reaching Conclusions on Self-Defence Based on a Dubious Reading of Resolution 2249' (2016) 3 *Journal on the Use of Force and International Law* 217; T Christakis, 'Challenging the 'Unwilling or Unable' Test' (2017) 77 *Heidelberg Journal of International Law* 19.

operating from the territory of states that are unable or unwilling to prevent the threats. The theory was put forward by the US in the context of their incursion into Cambodia in 1970 to counter North Vietnam's blatant violation of Cambodia's neutrality, since Cambodia was unwilling or unable to defend its neutral status.[24]

It has also been used as a questionable form of using force to justify collective military operations within a state that is not able to prevent terrorist violations within its territory, which is contrary to the UN Charter. It seems that this is an objective approach to the unwillingness or inability of the host state to prevent terrorist violations. This is an approach that might undermine stability and international peace and security. Accordingly, the world powers used this theory as a basis for their military presence within the territories of states that host violent ANSAs. However, it appears that use of force under the 'unwilling or unable theory' as a legal discourse has impoverished state sovereignty. In other words, this is proof that the 'unwilling or unable theory' has been used as a standard to simplify a change in the international laws protecting state sovereignty.

According to the 'unwilling or unable theory', the ineffectiveness of the host state to prevent its territory from being used by groups to launch an armed attack against another state will require the victim state to take action within its territory. Considering the ambiguous state practice, use of military force by victim states within the sovereign territory of host states is justified by some states under the 'unwilling or unable theory'. For instance, Israel's use of military force against the Palestinian Liberation Organisation (PLO) and Hezbollah,[25] the use of military force against the Kurdish Workers' Party (*Partiya Karkerên Kurdistanê*, PKK) in Iraq by Turkey in 2011,[26] the use of military force by the UK against suspected militants in Afghanistan,[27] and the use of military force by Russia in Georgia against Chechen rebels in response to their violent attacks in Russia[28] have all been justified by the unwillingness or inability of the host states to suppress rebel armed attacks. In a situation in which a host state is

[24] B Cuddy, *Wider War: American Force in Vietnam, International Law, and the Transformation of Armed Conflict, 1961–1977* (PhD Dissertation, University of Cornell, 2016), 84; B Cuddy, 'Was It Legal for the US to Bomb Cambodia?', *New York Times* (12 December 2017), www.nytimes.com/2017/12/12/opinion/america-cambodia-bomb.html.

[25] From a Russian perspective, the unwillingness or inability of the host state to prevent the use of its territory to attack another state is the legal basis for the taking all necessary measures in defence by all members of the UNSC. See Letter dated 17 July 1981 from the Chargé d'affairs a.i. Mission of Lebanon to the United Nations addressed to the President of the Security Council (S/14596), UN SCOR, 36th session, 2292d meeting at 5, UN Doc S/PV.2292 (17 July 1981).

[26] For more information, see Letter of Turkish Ministry of Foreign Affairs addressed to the UN Secretary-General and to the President of the UN Security Council, UN Doc S/1996/479 (2 July 1996).

[27] For a detailed assessment of the UK's operations in Afghanistan, see J Quigley, 'The Afghanistan War and Self-Defense' (2003) 37 *Valparaiso University Law Review* 541; PCR Terry, 'The War in Afghanistan – Was the Use of Force Legal and/or Wise?' (2011) 9 *New Zealand Yearbook of International Law* 969; L Brooke-Holland, *Unmanned Aerial Vehicles (Drones): An Introduction* (London, House of Commons Library, 2012).

[28] See Letter of Permanent Representative of the Russian Federation to the UN addressed to the UN Secretary-General, Annex, UN Doc S/2002/1012/Annex (12 September 2002).

unable or unwilling to prevent its territory from being used as a base of terrorist attacks of violent ANSAs, the victim states are left with little choice, contrary to their obligations under the customary international law. Either they respect the host state's territorial integrity at great risk to their own security, or they violate the host state's sovereignty and territorial integrity.[29] Parallel to this, the ICJ *Nicaragua* case reaffirmed that 'if self-defence is advanced as a justification for measures which would otherwise be in breach of both the principle of customary international law and of that contained in the Charter, it is to be expected that the conditions of the Charter should be respected'.[30]

In November 2015, British Prime Minister David Cameron noted that 'the Assad regime is unwilling and/or unable to take action necessary to prevent [Islamic State's] continuing attack on Iraq or indeed attacks on us'.[31] Responding to Islamic State's cross-border terrorist operations, the US-led coalition used force inside Syria based on the right of collective self-defence.

The US informed the UNSC in September 2014 that it relied on Article 51 of the UN Charter as the legal basis for conducting airstrikes against Islamic State in Syria in support of Iraq, which hosts thousands of US forces.[32] According to the US, Islamic State and other terrorist groups in Syria are a threat not only to Iraq but also to many other countries, including the US and their partners in the region and beyond. States must be able to defend themselves in accordance with the inherent right of individual and collective self-defence, as reflected in Article 51 of the UN Charter, when, as is the case here, the government of the state where the threat is located is 'unwilling or unable' to prevent the use of its territory for such attacks. The Syrian regime has shown that it cannot, or will not, effectively confront these terrorist safe havens itself. Accordingly, the US initiated necessary and proportionate military actions in Syria in order to eliminate the ongoing threat by Islamic State to Iraq, including the protection of Iraqi citizens from further attacks and by enabling Iraqi forces to regain control of its borders. In addition, the US initiated military actions in Syria against al-Qaeda elements known as the Khorasan Group to address terrorist threats that they posed to the US and their partners and allies.[33]

[29] KN Trapp, 'Back to Basics: Necessity, Proportionality, and the Right of Self-Defence against Non-State Terrorist Actors' (2007) 56 *International and Comparative Law Quarterly* 141, 147.

[30] *Case Concerning Military and Paramilitary Activities in and against Nicaragua* (27 June 1986), above n 4 at para 200.

[31] See 'PM Statement Responding to FAC Report on Military Operations in Syria', *UK Prime Minister's Office* (26 November 2015), www.gov.uk/government/speeches/pm-statement-responding-to-fac-report-on-military-operations-in-syria.

[32] S Arrington Sliney, 'Right to Act: United States Legal Basis Under the Law of Armed Conflict to Pursue the Islamic State in Syria' (2015) 6 *University of Miami National Security & Armed Conflict Law Review* 1, 19–22; S Sengupta, 'US Invokes Iraq's Defense in Legal Justification of Syria Strikes', *New York Times* (23 September 2014), www.nytimes.com/2014/09/24/us/politics/us-invokes-defense-of-iraq-in-saying-strikes-on-syria-are-legal.html.

[33] See Letter dated 23 September 2014 from the Permanent Representative of the United States of America to the United Nations addressed to the Secretary-General, UN Doc S/2014/695 (23 September 2014).

The point here is that the Syrian government has not consented to such operations within its territory and has therefore characterised them as an unlawful act, and a violation of its sovereignty and territorial integrity.[34] Considering that all the states participating in the US-led coalition challenge the legitimacy of Bashar al-Assad's regime, Syria reacted strongly to the US airstrikes, declaring that any action of any kind without the consent of the Syrian government would be an attack on Syria itself.[35]

To better articulate the US-led coalition's armed operations against Islamic State in Syria as collective self-defence, the conditions in which the use of armed force is accepted need to be evaluated as a matter of contemporary international law. As a practical matter, there is a generally accepted prohibition of the use of armed force clarified by Article 2(4) of the UN Charter. The most commonly held opinion is that there are just two exceptions to this prohibition outlined in the UN Charter, namely individual and collective self-defence (Article 51) and the use of force authorised by the UNSC in order to maintain or restore international peace and security (Article 39).[36] Aside from the above-mentioned exceptions, the use of force to end human rights violations and humanitarian crises within the state in which it takes place (humanitarian intervention) is still considered to be an unlawful act by a majority of states and scholars, and therefore remains controversial.[37]

Despite the generally accepted exceptions to the prohibition on the use of force, military intervention in the Iraqi and Syrian civil wars to prevent the growing threat from Islamic State has been a subject of controversy. Civil wars have already been classified as non-international armed conflicts. According to the International Committee of the Red Cross (ICRC), in all cases of armed conflict which are not of an international character, especially cases of civil war, colonial conflicts or religious wars, which may occur in the territory of one or more of the High Contracting Parties, the implementing of the principles of the Third Geneva Convention shall be obligatory on each of the adversaries.[38] However, there is no general consensus among the international community or among academic scholars on the legality of military interventions, both by request and for humanitarian purposes in civil wars.

[34] See Identical Letters dated 16 September 2015 from the Permanent Representative of the Syrian Arab Republic to the United Nations addressed to the Secretary-General and the President of the Security Council, UN Doc S/2015/718 (17 September 2015).

[35] Bannelier-Christakis, 'Military Interventions' (2016), above n 2 at 770; I Black, 'ISIS Air Strikes: Obama's Plan Condemned by Syria, Russia and Iran', *The Guardian* (12 September 2014), www.theguardian.com/world/2014/sep/11/assad-moscow-tehran-condemn-obama-isis-air-strike-plan.

[36] R Wolfrum and C Philipp, *United Nations: Law and Policies and Practice – Volume II* (Verlag CH, Beck Munchen, 1995) 1162.

[37] NS Rodley, 'Collective Intervention to Protect Human Rights and Civilian Populations: The Legal Framework' in N Rodley (ed), *To Loose the Bands of Wickedness: International Intervention in Defence of Human Rights* (London, Brassey's, 1992) 29; A Roberts, 'Humanitarian War: Military Intervention and Human Rights' (1993) 69 *International Affairs* 429, 445.

[38] JS Pictet (ed), *Commentary on the Third Geneva Convention* (Geneva, ICRC Press, 1960) 31.

It seems, therefore, that military interventions in civil wars must have a legal justification for taking necessary action. Otherwise, they would be characterised as a violation of the principle of the prohibition on the use of force under Article 2(4) of the UN Charter, which calls for the prohibition of threats or use of force against the territorial integrity or political independence of any state.[39] In this case, it seems that the request or consent of the territorial state involved in an armed conflict is the only justification that constitutes a legal basis for military intervention by a third party to assist the host state in self-defence.

At its core, military intervention by request is the consent given by the legitimate government of a victim state confronted with an internal armed conflict to an external power (or powers) to use armed force within the victim state's territory to support it against insurgency, terrorism or other violent groups. In addition, it could also mean an invitation for allies to assist the victim state in using military aggression for self-defence. The legality of military intervention by request has been confirmed by UNGA Resolution 3314 (1974), in which the UNGA has indirectly recognised the validity of military intervention by request. According to Article 3(e) of the Resolution, the use of the armed forces of one state, which are within the territory of another state with the agreement of the receiving state is an act of aggression where it is in contravention of the conditions provided for in the agreement or any extension of their presence in such territory beyond the termination of the agreement.[40]

Military intervention at the request, or with the consent, of the legitimate government of the requesting state engaged in a civil war has already been clarified in the ICJ *Nicaragua* case. The ICJ provides an elaborate and conducive account where it confirms that, contrary to the incompatibility of the military intervention by a mere request for assistance made by an opposition group in another state with the principle of non-intervention (as a customary international law), military intervention is permissible at the request of the legitimate government of a state.[41] Therefore, it is clear that intervention by request is not inconsistent with the principle of the sovereign equality of states,[42] according to which the territorial integrity and political independence of the states are inviolable.

In light of this analysis, therefore, no state can legally intervene in another state's internal affairs under any circumstance except under self-defence, UNSC authorisation and the host state's consent or when a state requests military assistance. As noted above, there is no rule permitting the use of force in collective

[39] ILC, 'Draft Articles on the Law of Treaties' (1996) 2 *Yearbook of the International Law Commission* 187, 247.

[40] UNGA, Resolution 3314, Definition of Aggression, UN Doc 3314 (XXIX) (14 December 1974).

[41] *Case Concerning Military and Paramilitary Activities in and against Nicaragua* (27 June 1986), above n 4 at para 246.

[42] See Declaration on Principles of International Law Concerning Friendly Relations and Co-operation Among States in Accordance with the Charter of the United Nations. UNGA, Resolution 2625, UN Doc A/RES/25/2625 (24 October 1970).

self-defence in the absence of a request by the territorial state (or where the host state consents to another state's use of force in its territory) which regards itself as the victim of an armed attack. Within this context, there is no question of violating the obligation to refrain from the use of force when consent is given by the host state. At this point, the third parties can justify their military intervention in armed conflicts by referring to the deliberate exception provided by Article 51 of the UN Charter, which provides for the right of collective self-defence by invitation of the victim state.[43]

In the absence of an invitation or consent of the host state, therefore, no state can use military aggression against any armed group that is active within another state's territory. Simply put, it is difficult to accept that states have the legal right to intervene in another state's national affairs contrary to the general principles of international law, including the obligation to respect the sovereignty, territorial integrity and non-intervention in the internal affairs of states.

As pointed out by the ICJ in the *Nicaragua* case, the principle of non-intervention involves the right of every sovereign state to conduct its affairs without outside interference. Although there are frequent violations of this principle, the Court considers that it is part and parcel of customary international law. According to the Court, respect for territorial sovereignty between independent states is an essential foundation of international relations,[44] and international law also requires political integrity to be respected. Expressions of an *opinio juris* regarding the existence of the principle of non-intervention in customary international law are numerous and easy to find.[45]

With regard to the unwillingness or inability of Syria to suppress the threat of violent ANSAs, it might be argued that it has not been successful in fighting the terrorist activities of Islamic State and the other terrorist groups within its sovereign territory. Yet external interventions in self-defence against ANSAs within the territory of the host state could only be justified if the victim states had already reported their ineffectiveness to the UNSC.[46] In this way, the UNSC can determine the existence of any threat to the victim state. In other words, the UNSC would make an appropriate decision regarding the host state's inability or unwillingness to suppress the threat.

[43] E Lumsden, 'An Uneasy Peace: Multilateral Military Intervention in Civil Wars' (2003) 35 *New York University Journal of International Law and Politics* 795, 800. See also L Doswald-Beck, 'The Legal Validity of Military Intervention by Invitation of the Government' (1985) 56 *British Yearbook of International Law* 189.

[44] *Corfu Channel Case*, Judgement, ICJ Reports (9 April 1949), 35.

[45] *Case Concerning Military and Paramilitary Activities in and against Nicaragua* (27 June 1986), above n 4 at para 202. For a discussion, see S Talmon, 'Determining Customary International Law: The ICJ's Methodology between Induction, Deduction and Assertion' (2015) 26 *European Journal of International Law* 417, 419–23.

[46] See in general, JA Green, 'The Article 51 Reporting Requirement for Self-Defense Actions' (2015) 55 *Virginia Journal of International Law* 563; N van der Steenhoven, 'Conduct and Subsequent Practice by States in the Application of the Requirement to Report Under UN Charter Article 51' (2019) 6 *Journal on the Use of Force and International Law* 242.

Ostensibly, using force against violent groups and ANSAs within the territory of another state based on the unwillingness or inability of the state in question to halt the threat from these groups, is an action beyond the current international legal system and is leading to the creation of new laws regarding the use of force. Considering the adverse consequences of military interventions based on this theory (ie an increase in the number of recorded casualties), it is difficult to allege that the external powers' desire to play the role of 'saviours' in civil wars and internal conflicts without the host state's consent and in the absence of UNSC authorisation is deeply rooted in their humanitarian objectives. In such a tense atmosphere of mistrust, therefore, the humanitarian impacts of a non-international armed conflict, insurgency or repression in the territory of a state that is unwilling or unable to counteract it might not be sufficient to justify the violation of that state's sovereignty. Instead, the warring states must take steps to enhance the effectiveness and the primary function of the UNSC in the maintenance and restoration of international peace and security.[47]

Having discussed the legal framework of the external interventions in civil wars and non-international conflicts, the first issue to be considered is the 'unwilling and unable' theory as a motivating factor in the war with Islamic State in Iraq and Syria.

B. Motivating Factors in the War with Islamic State

i. The US-led Coalition's Intervention against Islamic State in Syria

One of the primary justifications of the US-led coalition for military intervention in Syria has been the use of force in self-defence against an 'imminent armed attack' by Islamic State. According to the UK's Attorney-General, Jeremy Wright, 'Self-defence includes the right to use force in response to both an actual and imminent armed attack by [the ANSAs]'.[48] These statements are reminiscent of Attorney-General Lord Goldsmith's declaration on 21 April 2004 on Britain's position on the right to preventive self-defence, when he stated that 'It is … the Government's view that international law permits the use of force in

[47] This also indicates that the UNSC is primarily responsible for the maintenance of international peace and security and is therefore the primary agent for interpreting and identifying conflict situations, and the necessity and consequences of the use of force in self-defence. Otherwise, devising and applying the theory in simulated civil wars and non-international conflicts would undermine the sovereignty of independent states. Such a practice would also bring the international community back to imperialism as a process to extend powerful states' rule over weak and failed states by using armed force, which would enable them to take political and economic control of the states in question. For a more general assessment, see V Lowe (2010), *The United Nations Security Council and War: The Evolution of Thought and Practice since 1945* (Oxford, Oxford University Press, 2010) 5.

[48] See The Rt Hon Jeremy Wright QC MP, 'The Modern Law of Self-Defense', *EJIL: Talk!* (11 January 2017), https://www.ejiltalk.org/the-modern-law-of-self-defence/.

self-defence against an imminent attack, but does not authorise the use of force to mount a pre-emptive strike against a threat that is more remote'.[49]

At its core, this is a 'preventive war', which can be defined as the use of force by a state to repel an attacker before an actual armed attack has taken place, before the enemy army has crossed its border, and before the bombs of the enemy fall upon its territory – or an anticipatory war to prevent future attacks on the state itself.[50] This raises the realisation that Article 51 of the UN Charter only highlights one form of self-defence (a response to an armed attack) without negating other patterns of permissible action in self-defence vouchsafed by customary international law.[51] In that respect, it seems likely that the ICJ does not take a position on the use of force against the imminent threat of an armed attack by ANSAs based on extraterritorial self-defence. In this regard, the ICJ clarified its position in its judgment in the *Nicaragua* case, where the Court stated that:

> In view of the circumstances in which the dispute has arisen, reliance is placed by the parties only on the right of self-defence in the case of an armed attack which has already occurred, and the issue of the lawfulness of a response to the imminent threat of armed attack has not been raised.[52]

The ICJ has also stipulated that:

> The exercise of the right of collective self-defence presupposes that an armed attack has occurred; and it is evident that it is the victim state, being the most directly aware of that fact, which is likely to draw general attention to its plight.[53]

Emphasising the importance of the fight against terrorism, an expansive reading of the right of self-defence under Article 51 of the UN Charter must not prepare the ground for this realistic idea that 'international treaties are enforced only in order to serve the interests of the powerful states'.[54] Pertinently, the UNGA stated in Resolution 3314 (1974) that 'nothing in this Definition shall

[49] 'Statement of the UK Attorney-General, Lord Goldsmith, Speaking in the House of Lords' (21 April 2004), https://publications.parliament.uk/pa/ld200304/ldhansrd/vo040421/text/40421-07.htm.

[50] MF Lohr, 'Legal Analysis of US Military Responses to State-Sponsored International Terrorism' (1985) 34 *Naval Law Review* 1, 16; A Colonomos, 'War in the Face of Doubt: Early Modern Classics and the Preventive Use of Force' in S Recchia and JM Welsh (eds), *Just and Unjust Military Intervention: European Thinkers from Vitoria to Mill* (Cambridge, Cambridge University Press, 2013) 49.

[51] See DW Bowett, *Self-Defense in International Law* (Manchester, Manchester University Press, 1958) 187–92.

[52] *Case Concerning Military and Paramilitary Activities in and against Nicaragua* (27 June 1986), above n 4 at para 194.

[53] Ibid, at para 232.

[54] OA Hathaway, 'Between Power and Principle: A Political Theory of International Law' (2005) 72 *The University of Chicago Law Review* 469, 478. For further discussion, see N Krisch, 'International Law in Times of Hegemony: Unequal Power and the Shaping of the International Legal Order' (2005) 16 *European Journal of International Law* 369; O Schachter, 'The Role of Power in International Law' (1999) 93 *Proceedings of the Annual Meeting (American Society of International Law)* 200.

be construed as in any way enlarging or diminishing the scope of the Charter, including its provisions concerning cases in which the use of force is lawful'.[55]

In the case of Islamic State, the above-mentioned justification used by the external powers for the use of force against imminent threats posed by ANSAs stems from the unwillingness or inability of Syria, as the host state, to counter the threat posed by Islamic State.[56]

The absence of the express authorisation of the UNSC and the consent of the Syrian government to use force against Islamic State in Syria has not been a pleasant situation for the US, as it has generally maintained international security through its military presence in various regions based on the UNSC resolutions. Therefore, the US attempted to justify the coalition's military actions in Syria by using the conception of the unwillingness or inability of the host state, along with a broad interpretation of the right of self-defence contained in Article 51 of the UN Charter. The US-led coalition's involvement in the Syrian civil war has been a most effective venture for seizing the initiative in Syria, which has allegedly been both unwilling and unable to suppress Islamic State's terrorist attacks. However, the US-led intervention in Syria is a subject of controversy given that the nature of the 'unwilling or unable theory' is still disputed. There remains a lack of consensus between states regarding the legality and acceptability of the theory as a justification for the extraterritorial use of military force.

There is debate concerning state practice regarding the acceptability of self-defence against ANSAs in foreign territories as a result of the unwillingness or inability of the host state to suppress the threats posed by these groups. According to the International Law Association report released in 2018, the letters sent to the UNSC by Australia and eight other NATO members – the UK, Canada, Turkey, France, Denmark, Norway, Belgium and the US – concerning the use of military force in collective and individual self-defence against Islamic State in Syria is a demonstration of state practice regarding the self-defence against ANSAs in foreign territory.[57] Some scholars have gone so far as to assert that, whether or not the rule is customary international law, state practice affirms that it is a well-entrenched norm, and the official manuals of the US, UK and Canadian militaries refer to the 'unwilling or unable theory' in the law of neutrality.[58]

[55] UNGA, Resolution 3314, Definition of Aggression, UN Doc 3314 (XXIX) (14 December 1974), Art 6.

[56] Considering state practice, however, it is difficult to claim that the *opinio juris* of states concerning the use of military force against ANSAs in the territorial sovereignty of another state under the 'unwilling or unable theory' has been formed. See in general, SJ Lynn, 'Opinio Juris in Customary International Law' (1990) 15 *Oklahoma City University Law Review* 603.

[57] International Law Association, Final Report on Aggression and the Use of Force (Sydney Conference, 2018) 14–15, www.ila-hq.org/images/ILA/DraftReports/DraftReport_UseOfForce.pdf. See also N Lubell and M Wood, 'The ILA's 2018 Report on Aggression and the Use of Force' (2019) 6 *Journal on the Use of Force and International Law* 4.

[58] AS Deeks, 'Unwilling or Unable: Toward a Normative Framework for Extraterritorial Self-Defense' (2012) 52 *Virginia Journal of International Law* 483, 500. For a critical point of view, see C Martin, 'Challenging and Refining the "Unwilling or Unable" Doctrine' (2019) 52 *Vanderbilt Journal of Transnational Law* 387.

However, this does not provide sufficient justification and evidence for the general acceptance of the theory, and one cannot claim that the right to extraterritorial self-defence against ANSAs whose attacks and armed operations cannot be attributed to the host state has been widely recognised by the international community. For example, the theory is unacceptable to many countries that consider this kind of use of force to be a clear violation of a state's sovereignty and territorial integrity. In a more practical instance, there is clear evidence that the members of the Rio Group (Argentina, Belize, Bolivia, Brazil, Chile, Colombia, Costa Rica, Dominican Republic, Ecuador, El Salvador, Guatemala, Guyana, Honduras, Mexico, Nicaragua, Panama, Paraguay, Peru, Uruguay and Venezuela) did not support any form of the 'unwilling or unable theory' to sanction the use of force against ANSAs in foreign territory when they condemned and opposed the 2008 Colombian attacks of a Fuerzas Armadas Revolucionarias de Colombia (Revolutionary Armed Forces of Colombia) (FARC) camp in Ecuador's territory.[59] In the same way, the Non-Aligned Movement has already rejected the 'unwilling or unable theory' as a justification for military intervention in foreign territory. In 2000, the members of the Movement condemned Turkish military intervention in Iraq against the PKK, mentioning that the actions of the Turkish Armed Forces, conducted under the pretext of fighting guerrilla elements hiding inside Iraqi territory, were in violation of the territorial integrity of Iraq.[60]

In light of this, the actions of the nine members of the North Atlantic Treaty Organisation (NATO) based on factors that are completely arbitrary and unrelated to international law cannot be considered as evidence of the formation of a new customary rule in international law which is legally binding for all states. Accordingly, the lack of consensus among states on the legality of the 'unwilling or unable theory' would be the main obstacle to the establishment of an *opinio juris* regarding the theory's acceptability.[61] Furthermore, under the UN Charter, the use of force is legal only in cases of individual or collective self-defence provided by Article 51 of the Charter, or when the use of force has been authorised by the UNSC under Chapter VII to maintain or restore international peace and security. In this regard, the UNSC has adopted Resolution 2249 (2015), which states that Islamic State is an 'unprecedented threat to international peace and security'.[62] The Resolution calls upon member states that have the capacity to do so to take all necessary measures, in compliance with international law,

[59] See A Gurmendi, 'State Practice Regarding Self-Defence against Non-State Actors: An Incomplete Picture', *Opinio Juris* (17 October 2018), www.opiniojuris.org/2018/10/17/state-practice-regarding-self-defence-against-non-state-actors-an-incomplete-picture/.

[60] T Ruys, *'Armed Attack' and Article 51 of the UN Charter: Evolutions in Customary Law and Practice* (Cambridge, Cambridge University Press, 2010), 432. See also Kevin Jon Heller, 'Do Attacks on ISIS in Syria Justify the "Unwilling or Unable" Test?', *Opinio Juris* (13 December 2014), www.opiniojuris.org/2014/12/13/attacks-isis-syria-justify-unwilling-unable-test/.

[61] See Martin (2019), above n 58 at 412–15.

[62] UNSC, Resolution 2249, UN Doc S/RES/2249 (20 November 2015).

and in particular with the UN Charter, as well as international human rights, refugee and humanitarian law, on the territory under the control of Islamic State also known as [Islamic State], in Syria and Iraq, to redouble and coordinate their efforts to prevent and suppress terrorist acts committed specifically by Islamic State, also known as Da'esh. As there does not seem to be any reference in Resolution 2249 (2015) to Chapter VII of the Charter, this means that the use of force in collective self-defence was not the aim that the UNSC had predicted for the prevention and suppression of terrorist acts committed by Islamic State. The point is that the UNSC used clear language regarding the use of military force by member states against another state in its previous decisions. For instance, on 7 July 1950, the UNSC recommended in Resolution 84[63] that member states provide military force and other assistance and should make this available to a unified command under the US.

In the same way, on 6 August 1990 in Resolution 661,[64] the UNSC affirmed the inherent right of individual or collective self-defence in response to the armed attack by Iraq against Kuwait in accordance with Article 51 of the UN Charter. Accordingly, it seems clear that if the UNSC had directed any military action within the territory of another state, it would have emphasised the necessity of using military force.

In contrast, Resolution 2249 (2015) has called on all member states to be compliant with international law. However, as mentioned above, members of the US-led coalition members – mainly British authorities – tried to justify military intervention in Syria by using a broad interpretation of the UNSC Resolution, since the language of the Resolution regarding the legality of the use of military force in Syria is somewhat ambiguous.[65] Accordingly, they resorted to military force in self-defence under the notion of 'all necessary measures' stipulated in Resolution 2249 (2015). In this respect, the British Ambassador to the UN, Matthew Rycroft, had already stated that 'Today we sent a clear, unambiguous message that there will be no respite for our collective efforts to stop, suppress and destroy [Islamic State]'.[66] However, he adroitly avoided clarifying the legality of the military intervention in Syria within the context of UNSC Resolution 2249 (2015).

Notwithstanding, it must be noted that international law cannot be read in line with the concerns of individual states since international law consists of principles and general rules that restrict the freedom of action of all states based

[63] UNSC, Resolution 84, UN Doc S/RES/84 (7 July 1950).

[64] UNSC, Resolution 661, UN Doc S/RES/661 (6 August 1990).

[65] A Lang, 'Legal Basis for UK Military Action in Syria' (2015) 7404 *House of Commons Library, Briefing Paper* 7, 7–11; H Moynihan, 'Assessing the Legal Basis for UK Military Action in Syria', *Chatham House* (26 November 2015), www.chathamhouse.org/expert/comment/assessing-legal-basis-uk-military-action-syria.

[66] See 'Statement by Ambassador Matthew Rycroft of the UK Mission to the UN at the Security Council adoption of Resolution 2249 on ISIL', *Foreign & Commonwealth Office* (23 November 2015), www.gov.uk/government/speeches/today-we-sent-a-clear-unambiguous-message-that-there-will-be-no-respite-for-our-collective-efforts-to-stop-suppress-and-destroy-isil.

on their own assessments. In that sense, the military intervention by the US-led coalition in Syria, which was not approved by the UNSC, obliquely highlights the fact that military intervention debates largely concern powerful 'first-world' states' illegal interventions in 'third-world' states in a constrained and subordinated position within an asymmetrical global order.[67]

Regarding the contemporary international legal system, those states which intend to use military force against violent armed ANSAs or terrorist groups based within the territory of another state need to prove that military intervention within another state is necessary and that the state in question is not able to suppress for itself the threat posed by violent groups to international peace and security. In doing so, the UNSC's endorsement would politically legitimise any military interventions based on the intervening state's justifications. For this very reason, the US-led coalition would need to bring any evidence for intervention before the UNSC in order to obtain the authorisation of the permanent members as a primary requirement to using force within Syrian territory as an effective international legal response. In the case of Islamic State, Syria has been brought before the UNSC multiple times to give its authorisation for the use of force by way of a UNSC resolution. However, Russia and China have continually blocked the UNSC from authorising military force against Islamic State in Syria, with Russia vetoing thirteen times and China seven times.[68] In essence, if the UNSC decides that the situation represents a breach or threat to international peace and security, the Council will decide to use military means, including authorising other states to intervene militarily to restore peace and security. This means that the legality of military intervention without the UNSC's clear approval would be problematic. In accordance with the UN Charter, although states have an obligation to promote security, stability and respect for fundamental human rights, military intervention without UNSC approval and the host state's consent would contradict legal claims regarding states' sovereignty, political independence and territorial integrity used to justify the use of force within a foreign territory.

Although the 'unwilling or unable theory' has been considered to be a well-entrenched norm based on some states' practice, a victim state need not conduct an 'unwilling or unable' inquiry when it obtains a host state's consent to use force within its borders.[69] As Ashley Deeks has argued, obtaining the host state's

[67] Je Pitts, 'Intervention and Sovereign Equality: Legacies of Vattel' in Recchia and Welsh (2013), above n 50, 133.

[68] A Deeks, 'US Airstrikes against ISIS in Syria? Possible International Legal Theories', *Lawfare Blog* (23 August 2014), www.lawfareblog.com/us-airstrikes-against-isis-syria-possible-international-legal-theories; 'Security Council: Two Draft Resolutions, Zero Consensus on Ceasefire in Syria's Idlib', *UN News* (19 September 2019), https://news.un.org/en/story/2019/09/1046802. For further discussion, see Scharf (2016), above n 18 at 9; G Melling and A Dennett, 'The Security Council Veto and Syria: Responding to Mass Atrocities Through the 'Uniting for Peace' Resolution' (2017) 57 *Indian Journal of International Law* 285.

[69] Deeks (2012), above n 58 at 519.

permission for military intervention would reduce the overall number of cases in which the victim state uses force unilaterally in a host state's territory. Even if the host state declines to give the victim state consent to use force unilaterally, the victim state should, as a rule, explore whether there is an opportunity to work cooperatively with the territorial state to suppress the threat.[70] From this perspective, obtaining the consent of the host state or a cooperation proposal would legitimise military intervention against any ANSAs within a foreign territory. The proof that this element has been ignored can be found in the Syrian case, as the Syrian regime has not given valid informed consent to the US-led coalition to use force within its territories to combat Islamic State.[71]

More importantly, given that Syrian government forces have been engaged in the fight against Islamic State, the Syrian government cannot be accused of supporting terrorist groups, or even of remaining passive or unwilling to stop Islamic State's armed activities. In this sense, if it is accepted that Syria, as a territorial state, has been shown to have taken effective action against Islamic State, any measure that is aimed at preventing ANSAs from posing a continuous threat of continuous attacks would mean that any aggressive action taken by victim states – in this case, the US-led coalition – would not be justifiable.[72] Evidence shows that the Syrian authorities have fought Islamic State by using a wide range of military means and by calling upon its regional and strategic allies, including Russia and Iran, to support its forces in the fight.[73] Accordingly, it is therefore difficult to claim that the Syrian government has been unable to fight Islamic State. However, in its letter to the UNSC, dated 23 September 2014, the US reiterated its claim that the Syrian regime has shown that it cannot, and will not, confront the growing threat effectively.

Accordingly, as reflected in Article 51 of the UN Charter, the US has initiated what it considers to be necessary and proportionate military actions in Syria in order to eliminate the ongoing threat posed by Islamic State to Iraq. These measures include protecting Iraqi citizens from further attacks and enabling Iraqi forces to regain control of its borders.[74] This is the US's own assessment of the situation, which stems from the Syrian government's failure to suppress the threat from Islamic State. As Corten points out, the Syrian regime's 'objective inability' (a lack of results 'on the ground') or failure to eradicate Islamic State has allowed the US authorities to justify military intervention in Syria on grounds of self-defence in favour of Iraq and many other countries.[75]

[70] Ibid, at 520.

[71] Corten (2016), above n 21 at 779.

[72] N Lubell, *Extraterritorial Use of Force against Non-State Actors* (Oxford, Oxford University Press, 2010) 46. See also Scharf (2016), above n 18 at 20–21.

[73] Corten (2016), above n 21 at 778.

[74] Letter dated 23 September 2014 from the Permanent Representative of the United States of America to the United Nations addressed to the Secretary-General, UN Doc S/2014/695 (23 September 2014). For a discussion, see Scharf (2016), above n 18 at 20–21.

[75] Corten (2016), above n 21 at 778; Scharf (2016), above n 18 at 3.

Having looked at the US's position in the war with Islamic State, the Syrian case has shown that although the 'unwilling or unable theory' has not yet been recognised in international law, it has been firmly rooted and well established in the US legal approach, upon which '… the refusal of the host to provide its consent will not necessarily vitiate the right of the threatened state to take self-defence use of force measures'.[76] The US government has already asserted that a country has the right to use force to protect itself from attacks from a neighbouring country if the neighbouring state is unwilling or unable to prevent the use of its own territories for such an attack.[77]

However, the US approach does not necessarily indicate that using force against ANSAs within a foreign territory based on the 'unwilling or unable theory' has a precise basis in *jus ad bellum*. Considering that the theory has not been generally accepted by the majority of states and that the ICJ has refrained from recognising the theory, it seems clear that the 'unwilling or unable theory' is still considered to be vague and extremely arbitrary. Furthermore, in order for something to become part of customary international law, there must be widespread state practice and the *opinio juris* – a subjective element that is related to the consent of the states in the legal status of the conduct in question – or there must be a belief that such practice reflects international law.[78] At its core, however, *opinio juris* is not sufficient for establishing a customary international law and any rules established that are purely based on *opinio juris* can develop or change as easily and as quickly as *opinio juris* itself.[79] More importantly, the determination of a customary international law always requires a sufficient degree of clarity as to the content of the particular rule.[80] Therefore, as pointed out by Deeks, it appears that the 'unwilling or unable theory's 'lack of content' undermines the legitimacy of the theory as it is currently framed, and suggests that it is not, in its current form, imposing effective constraints on a state's use of force.[81] This would induce a certain reluctance to accept the theory as a favourable and legitimate basis for the use of force within a foreign territory. Ultimately, such a scenario would not create common *opinio juris* with

[76] G Travalio and J Altenburg, 'Terrorism, State Responsibility, and the Use of Military Force' (2003) 4 *Chicago Journal of International Law* 97, 116. See also M Byrne, 'Consent and the Use of Force: An Examination of "Intervention by Invitation" As a Basis for US Drone Strikes in Pakistan, Somalia and Yemen' (2016) 3 *Journal on the Use of Force and International Law* 97, 107.

[77] See Ruys (2010), above n 60 at 431; Scharf (2016), above n 18 at 21.

[78] A Cassese, *International Law* (Oxford, Oxford University Press, 2005) 156. See also M Mendelson, 'The Subjective Element in Customary International Law' (1995) 66 *British Yearbook of International Law* 177; O Elias, 'The Nature of the Subjective Element in Customary International Law' (1995) 44 *International and Comparative Law Quarterly* 501.

[79] AT Guzman, 'Saving Customary International Law' (2005) 27 *Michigan Journal of International Law* 115, 159. See also J Kammerhofer, 'Uncertainty in the Formal Sources of International Law: Customary International Law and Some of Its Problems' (2004) 15 *European Journal of International Law* 523, 533–36.

[80] O Dörr and K Schmalenbach (eds), *Vienna Convention on the Law of Treaties: A Commentary* (Heidelberg, Berlin & Verlag, Springer, 2012) 664.

[81] Deeks (2012), above n 58 at 487.

regard to the 'unwilling or unable theory'. Even if the theory is accepted as an exception to the general prohibition on the use of force contained in Article 2(4) of the UN Charter, it should also be recognised as an expanded form of the right of self-defence as an existing exception to the use of force contained in Article 51. In that case, the theory might be considered a justification for self-defence in order to improve the scope of the existing rules on the law of self-defence, which would adversely affect the integrity of the law on its use, and by extension, the future of international peace and security.

ii. Turkish Military Intervention against Islamic State

a. Constitution-based Requirement for Turkish Military Interventions

The Constitution of the Republic of Turkey (1982)[82] has explicitly identified a requirement, determinative in relation to the measures taken in self-defence, and the use of military force and deployment of military forces in foreign territory. The requirement is explicitly enshrined in Article 92 of the Turkish Constitution, which states:

> The power to authorise the declaration of a state of war in cases deemed legitimate by international law and except where required by international treaties to which Turkey is a party or by the rules of international courtesy to send the Turkish Armed Forces to foreign countries and to allow foreign armed forces to be stationed in Turkey, is vested in the Grand National Assembly of Turkey.
>
> If the country is subjected to sudden armed aggression, while the Grand National Assembly of Turkey is adjourned or in recess, and it thus becomes imperative to decide immediately on the use of the armed forces, the President of the Republic can decide on the use of the Turkish Armed Forces.

In itself, this is a source of constitutional controversy, particularly when Turkey provides justifications for using force and military intervention in foreign territory. An analytical reading of Article 92 will inform the way and extent to which Turkey interprets and applies *jus ad bellum* principles.

Article 92 explicitly refers to international law as the primary legal authority that legitimises the deployment of military forces. However, the Turkish Constitution does not suggest an accurate solution if there is a conflict between the norms of domestic and international laws. In the absence of obvious provisions and mechanisms to detect and resolve normative conflicts Article 92 is limited. Its focus is on the outcome rather than process and mechanism that needs to be used in conflict resolution. The most relevant example of this limitation is perhaps the phrase 'cases deemed legitimate by international law' in the first paragraph of Article 92. That paragraph indicates that the Grand National Assembly of Turkey is the only power that can authorise the declaration of

[82] Constitution of the Republic of Turkey (7 November 1982) (with amendments through 2017), www.constituteproject.org/constitution/Turkey_2017.pdf?lang=en.

a state of war and deployment of military forces in foreign territory. Experience shows that the Grand National Assembly of Turkey has taken different measures depending on the conditions of the particular case[83] due to the lack of consensus on the interpretation and application of Article 92, which does not make clear what 'cases deemed legitimate by international law' means and which mechanism and circumstances would determine whether cases are to be deemed legitimate under international law.

Regardless of what the majority positions of the Turkish authorities, politicians and scholars are with regard to the interpretation of 'cases deemed legitimate by international law' in Article 92, it would be convenient to merely assume that the phrase refers to *jus ad bellum* as the only branch of international law that governs the conditions under which states may resort to war or use of military force in general. In itself, *jus ad bellum* is governed by treaty law (including Article 2(4), 39–42, and 51 of the UN Charter) and customary international law.

The general prohibition on the use of force and the exceptions to it (use of force in self-defence and use of force with the UNSC authorisation) that have been set out in Chapter VII of the UN Charter are the core components of *jus ad bellum*. The prohibition on the use of force is generally considered to be a *jus cogens* rule that does not permit derogation, either by consent or by treaty.[84] In order to curtail the freedom of states to use force to settle international disputes, the use of force in international law has been prohibited for the first time by the UN Charter. In accordance with the Charter, to maintain international peace and security, all members of the UN shall settle their international disputes peacefully.

Even though the use of force is widely prohibited under international law, it might be justified under the exceptional conditions enshrined in Article 51 of the UN Charter, as use of force in self-defence and use of force authorised by the UNSC.

As discussed earlier, the wording of Article 51 is clear enough to allow the exercise of the right of self-defence by a state only if it has been the victim of an 'armed attack'. As the ICJ has pointed out in the *Oil Platforms* case, the defending state 'must … show that its actions were necessary and proportional to the armed attack made on it and that the platforms were a legitimate military target

[83] See for instance, KN Trapp, 'The Turkish Intervention against the PKK in Northern Iraq – 2007–08' in T Ruys et al (eds), *The Use of Force in International Law: A Case-Based Approach* (Oxford, Oxford University Press, 2018) 689–701; P Beaumont, 'Turkish MPs Pass Bill to Send Troops to Support Libyan Government', *The Guardian* (2 January 2020), www.theguardian.com/world/2020/jan/02/turkish-parliament-to-vote-on-sending-troops-to-libya; F Ní Aoláin, 'Authorizing Force: A Review of Turkish, Dutch and French Action', *Just Security* (16 October 2014), www.justsecurity.org/16282/authorizing-force-review-turkish-dutch-french-action/.

[84] A De Hoogh, 'Jus Cogens and the Use of Armed Force' in M Weller (ed), *The Oxford Handbook of the Use of Force in International Law* (Oxford, Oxford University Press, 2015) 1161–86; K Hossain, 'The Concept of Jus Cogens and the Obligation Under the UN Charter' (2005) 3 *Santa Clara Journal of International Law* 72; Kahgan (1997), above n 4 at 767–827.

open to attack in the exercise of self-defence'.[85] In other words, the ICJ has explicitly identified a standalone *jus ad bellum* targeting requirement.[86]

Some scholars and states argue that self-defence would also be the case when an 'imminent threat' of attack clearly exists.[87] Self-defence in that sense would be 'pre-emptive', which relies on the mere possibility of an armed attack at some unspecified, future period of time. Although Article 2(4) of the UN Charter does restrict the use of military force to resolve international disputes, it nevertheless recognises the 'inherent right' of states to act in self-defence in Article 51. From this point of view, it has been argued that pre-emptive self-defence is fully consistent with Article 51 of the UN Charter in asymmetrical warfare, particularly when combatting ANSAs.[88] This would, particularly, be the case for the Turkish military intervention against Islamic State in Iraq and Syria.

One can determine the scope of the 'legitimate force' highlighted in Article 92 of the Turkish Constitution and the extent to which legitimate force must be restricted in line with the applicable international law norms. The legitimisation of military force used by Turkey would be interpreted under the relevant rules of the international law governing the right to use military force. In that sense, the compliance of the use of military force with *jus ad bellum* rules would be the case if Turkey, as a victim of an armed attack, exercises its inherent right of self-defence, or if it exercises the right to use military force in cooperation with a group of states authorised by the UN Security Council.

For the present purpose, attention should be paid to the phrase 'where required by international treaties to which Turkey is a party' that is contained in the first paragraph of Article 92. The Grand National Assembly of Turkey, according to this provision, authorises the declaration of a state of war where required by international treaties to which Turkey is a party, or to send the Turkish Armed Forces to foreign countries and to allow foreign armed forces to be stationed in Turkey. It is, therefore, enough to note here that the right to use force would be implemented in accordance with the international treaties that regulate resort to military force in foreign territory. The primary instances that

[85] *Case Concerning Oil Platforms (Islamic Republic of Iran v United States of America)*, Judgment. ICJ Reports (6 November 2003), para 51. See also D Akande and T Liefländer, 'Clarifying Necessity, Imminence, and Proportionality in the Law of Self-Defense' (2013) 107 *American Journal of International Law* 563; D Kretzmer, 'The Inherent Right to Self-Defence and Proportionality in Jus Ad Bellum' (2013) 24 *European Journal of International Law* 235.

[86] JA Green and CPM Waters, 'Military Targeting in the Context of Self-Defence Actions' (2015) 84 *Nordic Journal of International Law* 3, 9; JA Green, 'The Oil Platforms Case: An Error in Judgment?' (2004) 9 *Journal of Conflict and Security Law* 357, 380.

[87] See for instance, Arend (2003), above n 7 at 89–103; M Wood, 'The Caroline Incident – 1837' in T Ruys et al (eds), *The Use of Force in International Law: A Case-Based Approach* (Oxford, Oxford University Press, 2018) 5–16.

[88] P Kelly, 'Preemptive Self-Defense, Customary International Law, and the Congolese Wars', *E-International Relations* (3 September 2016), www.e-ir.info/2016/09/03/preemptive-self-defense-customary-international-law-and-the-congolese-wars/. See also WM Reisman and A Armstrong, 'The Past and Future of the Claim of Preemptive Self-Defense' (2006) 100 *American Journal of International Law* 525; Arend (2003), above n 7 at 89–102.

might fall in this category are the use of force in self-defence under Article 51 of the UN Charter, and sending the Turkish Armed Forces to foreign countries under Article 5 of the NATO Agreement to which Turkey is a party. Article 5 requires collective self-defence where there is an attack against one ally since an attack against one ally is considered an attack against all allies.[89]

It is also worth noting that Turkey's military intervention in Iraq and Syria, justified under bilateral treaties, has made it clear that the phrase 'where required by international treaties to which Turkey is a party' also refers to binding bilateral or multilateral treaties to which Turkey is a party. In order to bring clarity to the legal justifications addressed by the Turkish authorities in this context, it should be explored whether and to what extent the bilateral treaties to which Turkey is a party authorise the use of force and military intervention in foreign territory.

While the precise relationship between Turkey's constitutional authorisation for use of military force and the use of force in international law is not the primary focus of this research, it would be convenient to explore how Turkey has used military force in foreign territory based on international treaties to which Turkey is a party. This would allow us to determine how the Turkish authorities interpret and implement the phrase 'cases deemed legitimate by international law' as a legally identified basis of the right to use force in foreign territory. In this particular context, the most beneficial way to explore Turkey's practice relating to the right to use force in foreign territory is to examine Turkey's justifications in using force against Islamic State and Kurdish fighters in Iraq and Syria.

b. Military Intervention in Syria

Turkey shares its longest common border (911 km) with Syria in the south-eastern part of the country. The border between Turkey and Syria has historically been contentious and has been one of the major causes of tension between the two countries. The joining of the Turkish- and Arabic-speaking province of Hatay with Turkey in 1939; Turkey's damming of the Euphrates River as part of the Southeast Anatolia Project (SAP), which has long been criticised for its negative effects on the natural environment, cultural heritage and the local population[90] since the 1970s; and most importantly, the Syrian government's support of the

[89] For further discussion on use of force and self-defence requirements under Article 5 of the NATO agreement, see BC Grady, 'Article 5 of the North Atlantic Treaty: Past, Present, and Uncertain Future' (2002) 31 *Georgia Journal of International and Comparative Law* 167; B Simma, 'NATO, the UN and the Use of Force: Legal Aspects' (1999) 10 *European Journal of International Law* 1; B Tertrais, 'Article 5 of the Washington Treaty: Its Origins, Meaning and Future' (2016) 130 *NATO Defense College Research Paper* 1, 1–8, www.css.ethz.ch/content/dam/ethz/special-interest/gess/cis/center-for-securities-studies/resources/docs/NDC-Article%205%20of%20the%20Washington%20Treaty.pdf.

[90] See G Conde, 'Water and Counter-Hegemony: Kurdish Struggle in the Tigris and Euphrates in Turkey' (2016) 9 *Revista de Paz y Conflictos* 43.

PKK and its leader, Abdullah Öcalan, in 1980, have been the major reasons for the tensions between the two countries over the years. However, following the Adana Security Agreement, which was signed by Turkey and Syria on 20 October 1998, and which obliged the Syrian government to expel Abdullah Öcalan, both countries have turned over a new leaf in their relations. In order to eliminate the existing tensions between the two countries and to stabilise the border region, the agreement entailed the following commitments:

> As of now, Öcalan was not in Syria and he definitely will not be allowed to enter Syria; the PKK elements abroad will not be permitted to enter Syria; as of now, the PKK camps are not operational and definitely will not be allowed to become active; and many PKK members have been arrested and have been taken to court.[91]

Given these commitments, it seems clear that Turkey's geopolitical position has made it more vulnerable to the significant cross-border security threats emanating from terrorist groups and other violent ANSAs, including the PKK, the Kurdish People's Protection Units or *Yekîneyên Parastina Gel* (YPG), the Democratic Union Party or *Partiya Yekîtiya Demokrat* (PYD), the Kurdish Democratic Confederalist political party established in 2003, and Islamic State based in Syria. Following the emergence of Islamic State, Turkey has suffered terrorist attacks not only in the Turkish-Syrian border area but also in major cities including Ankara and Istanbul. The attacks' targets have almost always been against the Turkish state, civilians and demonstrations.[92]

In view of all these elements, it appears that Turkey has been repeatedly targeted by Islamic State. Regardless of the justifications for military intervention in a foreign territory, the anxiety of the Turkish authorities regarding Islamic State's frequent attacks seems understandable. As a result, although Turkey is one of the members of the US-led coalition fighting Islamic State, the Turkish Armed Forces also unilaterally intervened in Syria to attempt to halt Islamic State's terrorist actions.

On 24 July 2015, Turkey sent the following letter to the President of the UNSC justifying its use of military force against Islamic State in Syria.

> With the emergence of [Islamic State], the threats from Syria gained new dimensions. Syria has become a safe haven for [Islamic State]. This area is used by Islamic State for training, planning, financing, and carrying out attacks across borders. Also, Security Council Resolutions 2170 (2014) and 2178 (2014) have underscored the threat posed

[91] The Adana Security Agreement signed by Turkey and Syria in Adana (1998), *Voltaire Network* (20 October 1998), www.voltairenet.org/article208057.html.

[92] The conflict in Syria and the threat of Islamic State emanating from northern Syria have also been the major causes of the largest number of displaced people and refugees in the world today. According to the UN Refugee Agency, in September 2018, 5.64 million Syrian refugees were registered in neighbouring countries. Since the beginning of the crisis in Syria, Turkey has been the country hosting over 3.6 million registered Syrian refugees. See 'Refugees and Asylum Seekers in Turkey: 2019 Planning Summary', *UNHCR* (15 February 2019), https://reporting.unhcr.org/sites/default/files/pdfsummaries/GA2019-Turkey-eng.pdf; UNHCR, 'Operational Portal: Turkey' (last updated on 9 December 2020), https://data2.unhcr.org/en/situations/syria/location/113.

> by Islamic State and the resolve of the international community to combat Islamic State. The terrorist attack that took the lives of 32 Turkish citizens in Suruç on 20 July 2015 reaffirms that Turkey is under a clear and imminent threat of continuing attack from Islamic State. Most recently, on 23 July 2015, Islamic State attacked the border military post in Elbeyli and killed a Turkish soldier. It is apparent that the regime in Syria is neither capable of nor willing to prevent these threats emanating from its territory, which clearly imperil the security of Turkey and the safety of its nationals. Individual and collective self-defence is our inherent right under international law, as reflected in Article 51 of the UN Charter. On this basis, Turkey has initiated necessary and proportionate military actions against Islamic State in Syria, including in coordination with individual members of the Global Coalition, in order to counter the terrorist threat and to safeguard its territory and citizens.[93]

It should be emphasised from the outset that Turkey's initial military attack against Islamic State in January 2014 and its joining of the US-led coalition's armed operations under the 'unwilling or unable theory' led to an intensification of Islamic State's terrorist operations against them. As their primary justification, the Turkish authorities declared that Syria, as the host state, had been unwilling or unable to control its territories, which were under the effective control of Islamic State and were being used as a base for its terrorist operations. Therefore, in order to protect itself against these threats, the Turkish Armed Forces entered Syria based on the right of self-defence.

As discussed earlier with regard to the US-led coalition's airstrikes in Syria, Turkey deployed its armed forces within Syrian territory with neither the consent of the Syrian government nor UNSC authorisation. In short, the use of force based on the Syrian government's supposed unwillingness or inability to act for itself is still unacceptable; and that no state is permitted to use military force against any armed group that is active within a foreign territory without the consent of the host state or UNSC authorisation. While the UNSC should determine the existence of any threat to the victim state and should make an appropriate decision regarding the unwillingness or inability of the territorial state, the unwillingness or inability of the Syrian government to suppress the threat posed by Islamic State has almost been a controversial matter for the international community. Specifically, it would be unfair to say that Syria has not fought against Islamic State or other terrorist groups within its territory, given that it has launched many operations against Islamic State and other terrorist targets both unilaterally and with the comprehensive support of its regional and strategic allies, including Iran and Russia.

What is clear, however, is that Turkey initially resorted to military action against Islamic State in Syria based on the 'unwilling or unable theory'. In the aforementioned letter to the UNSC, Turkey referred to its inherent right to individual and collective self-defence against Islamic State due to the

[93] Letter dated 24 July 2015 from the Chargé d'affaires a.i. of the Permanent Mission of Turkey to the United Nations addressed to the President of the Security Council, UN Doc S/2015/563 (24 July 2015).

Syrian government's unwillingness or inability to combat Islamic State, which has posed a serious threat to Turkey's national security.

As can be seen, there is a major difference in the key elements and motivating factors of the US and Turkey's military intervention in Syria. Turkey has initially justified its military presence in Syria based on the war with Islamic State. However, it appears that Turkey has also used the Islamic State crisis as an opportunity to expand its operations against the PKK, the YPG and the PYD, which pose a threat to the Turkish national security. Therefore, their victories in the region could enhance consolidation of Kurdish territories that may lead to the creation of a 'Kurdish corridor'.[94] This is probably the most likely hypothesis as to why Turkey intervened in Syria: it is concerned that the area of northern Syria controlled by the YPG could become part of a potential Kurdish state.

The axis around which Turkey's recent activities in Syria revolves, therefore, is directly related to terrorism being Turkey's major domestic issue. In a sense, the growing threat of both Islamic State and Kurdish militants provided justification for the Turkish military to intervene against both groups.

Following the outbreak of the Syrian civil war in 2011, Turkey endeavoured to protect its border from illegal migration. However, the invasion and occupation of northern Syria by Islamic State and YPG militants compelled Turkey to take the drastic measures to protect its border with Syria. As a security-enhancing measure, Turkey started to construct a wall along its entire south-eastern border with Syria and deployed its troops and equipment near the border in 2015. However, this strategy did not work out as a protective strategy. The Istanbul nightclub massacre[95] and the Russian ambassador's assassination in Ankara[96] are the most important indications that the wall policy and the deployment of Turkish troops to the border per se were unable to protect Turkey from the cross-border threats of Islamic State and YPG. The threats of Islamic State and YPG, therefore, led to the Turkish military crossing the border in order to counteract the threats posed by Islamic State and to prevent the PKK and its extensions in Syria from establishing themselves west of the Euphrates along Turkey's borders.[97]

[94] S Dapkus, 'Turkey's Security Dilemma on the Border with Syria: Situation Assessment and Perspectives of the Intervention' (2016) 33 *Lithuanian Foreign Policy Review* 48, 53; F Itani and A Stein, 'Turkey's Syria Predicament', *Atlantic Council Issue Brief* (3 May 2016) 6, www.atlanticcouncil.org/wp-content/uploads/2016/05/Turkey_s_Syria_Predicament.pdf.

[95] See N Soliev, 'The Terrorist Threat in Turkey: A Dangerous New Phase' (2017) 9 *Counter Terrorist Trends and Analyses* 24; K Shaheen, 'Turkey Nightclub Shooting: Istanbul on Alert after Aunman Kills Dozens', *The Guardian* (1 January 2017), www.theguardian.com/world/2016/dec/31/turkey-armed-attacker-opens-fire-in-istanbul-nightclub-reports.

[96] PK Baev and K Kirişci, 'An Ambiguous Partnership: The Serpentine Trajectory of Turkish-Russian Relations in the Era of Erdoğan and Putin' (2017) 13 *Brookings Policy Paper* 1, 10; S Walker, 'Russian Ambassador to Turkey Shot Dead by Police Officer in Ankara Gallery', *The Guardian* (20 December 2016), www.theguardian.com/world/2016/dec/19/russian-ambassador-to-turkey-wounded-in-ankara-shooting-attack.

[97] For more details, see PM Butchard, 'Digest of State Practice: 1 July–31 December 2018' (2019) 6 *Journal on the Use of Force and International Law* 131.

In the wake of the threats mentioned above, Turkey launched three major operations in northern Syria. The Turkish Armed Forces carried out the first operation, 'Operation Euphrates Shield', in August 2016 in the triangle between Azaz, Jarablus and al-Bab in northern Syria.[98] The second operation, 'Operation Olive Branch', was launched in January 2018 in northern Syria to protect Turkey's national security.[99] The final operation, 'Operation Peace Spring',[100] began on 9 October 2019 in order to eradicate the terrorist threat. The Turkish authorities justified the operations as self-defence measures against Islamic State and the Kurdish militants in Syria, which would ensure Turkey's continued existence and security by clearing terrorists from the region.[101]

In its last statement, Turkey stated that the ultimate goal of Operation Peace Spring, which was launched:

> in the face of multi-dimensional terror threats emanating from Syria against our national security, [was] to ensure the security of our borders, to neutralise terrorists in the region and to save the Syrian people from the oppression of terrorists … The Operation [was] being conducted on the basis of international law, in accordance with our right of self-defence under Article 51 of the UN Charter and resolutions of the UNSC on the fight against terrorism.[102]

Turkey has been a key target of Islamic State since the group first appeared in Syria and since Turkish Armed Forces fought against them there. Islamic State has targeted Turkey more than any other country. A further concern, however,

[98] See J Jager, 'Turkey's Operation Euphrates Shield: An Exemplar of Joint Combined Arms Maneuver', *Small Wars Journal* (17 October 2016), www.smallwarsjournal.com/jrnl/art/turkey%E2%80%99s-operation-euphrates-shield-an-exemplar-of-joint-combined-arms-maneuver; O Ajjoub and MHCK Williams, 'Crushing Rojava: Turkey's War in Syria', *The Conflict Archives* (23 October 2019), www.theconflictarchives.com/news/2019/10/23/crushing-rojava-turkeys-war-in-syria.

[99] A Peters, 'The Turkish Operation in Afrin (Syria) and the Silence of the Lambs', *EJIL: Talk!* (30 January 2018), www.ejiltalk.org/the-turkish-operation-in-afrin-syria-and-the-silence-of-the-lambs/; S Marinelli, 'The Use of Force of Turkey in Rojava after the Capture of Afrin: Consequences for International Law and for the Syrian Conflict', *International Law Blog: Fresh Perspectives on international Law* (26 March 2018), www.internationallaw.blog/2018/03/26/the-use-of-force-of-turkey-in-rojava-after-the-capture-of-afrin-consequences-for-international-law-and-for-the-syrian-conflict/; Ajjoub and Williams (2019), above n 98.

[100] See B McKernan, 'Turkey Unleashes Airstrikes against Kurds in North-East Syria', *The Guardian* (9 October 2019), www.theguardian.com/world/2019/oct/09/turkey-launches-military-operation-in-northern-syria-erdogan.

[101] See Identical Letters dated 20 January 2018 from the Chargé d'affaires a.i. of the Permanent Mission of Turkey to the United Nations addressed to the Secretary-General and the President of the Security Council, UN Doc S/2018/53 (22 January 2018). For further discussion, see D Schmidt, 'Turkey's Syria Invasion: German Research Report Says Illegal on All Counts', *Just Security* (15 November 2019), www.justsecurity.org/67219/turkeys-syria-invasion-german-research-report-says-illegal-on-all-counts/; Peters (30 January 2018), above n 99.

[102] Republic of Turkey Ministry of Foreign Affairs, Press Release Regarding Certain Comments in the International Community on Operation Peace Spring, No 297 (11 October 2019), www.mfa.gov.tr/no_297_-baris-pinari-harekati-ni-hedef-alan-yorumlar-hk.en.mfa. See also V Todeschini, 'Turkey's Operation "Peace Spring" and International Law', *Opinio Juris* (21 October 2019), www.opiniojuris.org/2019/10/21/turkeys-operation-peace-spring-and-international-law/; AS Yayla and CP Clarke, 'Turkey's Double ISIS Standard', *Foreign Policy* (12 April 2018), www.foreignpolicy.com/2018/04/12/turkeys-double-isis-standard/.

relates to whether or not Turkey's justifications for military intervention in Syria have a legal basis, even though the situation in Syria poses a direct threat to Turkey as a neighbouring state.

Turkish military intervention in Syria under the 'unwilling or unable theory' is still disputed. Furthermore, the contractually based grounds alleged by Turkish authorities to justify cross-border operations in Syrian territory is the subject of controversy. In terms of the legality of the three major operations within Syrian territory, the provisions of the Adana Security Agreement, which were amended in 2010, have provided the evidence that enabled Turkey to use force against Islamic State and other violent groups based in Syria.

On 19 and 20 October 1998, when Turkish and Syrian authorities discussed the defusion of border tensions between the two countries, they made a joint commitment to co-operate in combatting terrorism. According to the *Adana Security Agreement*, and on the basis of the principle of reciprocity, Syria will not permit any activity which emanates from its territory aimed at jeopardising the security and stability of Turkey. Syria will not allow the supply of weapons, logistical material, financial support, and propaganda activities of the PKK on its territory. Syria has recognised that the PKK is a terrorist organisation, and has prohibited all activities of the PKK and its affiliated organisations, along with those of other terrorist organisations, on Syrian territory. Syria will not allow the PKK to establish camps and other facilities for training and shelter or to have commercial activities on its territory. Syria will not allow the PKK to use its territory for transit to third countries, and Syria will take all necessary measures to prevent the leader of the PKK terrorist organisation from entering into Syrian territory and will instruct its authorities at border points to that effect.[103]

Turkey and Syria have already agreed upon a counterterrorism strategy through which both sides have an obligation to combat terrorism. Given that the main objective of the Adana Security Agreement is to fight the PKK and its extensions in Syrian territory, both sides have agreed to establish certain mechanisms for the effective and transparent implementation of the measures mentioned above.[104] The emergence of Islamic State in Syria, however, has shown that the Syrian government has not been effective in terms of the application of the major terms and conditions of the Adana Security Agreement. For this reason, Turkey and Syria reopened discussions on the agreement and created a revised document called the Joint Cooperation Agreement in 2010.[105] According to the Joint Cooperation Agreement, Syria is obliged to prevent any

[103] The Adana Security Agreement signed by Turkey and Syria in Adana (20 October 1998), above n 91.

[104] Ibid.

[105] Türkiye Cumhuriyeti ile Suriye Arap Cumhuriyeti Hükümeti Arasında Terör ve Terör Örgütlerine Karşı Ortak İşbirliği Anlaşması (unofficial title in English: Joint Cooperation Agreement on Counterterrorism between the Republic of Turkey and the Syria Arab Republic), Republic of Turkey Prime Ministry (21 December 2010), www2.tbmm.gov.tr/d23/1/1-1009.pdf.

type of activity that emanates from its territory which could jeopardise Turkey's national security and stability (Article 4). Although Turkish counterterrorism measures against Islamic State are generally justified within the scope of both the Adana Security Agreement and the Joint Cooperation Agreement, neither of the documents authorises military intervention and arbitrary operation. More precisely, the amended document only provides for 'joint cooperation' in the fight against terrorist organisations including the PKK and its extensions as well as any other violent groups active in Syria and Turkey (Article 2). The two agreements provide that the contracting parties will never allow any terrorist or other violent group to use their territory in order to violate their national security and stability. Importantly, the Joint Cooperation Agreement stipulates that both Syria and Turkey have made a commitment to pursue all terrorist groups in perpetuity and to take all necessary joint measures to a certain degree through identifying their resources and locations (Article 7).

However, it is difficult to claim that the Joint Cooperation Agreement or the Adana Security Agreement authorise military intervention as a necessary measure in fighting against terrorist groups, which does not seem to have been the intention of the contracting parties at the time of the negotiations. The most prominent examples of authorised external military interventions are the US intervention in Panama under the 1903 US-Panama Hay-Herrán Treaty (Article 7),[106] the Soviet intervention in Iran under the 1921 Treaty between the Soviet Union and Iran (Article 6),[107] and the intervention in Cuba legalised under the 1903 US-Cuba Treaty of Relations (Articles 3 and 7).[108] All these treaties authorised the use of force in the territory of the contracting parties. Even so, one might argue that treaty-based interventions might potentially be abused by powerful states.[109]

What is clear in the Syrian case is that the mentioned agreements do not authorise the use of force in the territory of the contracting parties and it appears clear, therefore, that Turkish military intervention in Syria is an approach that

[106] Convention for the Construction of a Ship Canal (Hay-Bunau-Varilla Treaty) (Panama, 18 November 1903), https://avalon.law.yale.edu/20th_century/pan001.asp#art7; R Jennings and A Watts, *Oppenheim's International Law – Vol 1: Peace* (London, Longman, 1996) 446. See also CD Ameringer, 'Philippe Bunau-Varilla: New Light on the Panama Canal Treaty' (1966) 46 *The Hispanic American Historical Review* 28.

[107] The 1921 Treaty of Friendship between Persia and the Russian Socialist Federal Soviet Republic (Moscow, 26 February 1921) (1922) 668 *League of Nations Treaty Series* 401; WM Reisman, 'Termination of the USSR's Treaty Right of Intervention in Iran' (1980) 74 *American Journal of International Law* 144, 146–47; Jennings and Watts (1996), above n 106 at 446.

[108] Treaty between the US and Cuba Embodying the Provisions Defining the Future Relations of the US with Cuba Contained in the Act of Congress (Platt Amendment) (Habana, 22 May 1903) in LH Woolsey, 'The New Cuban Treaty' (1934) 28 *American Journal of International Law* 530; RA Lecuona, 'International Law, Cuba, and the United States of America' (1997) 14 *International Journal on World Peace* 37, 39; Jennings and Watts (1996), above n 106 at 446.

[109] For general information, see D Wippman, 'Treaty-Based Intervention: Who Can Say No?' (1995) 62 *The University of Chicago Law Review* 607, 685; D Wippman, 'Prodemocratic Intervention by Invitation' in GH Fox and BR Roth (eds), *Democratic Governance and International Law* (Cambridge, Cambridge University Press, 2000) 312–13.

stems from the broad interpretation of the key provisions of the *Adana Security Agreement* and the *Joint Cooperation Agreement*, according to which the contracting parties consent to take 'necessary measures' for certain purposes.

Returning to treaty-based military interventions, even if the Turkish approach is accepted as a legal basis for military intervention, state practice indicates that although the use of force based on a bilateral treaty is one of the primary circumstances that may justify forcible intervention,[110] the intervening state is prohibited from taking any action in violation of the traditional rules of international law that developed for the purpose territorial protection.[111] In other words, states party to a treaty only assume obligations under the treaty that arise not just from the mere act of granting consent but from the international law principle of *pacta sunt servanda*. This is the primary requirement in the application of treaties regulated by Article 26 of the 1969 Vienna Convention on the Law of Treaties, which states that 'every treaty in force is binding upon the parties to it and must be performed by them in good faith'.[112]

The treaty-based intervention is an approach that has also been approved by Russia, which acts as the Syrian government's strategic ally in the region.[113] The consequence of this, therefore, would be that the Adana Security Agreement and the Joint Cooperation Agreement are used to legitimise Turkish cross-border military operation in Syria to prevent irregular armed groups conducting terrorist actions against Turkey from Syrian territory. According to Vladimir Putin, the president of the Russian Federation, '[the Adana Security Agreement] deals, in particular, with the fight against terrorism. I think that this is the base that closes many issues in terms of ensuring Turkey's security on its southern borders'.[114] Mevlut Çavuşoğlu, Turkey's Minister of Foreign Affairs, has interpreted this statement as a green light to move its forces into Syria, mentioning that 'we think [Putin] referred to the [Adana Security Agreement] implying that Turkey can intervene in [Syria]'.[115] Moreover, as mentioned earlier, such an

[110] AS Deeks, 'Consent to the Use of Force and International Law Supremacy' (2013) 54 *Harvard International Law Journal* 1, 18–20; Jennings and Watts (1996), above n 106 at 446.

[111] See C Marxsen, 'Territorial Integrity in International Law – Its Concept and Implications for Crimea' (2015) *Heidelberg Journal of International Law* 7.

[112] Vienna Convention on the Law of Treaties (concluded at Vienna on 23 May 1969) (1980) 1155 *United Nations Treaty Series* 331, 331–53. For a discussion, see also JM Iyi, *Humanitarian Intervention and the AU-ECOWAS Intervention Treaties Under International Law: Towards a Theory of Regional Responsibility to Protect* (Heidelberg, Springer, 2016) 254.

[113] N Koçak, 'Russia Open to Turkish Ops in Syria under Adana Agreement', *Daily News* (18 February 2019), www.hurriyetdailynews.com/russia-open-to-turkish-ops-in-syria-under-adana-agreement-141306; C Miller, 'Putin and Erdogan's Deal for Syria Can't Last', *Foreign Policy* (28 October 2019), www.foreignpolicy.com/2019/10/28/putin-erdogan-deal-syria-kurds-agreement-war-continues/.

[114] See 'Proposed Russian Control of Syria Border Unlikely to Appeal to Turkey', *The New Arab* (25 January 2019), https://english.alaraby.co.uk/english/indepth/2019/1/25/adana-not-an-option-for-turkey-in-northern-syria-1.

[115] Ibid. See also 'Russia Positive on Turkey's Plans to Secure Its Borders: FM Çavuşoğlu', *Daily News* (24 January 2019), www.hurriyetdailynews.com/russia-positive-on-turkeys-plans-to-secure-its-borders-fm-cavusoglu-140741.

approach provided Turkey with a golden opportunity to prevent Kurdish fighters from advancing along the Turkish border and in the Syrian territories recaptured from Islamic State.

Furthermore, war crimes committed by Kurdish fighters in northern Syria in territory recaptured from Islamic State have been the major motivating factor that provided the opportunity for Turkey to bring the bilateral counterterrorism agreements forward. In February 2015, Amnesty International reported that the YPG began demolishing houses and displacing villagers after taking control of Rojava, the de facto autonomous region in northern Syria which had been under the control of Islamic State.[116]

According to the report, and information from eyewitnesses, Kurdish fighters pulled people out of their homes before burning the buildings to the ground. The evidence also shows that the YPG fighters had accused the residents in villages south of the town of Suluk of supporting Islamic State and threatened to shoot them or call in airstrikes if they did not leave. According to the report, the majority of residents affected by the YPG's unlawful practices were Arabs and Turkmens. However, in some cases, including in the mixed town of Suluk, Kurdish residents had also been prevented by Kurdish fighters from returning to their homes.[117] As reported by the Syrian Network for Human Rights, the Syrian Democratic Forces (SDF), led by the YPG, carried out arbitrary arrests and enforced disappearances in areas under their control, targeting political activists and media journalists opposing their policies, as well as arrests with the aim of forced conscription. They also detained civilians, including women and children. As a means to advance in northern Syria, Kurdish fighters detained at least 2,705 individuals, largely of Arab and Turkmen descent, at the Turkish-Syrian border until March 2019, and justified their actions as being for the civilians' own protection.[118]

Given these actions, it appears that the terrorist threat embodied by the Kurdish military advance in northern Syria compelled Turkey to resort to military force including cross-border operations to suppress the threat, particularly

[116] See 'Syria: US Ally's Razing of Villages Amounts to War Crimes', *Amnesty International* (13 October 2015), www.amnesty.org/en/latest/news/2015/10/syria-us-allys-razing-of-villages-amounts-to-war-crimes/.

[117] See 'We Had Nowhere Else to Go: Forced Displacement and Demolitions in Northern Syria', *Amnesty International* (12 October 2015), www.amnestyusa.org/reports/we-had-nowhere-else-to-go-forced-displacement-and-demolitions-in-northern-syria/. See also B Hubbard et al, 'Abandoned by US in Syria, Kurds Find New Ally in American Foe', *New York Times* (13 October 2019), www.nytimes.com/2019/10/13/world/middleeast/syria-turkey-invasion-isis.html.

[118] UNGA, 'Report of the Independent International Commission of Inquiry on the Syrian Arab Republic submitted to the Human Rights Council', UN Doc A/HRC/28/69 (5 February 2015), paras 41–42. See also 'Eight Years Since the Start of the Popular Uprising in Syria, Terrible Violations Continue: From Minority Ruel, Repression and Dictatorship Towards Pluralism, Human Rights and Democracy', *The Syrian Network for Human Rights* (11 March 2019), 6, www.sn4hr.org/wp-content/pdf/english/The_eighth_year_of_the_start_of_the_popular_movement_in_Syria_and_the_terrible_violations_continue_en.pdf; 'Under Kurdish Rule: Abuses in PYD-run Enclaves of Syria', *Human Rights Watch* (19 June 2014), www.hrw.org/node/256559/printable/print.

in the aftermath of Islamic State. One might argue that the fight against Islamic State's terrorist actions in the broad meaning of the phrase seems less of a rational explanation for Turkey's presence in Syria. What is clear, however, is that the necessary steps taken by Turkey in Syria stem from the Turkish authorities' interpretation of necessary counterterrorism measures as a certain framework to safeguard Turkey's national security and stability. From this point of view, it is logical to say that there is a relationship between the Syrian government's obligations and the YPG and Islamic State's terrorist operations against Turkey; however, it does not justify military intervention in Syria. In practice, it seems that Syria's failure to comply with its obligations has prepared justifiable grounds for Turkey to use force against the mentioned groups in northern Syria as a last resort by utilising a broad reading of the Adana Security Agreement and the Joint Cooperation Agreement in the direction of Turkey's own assessment of the situation.

The conditions that justified Turkey's right to use force against the Kurdish fighters in northern Syria, particularly under Operation Peace Spring, are a matter of great importance. According to the decision (2018/3775 E, 2018/5600 K)[119] made by the Sixteenth Criminal Division of the Court of Cassation (Supreme Court of Appeals of Turkey), Islamic State and the PKK/YPG/PYD have organised numerous terrorist attacks against Turkey, of which the major ones are listed below.

(1) terrorist attacks launched by Islamic State: bomb attack in Sultanahmet (6 January 2015); bomb attack on the People's Democratic Party (Halkların Demokratik Partisi (HDP)) in Adana and Mersin (18 May 2015); Suruç attack (20 July 2015); Ankara explosion (10 October 2015); Taksim attack (19 March 2016); Gaziantep Şehitkâmil attack (1 May 2016); Atatürk Airport attack (28 June 2016); the attack on a wedding in Gaziantep Şahinbey District (20 August 2016); and Ortakoy Reina armed attack (1 January 2016).[120]
(2) terrorist attacks launched by the PKK/YPG/PYD: Sabiha Gökçen Airport attack (23 December 2015); Ankara Military Service vehicle attack (18 February 2016); Ankara Kizilay attack (13 March 2016); Beşiktaş attack (10 December 2016); and Kayseri attack (17 December 2016).[121]

More specifically, the Court of Cassation has considered Islamic State and the Kurdish groups active in both Turkey and Syria to be equal in terms of their political ideologies and their threat to Turkey's national security and stability. Having compared the facts of the two cases, the Court emphasised that the PKK,

[119] Türkiye Cumhuriyeti, Yargitay 16. Ceza Dairesi, Esas No: 2018/3775, Karar No: 2018/5600 (31 December 2018), 10, https://karararama.yargitay.gov.tr/YargitayBilgiBankasiIstemciWeb/. See also Wave of Terror Attacks in Turkey Continue at a Steady Pace', *New York Times* (5 January 2017), www.nytimes.com/interactive/2016/06/28/world/middleeast/turkey-terror-attacks-bombings.html.
[120] Türkiye Cumhuriyeti, Yargitay 16. Ceza Dairesi, above n 119 at 10.
[121] Ibid, at 11.

PYD, YPG and the Kurdistan Freedom Hawks or Teyrebazen Azadiya Kurdistan (TAK) all are one and the same for Turkey since they pursue the common goal of creating a self-governing Kurdish state through organising terrorist attacks against Turkey in the northwest of the country. More importantly, the same ideology between Islamic State and al-Qaeda could be determined between the PKK, YPG, PYD and TAK. In this sense, the above-mentioned terrorist attacks are all claimed to be cumulative attacks against Turkey. All these continuous attacks, which have reached the threshold of armed attacks, have compelled Turkey to take necessary measures within the Syrian territory in the direction of the Adana Security Agreement and the Joint Cooperation Agreement provisions.[122] For this very reason, in its letter dated 9 October 2019 to the UNSC, Turkey notified the Council that:

> The PKK/PYD/YPG units [as well as Islamic State] close to Turkish borders in the north-east of Syria, continue to be a source of direct and imminent threat as they opened harassment fire on Turkish border posts, by also using snipers and advanced weaponry such as anti-tank guided missiles.[123]

Having released this statement, the justifications propounded by Turkey bring two crucial arguments to the fore in terms of the legality of the intervention in northern Syria. First, it appears that the most controversial point in the letter is the 'imminent threat' allegation, which has often been criticised by scholars as an invalid argument for justifying the use of force in self-defence. This issue has also divided UN member states. They have explicitly disagreed about: whether they have the right to use military force pre-emptively, to defend themselves against imminent threats; and whether they have the right to use it preventively to defend themselves against latent or non-imminent threats.[124]

What is clear in this regard is that the lawfulness of the use of force in self-defence against the imminent threat of armed attack is still a subject of controversy, so much so that the ICJ has remained silent and has expressed no view on the issue. However, the ICJ has said that '… reliance is placed by the Parties only on the right of self-defence in the case of an armed attack which has already occurred'.[125] This is exactly the point that has already been underlined in the decision by Turkey's Court of Cassation and in the letter dated 9 October addressed to the UNSC. Moreover, not only have continuing operations reached the threshold of armed attack, and attacks have already occurred across the country, but also the imminent threat of attack by the aforementioned

[122] Ibid.

[123] Letter dated 9 October 2019 from the Permanent Representative of Turkey to the United Nations addressed to the President of the Security Council, UN Doc S/2019/804 (9 October 2019). For further discussion, see Schmidt (15 November 2019), above n 101; Todeschini (21 October 2019), above n 102.

[124] See UNGA, 'In Larger Freedom: Towards Development, Security and Human Rights for All', Report of the Secretary-General, UN Doc A/59/2005 (21 March 2005), paras 122–26.

[125] *Case Concerning Military and Paramilitary Activities in and against Nicaragua* (27 June 1986), above n 4 at para 194.

groups have compelled Turkey to use force in northern Syria. In short, even if one argues that the 'continuity' is not met in the present case, the risk of the provision of weapons to the PKK may still prove to be a justification for Turkish military intervention against the imminent threat stemming from the YPG in northern Syria. As the ICJ stated, it is almost inevitable that:

> The concept of 'armed attack' includes not only acts by armed bands where such acts occur on a significant scale but also assistance to rebels in the form of the provision of weapons or logistical or other support. Such assistance may be regarded as a threat or use of force ....[126]

Having moved in the same direction, Turkey has already expressed its concerns, saying that the weapons given by the US to the YPG to use against Islamic State in Syria, are ultimately finding their way to the PKK for use against Turkey[127] due to the weakness of Islamic State in Syrian territory.

The second argument is that even if the authorising factors mentioned above robustly justify Turkey's position in using force against the YPG and Islamic State as a last resort, its military response needs to have complied with the basic requirements of self-defence including 'necessity and proportionality' contained in Article 51 of the UN Charter as the core principles of international law regulating *jus ad bellum*. As the ICJ reaffirmed in the *Nicaragua* case, the lawfulness of any response to an attack depends on observance of the criteria of the necessity and the proportionality of the measures taken in self-defence.[128] Otherwise, any form of the military operation in self-defence that does not respect the mentioned conditions might be regarded as a violation of Article 2(4) of the UN Charter. From this particular perspective, therefore, it seems that the major challenge to Turkey's 'self-defence' military operations in northern Syria, particularly to Operation Peace Spring, might come from the indiscriminate use of force, mostly by the Turkish-backed armed forces from the Free Syrian Army, in violation of *jus in bello* and international human rights law. As reported by the Office of the UN High Commissioner for Human Rights (OHCHR), the aforementioned groups have been accused of the extrajudicial execution of multiple civilians, intimidation, ill-treatment, killing, kidnapping, looting and

[126] Ibid. For further discussion, see SA Alexandrov, *Self-Defense against the Use of Force in International Law* (The Hague, Kluwer Law International, 1996) 139–49; IM Lobo De Souza, 'Revisiting the Right of Self-Defence against Non-State Armed Entities' (2016) 53 *Canadian Yearbook of international Law* 202; B Michael, 'Responding to Attacks by Non-State Actors: The Attribution Requirement of Self-Defence' (2009) 16 *Australian International Law Journal* 133, 135–37.

[127] See T Gumrukcu, 'Turkey says US Support for Syrian Kurdish YPG a Big Mistake', *Reuters* (18 November 2018), www.reuters.com/article/us-mideast-crisis-syria-turkey-usa-idUSKCN1NN09I; K Shaheen, 'US Decision to Arm Kurds in Syria Poses Threat to Turkey, Says Ankara', *The Guardian* (10 May 2017), www.theguardian.com/world/2017/may/10/ankara-calls-us-arming-of-kurds-fighting-isis-in-syria-a-threat-to-turkey.

[128] *Case Concerning Military and Paramilitary Activities in and against Nicaragua* (27 June 1986), above n 4 at para 194.

seizure of property, and the operation has displaced thousands of civilians.[129] Following their disproportionately violent operations in northern Syria, the UN Office for the Coordination of Humanitarian Affairs (OCHA) expressed deep concern regarding the human suffering in northern Syria and urged all parties to exercise restraint and to act in line with their obligations under the UN Charter and *jus in bello*, which advocates the protection of civilians and civilian infrastructure.[130]

Overall, many of the reasons justifying Turkish military intervention in northern Syria are still controversial in terms of the interpretation of the right to use force, since imminent attack as justification for self-defence is also the subject of some debate. By itself, the right to use force in self-defence is preserved in Article 51 of the UN Charter where an actual armed attack occurs. However, there is an accepted view which provides that all states have a right to use force in self-defence in order to avert the threat of an imminent attack, since it cannot be accepted in practice that self-defence must await an actual attack in all cases.[131] For this reason, the UN Secretary-General's Report on the High-Level Panel Report on Threats, Challenges and Change offers an objective and verifiable basis for the use of force against imminent threats, when it mentions that:

> The language of [Article 51] is restrictive … However, a threatened state, according to long-established international law, can take military action as long as the threatened attack is imminent, no other means would deflect it and the action is proportionate.[132]

[129] R Colville, 'Press Briefing Note on Syria', *OHCHR* (11 October 2019), www.ohchr.org/EN/NewsEvents/Pages/DisplayNews.aspx?NewsID=25129&LangID=E. See also UNSC, 'Turkey's Military Operation Has Displaced Thousands of Civilians, Worsened Syria's Dire Humanitarian Crisis, Top Official Warns Security Council', 8645th meeting (PM), UN Doc SC/13994 (24 October 2019), www.un.org/press/en/2019/sc13994.doc.htm; M Chulov 'Syria: Videos of Turkey-Backed Militias Show Potential War Crimes', *The Guardian* (26 October 2019), www.theguardian.com/world/2019/oct/26/syria-turkey-arab-videos-torture-kurdish-bodies-militia.

[130] See UN Human Rights Council, 'Report of the Independent International Commission of Inquiry on the Syrian Arab Republic', UN Doc A/HRC/44/61 (2 July 2020), paras 109–11. See also 'Humanitarian Chief Concludes Visit to Ankara and Turkey/Syria Border', *OCHA* (11 October 2019), www.unocha.org/story/humanitarian-chief-concludes-visit-ankara-and-turkeysyria-border.

[131] This would be the case if responding to the armed attack is necessary now, regardless of when and how exactly the attack will take place. In that sense, an imminent attack is thus one where the attacker has committed to a particular aggressive course of action which they will not desist from absent some kind of intervention in the causal chain, such as a use of force in self-defence. See M Milanovic, 'The Soleimani Strike and Self-Defence against an Imminent Armed Attack', *EJIL: Talk!* (7 January 2020), www.ejiltalk.org/the-soleimani-strike-and-self-defence-against-an-imminent-armed-attack/; GH Brandis QC, 'The Right of Self-Defence against Imminent Armed Attack in International Law', *EJIL: Talk!* (25 May 2017), www.ejiltalk.org/the-right-of-self-defence-against-imminent-armed-attack-in-international-law/; Wilmshurst (2006), above n 8 at 4.

[132] UNGA, 'Report of the High-Level Panel on Threats, Challenges and Change: Note by the Secretary-General Follow-up to the Outcome of the Millennium Summit', UN Doc A/59/565 (2 December 2004), para 188. For further discussion, see D Bethlehem, 'Self-Defense against an Imminent or Actual Armed Attack by Nonstate Actors' (2012) 106 *American Journal of International Law* 770; Kretzmer (2013), above n 85 at 235–82; Akande and Liefländer (2013), above n 85 at 563–70.

However, this is still problematic and the major challenge that remains is to establish what kind of threat might be considered equivalent to an imminent attack and what criteria indicate imminence. There remains a contradiction, however, since the wording of Article 51 is ambiguous and it is not clear to what extent it prohibits the adverse effects of the use of force in self-defence against ANSAs based in another state's territory. Therefore, one cannot claim that a broad interpretation of Article 51 might be inconsistent with the primary objective of the right of self-defence, which ensures the national security, territorial integrity and political independence of all states against armed attacks by other states or any form of violent ANSAs and terrorist groups.

It appears, however, that the legality of the Turkish military intervention in northern Syria remains dubious because of the scale of and the threshold for using force in self-defence. At some point, the scope of any form of force used in response to an armed attack is limited to necessary, proportionate, measured and responsible operations, even if approval of the right of self-defence for the victim state has already been given.

It might be also argued that Turkey's continued military presence in Syrian territory under Operation Peace Spring has lost its legitimacy. As discussed above, the primary objective of the Adana Security Agreement was repelling the advances of terrorist groups in the Turkish-Syrian border area. Considering that Turkey's troops have already repelled the YPG and Islamic State fighters by seizing control of approximately 30–35 km of Syrian territory, its continued presence in Syria as an extension of the treaty-based intervention is contrary to the primary objective and purpose of both the Adana Security Agreement and the Joint Cooperation Agreement. Both agreements provide that Turkey has the right to repel terrorist and other violent groups from its borders so that they can no longer threaten Turkey's national security. Removing Kurdish fighters from approximately 35 km of Syrian territory adjacent to its borders indicates that Turkey has gone far beyond the purpose of the Adana Security Agreement, which in Annex 4 confines any conceivably necessary Turkish security measures to an area 5 km deep into Syrian territory. According to Annex 4 of the Agreement, 'The Syrian side understands that its failure to take the necessary measures and security duties, stated in this agreement, gives Turkey the right to take all necessary security measures within 5 km deep into Syrian territory'.[133]

Turkey's continued military presence within Syrian territory might, therefore, be considered as a violation of Syria's territorial integrity as it is now ignoring the legitimacy and authority of the Syrian government within its own territory. Consequently, this latest action elicited a harsh response from the Syrian government, which sent identical letters dated 31 October 2019 to both

[133] The Adana Security Agreement signed by Turkey and Syria in Adana (20 October 1998), above n 91. See also C Kreß, 'A Collective Failure to Prevent Turkey's Operation "Peace Spring" and NATO's Silence on International Law', *EJIL: Talk!* (14 October 2019), www.ejiltalk.org/a-collective-failure-to-prevent-turkeys-operation-peace-spring-and-natos-silence-on-international-law/.

the UN Secretary-General and the President of the UNSC.[134] The letters stated that Turkey has occupied several Syrian villages and its military aggression against the Syrian people continues unabated. Having reaffirmed the inviolability, sovereignty and integrity of its territory, Syria reiterated the government's unwavering determination to continue the war against terrorism and to liberate any territory, particularly in northern Syria, that terrorist groups continue to control.

c. Military Intervention in Iraq

Turkey's third-longest border is its 378-km-long common frontier with Iraq in the north-eastern part of the country, as stipulated by the 1926 Frontier Treaty,[135] also known as the Ankara Treaty. In the 1990s, Turkey deployed its troops in northern Iraq to fight against the PKK without the prior consent of the Iraqi government.[136] Since then, the Turkish Armed Forces have resorted to armed operations in self-defence against the PKK bases in northern Iraq. Moreover, the international community of states characterised Turkey's military operations against the PKK as necessary self-defence measures, as a targeted response to terrorist attacks.[137] Similarly, Turkey deployed hundreds of armed troops to the Iraqi town of Bashiqa, 12 km northeast of Mosul in northern Iraq, to fight against Islamic State in October 2016, but Iraqi authorities called for Turkey to withdraw its forces. One of the most important questions in this respect, therefore, is whether Turkey's military intervention against Islamic State in northern Iraq was legal.

[134] See Identical Letters dated 31 October 2019 from the Permanent Representative of the Syrian Arab Republic to the United Nations addressed to the Secretary-General and the President of the Security Council, UN Doc S/2019/856 (31 October 2019).

[135] Treaty between the United Kingdom and Iraq and Turkey Regarding the Settlement of the Frontier Between Turkey and Iraq (Signed at Angora, 5 June 1926) (1927) 21(4) *American Journal of International Law* Supplement: Official Documents 136, 136–43. For a discussion see N Coşar and S Demirci, 'The Mosul Question and the Turkish Republic: Before and after the Frontier Treaty, 1926' (2006) 42 *Middle Eastern Studies* 123.

[136] Turkey's right to use force against the PKK in northern Iraq was evident in a 'Security Protocol' signed between Ankara and Baghdad in October 1984. The Protocol allowed raids on the PKK encampments in northern Iraq. According to the Protocol, both parties had the right to pursue the PKK fighters in the other's country to a maximum depth of 5 km. See M Charountaki, 'Turkish Foreign Policy and the Kurdistan Regional Government' (2012) 17 *Perceptions* 185, 189; A Nachman, *Turkey: Facing a New Millennium: Coping with Intertwined Conflicts* (Manchester, Manchester University Press, 2003) 12.

[137] CJ Tams and JG Devaney, 'Applying Necessity and Proportionality to Anti-Terrorist Self-Defence' (2012) 45 *Israel Law Review* 91. In 1995, Turkey claimed that Iraq is unable to prevent the use of northern Iraqi territory for cross-border terrorist attacks, and therefore Turkey has a right to conduct trans-border operations targeting exclusively terrorist elements based in and operating from northern Iraq. See Letter dated 24 July 1995 from the Charge d'affaires a.i. of the Permanent Mission of Turkey to the United Nations addressed to the President of the Security Council, UN Doc S/1995/605 (24 July 1995).

Despite Turkey's military operations conducted against the PKK without the prior consent of the Iraqi central government, its military intervention in northern Iraq to fight against Islamic State has been quite contentious due to Turkey's controversial justifications.

Historically, Mosul was part of the Ottoman Empire until the end of World War I, but as a result of Britain's occupation in 1918, after oil was found in the region, the question of the settlement of the frontier between Turkey and Iraq was redirected to the League of Nations. The League found that Iraq should retain Mosul, and the new Republic of Turkey thereby reluctantly assented to the decision by signing the Frontier Treaty with Iraq in 1926 and was convinced to support the independence of Iraq. Turkey then agreed to act in accordance with the Treaty, mainly because Iraq agreed to give a 10 per cent royalty on Mosul's oil deposits to Turkey for 25 years in accordance with Article 14 of the Treaty. The Frontier Treaty, which was signed in Ankara on 5 June 1926 by the UK and Turkey, therefore determined the political borders between Turkey and Iraq and regulated relations between the two neighbours. The Treaty entered into force on 20 February 1926.

According to the common view among the majority of Turkish scholars, and as stated by former Turkish President Abdullah Gül, the signing of the Frontier Treaty meant that Turkey left Mosul to Iraq only on the condition of 'non-disruption of the national unity and territorial integrity of Iraq in any case'.[138] From this perspective, therefore, the national unity and territorial integrity of Iraq has since been disrupted as a result of Islamic State's terrorist actions, and the presence of this group in the region, and its terrorist actions in the frontier zone, also threatens Turkish national security and sovereignty. Beyond this, the occupation of Mosul and the capturing of dozens of hostages by Islamic State fighters after seizing the Turkish consulate in Mosul on 11 June 2014, were some of the primary motivating factors that compelled Turkey to join the US-led coalition against Islamic State (in August 2014) and to also begin unilateral operations in Mosul (in October 2016).[139]

As a legal basis, Turkish military intervention in Mosul was grounded in the statement, 'by all means in their power', of Article 6 of the Frontier Treaty, which reads:

> The High Contracting Parties undertake reciprocally to oppose by all means in their power any preparations made by one or more armed individuals with the object of committing acts of pillage or brigandage in the neighbouring frontier zone and to prevent them from crossing the frontier.

[138] See 'Abdullah Gül: Irak Bölünürse, Hakkımız Doğar', *Yeni Akit* (10 June 2014), www.yeniakit.com.tr/haber/abdullah-gul-irak-bolunurse-hakkimiz-dogar-20327.html. See also Coşar and Demirci (2006), above n 135 at 123–32.

[139] T Ruys and N Verlinden, 'Digest of State Practice 1 January–30 June 2014' (2014) 1 *Journal on the Use of Force and International Law* 357. See also 'ISIS Militants Kidnap Turkish Diplomats after Seizing Consulate in Mosul', *The Guardian* (11 June 2014), www.theguardian.com/world/2014/jun/11/isis-militants-kidnap-turkish-diplomats-consulate-mosul-iraq.

The Turkish authorities have argued that Article 6 allows the Turkish Armed Forces to intervene in Iraq in order to ensure the sovereignty and territorial integrity of Iraq in Mosul, which is primarily inhabited by ethnic Turkmens, who associate themselves with Turkic origins and mostly adhere to a Turkish heritage and identity. In other words, Turkey relates its intervention to the protection of its kinsmen (the Iraqi Turkmen) in the region. Furthermore, the occupation of, and the committing of terrorist attacks in the frontier zone between Turkey and Iraq could be interpreted as acts of pillage or brigandage in the frontier zone, as described in Article 6 of the Treaty.

However, the justifications are still controversial in legal terms. A broad interpretation of Article 6 in order to confer the right to military intervention in Iraq's territory is inconsistent with the Treaty's objectives and purpose, as it is clear that such an interpretation is not in compliance with the ordinary meaning that is given to the terms used in Article 6 of the Frontier Treaty.

According to Article 31(1) of the 1969 Vienna Convention on the Law of Treaties, 'A treaty shall be interpreted in good faith in accordance with the ordinary meaning to be given to the terms of the treaty in their context and in light of its object and purpose'. In the same way, Shaw argues that:

> … any true interpretation of a treaty in international law will have to take into account all aspects of the agreement, from the words employed to the intention of the parties and the aims of the particular document. It is not possible to exclude completely any one of these components.[140]

From this perspective, therefore, it would not be accurate to state that Article 6 of the Frontier Treaty allows the military intervention of the state parties in each other's internal affairs, since boundary treaties between states are based on the principles of respect for sovereignty and the respective rights and interests of the contracting parties. This means that boundary treaties cannot be interpreted broadly in favour of one side or the other. In simple terms, a broad interpretation of the provisions of boundary treaties between two or more states could cause them to go beyond international norms. Nevertheless, Turkish military intervention in Mosul could be examined in the context of some of the political justifications. As the Turkish authorities have argued, Turkey seeks to protect its economic and political interests in Mosul while fighting both the PKK and Islamic State. The fact is that the question of Mosul is very significant for Turkey, not only because Islamic State was occupying the city but also because the presence of the PKK in this region genuinely threatens Turkish national security in the Turkey-Iraq border region.[141]

[140] MN Shaw, *International Law* (Cambridge, Cambridge University Press, 2014) 676. For further discussion, see RK Gardiner, *Treaty Interpretation* (Oxford, Oxford University Press, 2015) 181–222; A Orakhelashvili, *The Interpretation of Acts and Rules in Public International Law* (Oxford, Oxford University Press, 2008) 301–92; C Fairman, 'The Interpretation of Treaties' (1934) 20 *Transactions of the Grotius Society* 123.

[141] It has been showed that the PKK established a de facto and military administration in Sinjar, west of Mosul, after entering Sinjar to fight against Islamic State under the banner of the Sinjar

From a legal point of view, as the ICJ has pointed out in the *Corfu Channel* case, 'alleged right of intervention as the manifestation of a policy of force, such as has, in the past, given rise to most serious abuses and as such cannot … find a place in international law …'.[142] Accordingly, respect by independent states for each other's territorial integrity and sovereignty forms the basis of international relations. However, one might argue from a political point of view that military intervention in Mosul by Turkey, as a country that has been confronted with the terrorist actions of the separatist militants of the PKK for more than 40 years, would be justifiable. From this perspective, it can be argued, at first glance, that Turkey's unilateral military intervention in Iraq based on the right of self-defence is justifiable by the inability or unwillingness of the host state, Iraq, to suppress the threats of the ANSAs on its territory. In this case, however, international law prohibits such an intervention under any circumstances. Although the Iraqi central government has not been able to take any action against the PKK or Islamic State within its territory, the right to the extraterritorial use of military force based on the states' own assessment of the situation has not been established in customary international law,[143] and the legality of such operations under the 'unwilling or unable theory' is a matter of controversy in international law.

In both cases, Turkey has relied on alternative and almost complementary grounds to justify its military intervention in Iraq (based on the 1926 Frontier Treaty) and in Syria (based on the 1998 Adana Security Agreement and the 2010 Joint Cooperation Agreement) rather than the 'unwilling or unable theory'. Even if it is accepted that Turkey's cross-border operations in northern Syria are justified under the bilateral counterterrorism agreements between Turkey and Syria, the legality of the Turkish military presence in Syria and its approach to the extraterritorial use of force against Islamic State in Iraq based is contentious given that Turkey has moved beyond *jus ad bellum* considerations.

Turkey's military presence in northern Syria has lost legitimacy, as the primary objective of the Adana Security Agreement is to repel the advances of terrorist groups across Turkish borders. Given that Turkey has already repelled the Kurdish and Islamic State fighters by seizing control of a buffer zone some 30–35 km deep, Turkey's continued presence could be contrary to the main purposes of both the Adana Security Agreement and the Joint Cooperation Agreement. Turkey has already expelled Kurdish and Islamic State fighters from the zone and, consequently, has achieved success according to the purposes of

Resistance. Turkey's main concern, therefore, has been the filling of any possible power gap emerging in northern Iraq by the PKK. In other words, although Sinjar has been liberated from Islamic State, the Iraqi central government is still unable to manage the region. See International Crisis Group, 'The PKK's Fateful Choice in Northern Syria' (2017) 176 *Middle East Report* 1, 1–35, www.refworld.org/pdfid/590b13ef4.pdf.

[142] *Corfu Channel Case* (9 April 1949), above no 44 at 35. See also *Case Concerning Military and Paramilitary Activities in and against Nicaragua* (27 June 1986), above n 4 at para 202.

[143] *Case Concerning Military and Paramilitary Activities in and against Nicaragua* (27 June 1986), above n 4 at para 195.

both agreements. A continued military presence on Syrian territory might therefore be considered a violation of Syria's territorial integrity and a usurpation of the authority of the Syrian government within its own borders. In essence, given that the exclusive purpose of self-defence actions is to halt and repel an armed attack, seizing control of part of Syria and the consequent displacement of local civilians is an example of excessive force by Turkey.[144]

C. The Effectiveness of the Extraterritorial Use of Force against Islamic State

Regardless of the consequences for intervening states who are victims of Islamic State's threats, it would appear that the extraterritorial use of armed force against Islamic State due to the failure, unwillingness or inability of host states to suppress the threat of ANSAs has led to changes in international law. Military intervention in Syria, in the absence of a UNSC resolution or the consent of the Syrian government, overwhelmingly undermines the UNSC's position as the primary international authority for maintaining and restorating of international peace and security. UNSC Resolution 2249 (2015), in which the Council refrained from referring to the extraterritorial use of force in Syrian territory, explicitly indicates that the Council should refrain from avoiding the principles of sovereignty, territorial integrity and political independence.

With an increasing number of military interventions based on the 'unwilling or unable theory', some arguments have been proposed in support of the US's position in Syria. For instance, Michael P Scharf argues that the US's justification for using force against Islamic State is based on the view that limited use of force in Syria, which is seen as a failed state, would not violate Syria's territorial integrity because Syria itself does not exercise meaningful control over its own borders or territory. Such an argument, however, constituted a radical departure from the traditional view that a state's legal status, rights and responsibilities do not evaporate just because it loses control over parts of its territory, such as during periods of civil war, insurgency or governmental collapse.[145]

Even in the context of the right of self-defence, it is still a subject of controversy as to how the extraterritorial use of force based on the 'unwilling or unable theory' without either a UNSC resolution or the consent of the host state would fulfil the necessary requirements for using reasonable force in self-defence.

[144] See for details, Green and Waters (2015), above n 86 at 11; JA Green, *The International Court of Justice and Self-Defence in International Law* (Oxford, Hart Publishing, 2009) 66–96. As Adam Roberts has argued, a military presence in a territory not fully sanctioned by valid agreement is a criterion which can help identify military occupation. See A Roberts, 'What Is Military Occupation' (1984) 55 *British Yearbook of International Law* 249.

[145] Given the large number of failed states – based on extensive areas within their borders outside government control – the creation of a new customary international law that would allow states to invade other states whenever they deem that 'state failure' has occurred would create a 'legion of loopholes' in the UN Charter and substantial potential for abuse. See Scharf (2016), above n 18 at 49.

Even if Islamic State's operations are entirely characterised as armed attacks that require necessary countermeasures, Syria's conditional consent to military intervention cannot be construed as a justification to resort to the unilateral use of force in Syrian territory.[146] As mentioned above, although the 'unwilling or unable theory' is well established in the US legal approach, the practice shows that the efforts made to create a new exception to the prohibition on the use of force in international law will cause problems regarding the application of *jus ad bellum* in future.

Regardless of the political considerations, it seems clear that the 'unwilling or unable theory' will increasingly be used as justification for states to use force in foreign territory based on their own assessment of a situation. Minimising the number of casualties and harm to civilians during both domestic and international armed conflicts is the primary objective of *jus in bello* when applied to warring parties. However, it seems clear that some states might feel pressured into using force under the 'unwilling or unable theory' without considering the possible impacts.

The US-led coalition has retaken a large part of the territories formerly occupied by Islamic State, and thousands of Islamic State fighters have been killed in the US-led airstrikes. However, it appears that the extraterritorial use of force against Islamic State has had severe humanitarian consequences.[147] For example, the US-led coalition failed to take precautions to minimise harm to civilians caused by the airstrikes. As a result, Amnesty International has reported that more than 1,600 civilians have been killed as a direct result of the US-led coalition's air campaign (34,502 strikes since 2014) against Islamic State in the northern Syrian city of Raqqa. According to the report, the coalition killed hundreds and injured thousands of Syrian civilians, and the city was obliterated. As a result of the coalition's indiscriminate use of artillery in densely populated areas, Raqqa's residents were trapped as fighting raged in the streets between Islamic State and the SDF, led by the YPG, while the coalition's airstrikes rained down.[148]

Therefore, even if the extraterritorial use of force based on the 'unwilling or unable theory' is accepted as a new exception to the prohibition on the use

[146] K Tibori-Szabó, 'The "Unwilling or Unable" Test and the Law of Self-Defence' in C Paulussen et al, *Fundamental Rights in International and European Law: Public and Private Perspectives* (The Hague, TMC Asser Press, 2016) 95.

[147] As pointed out by the UN Secretary-General, with respect to the Syrian civil war, 'fighting terrorism does not absolve warring parties of their core obligations under international law'. See 'Save Idlib from "Transforming into a Blood Bath", UN Chief Guterres Urges Fighters and Their Allies', *UN News* (11 September 2018), https://news.un.org/en/story/2018/09/1018992.

[148] See 'Thank You for Demanding Justice for Syrians Killed by US-led Coalition', *Amnesty International* (24 September 2019), www.amnesty.org.uk/syrians-us-led-coalition; 'Syria: Unprecedented Investigation Reveals US-led Coalition Killed More Than 1,600 Civilians in Raqqa "Death Trap"', *Amnesty International* (25 April 2019), www.amnesty.org/en/latest/news/2019/04/syria-unprecedented-investigation-reveals-us-led-coalition-killed-more-than-1600-civilians-in-raqqa-death-trap/.

of force, the force used in self-defence against the ANSAs in the territory of a so-called failed state must comply with the basic principles of *jus ad bellum*.

First, the force used in response to an attack must be proportionate. That is, the consequences of the force used in response must not be unreasonable or excessive in relation to the harm expected from the attack. In that sense, therefore, the principle of proportionality limits the power of states to resort to force, and states can only resort to force to defend themselves against an armed attack and only to such extent as is necessary to repel it.[149]

Second, the force used in self-defence must be necessary and must be strictly limited to military objectives (proportionality). The necessity and proportionality principles, in relation to military targeting, are asserted to be derived from the 1837 sinking of the steamship Caroline.[150] Military targeting, which stretches back to the very beginnings of customary international law governing self-defence,[151] notably refers to a restriction in the choice of targets in self-defence. In that sense, the necessity principle determines whether military force may be used, and where it must be directed. Proportionality proceeds to govern how much force is permissible to achieve a defensive purpose and guards against excessive reactions, such as attacks on civilian targets.[152] This is inferred from the 2003 *Oil Platforms* decision by the ICJ, in which the Court noted that 'one aspect of these criteria [necessity and proportionality] is the nature of the target of the force used avowedly in self-defence'.[153] As Green and Waters pointed out, this statement indicates that non-military targeting is contrary to the customary *jus ad bellum* necessity and proportionality criteria regulating self-defence.[154]

Indeed, the legality of the military force used by the US-led coalition in self-defence against Islamic State would rest on whether it was reasonable for the coalition to resort to self-defence in these circumstances in Iraq and Syria. While *jus ad bellum*, out of necessity and proportionality, only restricts the exercise of the right of self-defence to military targets connected with actual or imminent armed attack, it seems that the US-led coalition states' indiscriminate and uncontrolled attacks on the Iraqi and Syrian energy resources and installations controlled by Islamic State were punitive reactions. This means that their legality is a matter of controversy.

[149] See also Kretzmer (2013), above n 85 at 235–83; R van Steenberghe, 'Proportionality under Jus Ad Bellum and Jus in Bello: Clarifying Their Relationship' (2012) 45 *Israel Law Review* 107.

[150] For general information, see Jennings (1938), above n 7 at 82–99; Green (2006), above n 7 at 429–80; Wood (2018), above n 87 at 5–16.

[151] Green and Waters (2015), above n 86 at 10.

[152] K Okimoto, 'The Cumulative Requirements of Jus ad Bellum and Jus in Bello in the Context of Self-Defense' (2012) 11 *Chinese Journal of International Law* 45, 65; Green and Waters (2015), above n 86 at 12.

[153] *Case Concerning Oil Platforms* (6 November 2003), above n 85 at para 74. See also *Case Concerning Armed Activities on the Territory of the Congo (Democratic Republic of the Congo v Uganda)* (19 December 2005), above n 11 at para 147; *Case Concerning Military and Paramilitary Activities in and against Nicaragua* (27 June 1986), above n 4 at para 237; *Legality of the Threat or Use of Nuclear Weapons* (8 July 1996), above n 6 at para 30.

[154] Green and Waters (2015), above n 86 at 10.

Although the tragic humanitarian impacts of the airstrikes on Islamic State in Syria have not prevented the US-led coalition from targeting energy resources and installations controlled by Islamic State, their extensive and punitive operations, ostensibly in self-defence, were condemned by the Syrian government and some other states as unnecessary and, therefore, illegal conduct.[155] Importantly, inconsistency in state practice, and the ICJ's jurisprudence with respect to the levels of necessity and proportionality that are employed in identifying any excessive military force used in the exercise of self-defence, makes it quite difficult to determine the extent to which the coalition's self-defence operations against Islamic State in Syria have been lawful.[156] In contrast, the interpretation of the customary rules of *jus ad bellum*, which broadly authorise uncontrolled use of force in foreign territory in response to threats, would pave the way for the states to go beyond the boundaries of international law governing self-defence.

Bernard Brodie argues that the US is accustomed to regarding a treaty obligation for military intervention to be sufficient justification for such an intervention.[157] Therefore, given that the use of force under the 'unwilling or unable theory' is not provided for in treaty law, but is rather an argument that the US supports, one cannot claim that it reflects the view of the majority of the international community. Conversely, a generally accepted view is that the extraterritorial use of armed force without the consent of the territorial state or the UNSC must be justified under the conditions contained in Article 51 of the UN Charter.[158] This means that there is no right to use extraterritorial armed force in support of the UN Charter in terms of maintaining international peace and security except by an affirmative vote by the UNSC.[159] Otherwise, it might be expected that states would simply make arbitrary decisions to act in a foreign territory based upon their own assumptions and understanding of the situation in that particular state. The extraterritorial use of force against Islamic State within Syrian territory without UNSC approval and the consent of the territorial state indicates that intervening states have not respected the UNSC's primary responsibility for the maintenance of international peace and security, since the Council has already clarified its approach to the security mechanisms

[155] For more details, see Identical Letters dated 24 December 2019 from the Chargé d'affaires a.i. of the Permanent Mission of the Syrian Arab Republic to the United Nations addressed to the Secretary-General and the President of the Security Council, UN Doc S/2019/987 (24 December 2019). See also Corten (2016), above n 21 at 788–91, 796–97.

[156] See Green (2009), above n 144 at 95; Ruys (2010), above n 60 at 116; L Arimatsu and M Schmitt, 'The Legal Basis for the War against ISIS Remains Contentious', *The Guardian* (6 October 2014), www.theguardian.com/commentisfree/2014/oct/06/legal-basis-war-isis-syria-islamic-state.

[157] See B Brodie, *War and Politics* (London, Cassel Ltd, 1973) 153.

[158] D Kretzmer, 'Use of Lethal Force against Suspected Terrorists' in AMSD Frias et al (eds), *Counter-Terrorism: International Law and Practice* (Oxford, Oxford University Press, 2012) 623.

[159] Brodie (1973), above n 157 at 154. For a discussion, see Q Wright, 'The Legality of Intervention under the United Nations Charter' (1957) 51 *Proceedings of the American Society of International Law at Its Annual Meeting (1921–1969)* 79.

required to combat Islamic State through adopting Resolution 2249 (2015). What is clear, however, is that the Council reaffirmed that the necessity of combatting terrorism must comply with all the states' obligations under international law, particularly with regard to international human rights, refugee and humanitarian law. It has not authorised unilateral military intervention in Syria.

To make matters worse, the coalition has accepted responsibility for the civilian deaths as a result of the 2017 airstrikes (mainly in Raqqa), but Islamic State has not been eradicated and no compensation has been paid for the significant humanitarian consequences of the extraterritorial use of force justified by the 'unwilling or unable theory' in Syria. As a result, it seems that maintaining international peace and security is no longer the main priority.

III. MILITARY ASSISTANCE ON REQUEST IN THE WAR WITH ISLAMIC STATE

A. The Conceptual Framework of Military Assistance on Request

Military assistance at the request of another government is one of the most highly disputed and controversial subjects of international law. It is also one of the most important limits on state sovereignty and territorial integrity. It can be defined as when a state seeks assistance from other states to defend its borders from outside attacks, internal disturbances and isolated guerrilla or terrorist activities. However, military intervention in this vein has been accepted by the international community of states when consent has been granted by a state to 'reinforce its authority'.[160] As reaffirmed by UNSC Resolution 387 (1976), it is the 'inherent and lawful right of every state, in the exercise of its sovereignty, to request assistance from any other state or group of states'.[161] The jurisprudence of the ICJ provides some illustrations. According to the ICJ, and contrary to the incompatibility of military intervention by a mere request for assistance made by an opposition group in another state with the principle of non-intervention (as per customary international law), military intervention is permissible at the request of the government of a state. This is evidence that stems from the wording of the ICJ in the *Nicaragua* case: 'Indeed, it is difficult to see what would remain of the principle of non-intervention in international law if intervention, which is already allowable at the request of the government of a state, were also to be allowed at the request of the opposition'.[162]

[160] GH Fox, 'Intervention by Invitation' in M Weller (ed), *Oxford Handbook of the Use of Force in International Law* (Oxford, Oxford University Press, 2015) 821; TC Heller and AD Sofaer, 'Sovereignty: The Practitioner's Prospective' in SD Krasner (ed), *Problematic Sovereignty: Contested Rules and Political Possibilities* (New York, Colombia University Press, 2001) 24–25.

[161] UNSC, Resolution 387, UN Doc S/RES/387 (31 March 1976).

[162] *Case Concerning Military and Paramilitary Activities in and against* Nicaragua (27 June 1986), above n 4 at para 246.

Nevertheless, as Brownlie has argued, a problem arises when the legal status of the government that is alleged to have given consent is in doubt.[163] Further, doctrine and state practice limit the requests of the established and internationally recognised government of a state for assistance (which is often made in the form of detachments of armed forces or the supply of military equipment[164]) to particular circumstances. Given the unpredictable impacts of military intervention, the legitimacy of any intervention by request depends on the factual requirements of 'effective control of the state government over its territory' and the 'democratic legitimacy of the state government'.[165]

Regarding the first requirement, while there is no precise definition of effective control or what constitutes it, the most widely accepted view is that effective control, as the test for a government's capacity to represent the state, has largely been measured by the degree to which the government has a certain level of unconditional control and commands the obedience of the people within the state. In addition, all population groups and institutions within the jurisdiction of the state recognise and accept the incumbent government's superiority and its right to represent the state as a whole.[166]

The second requirement is democratic legitimacy – a criterion for the recognition of a government in international law. Although there is no precise definition of democratic legitimacy, it generally refers to a human rights-based conception of domestic governance and the capability of a government which came to power with the will of the people, expressed through a free and fair electoral process, to exert its power in a manner consistent with basic political freedoms and the rule of law.[167] What is significant here, however, is that customary international law, which permits states to consider the democratic legitimacy of a government for the purposes of recognition, does not yet require them to do so. In other words, customary international law does not oblige states to withhold recognition of a government that came into power through unconstitutional means.

[163] I Brownlie, *International Law and the Use of Force by States* (Oxford, Oxford University Press, 1963) 317. For further discussion, see L Visser, 'May the Force Be with You: The Legal Classification of Intervention by Invitation' (2019) 66 *Netherlands International Law Review* 21; Doswald-Beck (1985), above n 43 at 189–252; Byrne (2016), above n 76 at 107–10.

[164] Jennings and Watts (1996), above n 106 at 435.

[165] Broadly speaking, the authority which has come to power and exercises full control over the country would have to be regarded as the legitimate government of the state, and is therefore entitled to give consent to military assistance that may be regarded as valid under international law. See CJ Le Mon, 'Unilateral Intervention by Invitation in Civil Wars: The Effective Control Test Tested' (2003) 35 *New York University Journal of International Law and Politics* 741, 743–46; K Macak, *Internationalized Armed Conflicts in International Law* (Oxford, Oxford University Press, 2018) 112–19.

[166] SD Murphy, 'Democratic Legitimacy and the Recognition of States and Governments' (1999) 48 *International and Comparative Law Quarterly* 545, 566; D Wippman, 'Military Intervention, Regional Organizations, and Host-State Consent' (1996) 7 *Duke Journal of Comparative and International Law* 209, 212; E de Wet, 'From Free Town to Cairo via Kiev: The Unpredictable Road of Democratic Legitimacy in Governmental Recognition' (2014) 108 *AJIL Unbound* 201, 203.

[167] See J D'Aspremont, 'Legitimacy of Governments in the Age of Democracy' (2006) 38 *New York University Journal of International Law and Politics* 877, 899; J D'Aspremont, 'The Rise and Fall of Democracy Governance in International Law: A Reply to Susan Marks' (2011) 22 *European Journal of International Law* 549, 569–70.

Accordingly, it could be argued that the criterion of democratic legitimacy is only one of many factors to consider when recognising a government. Although the most important factor is still effective control as a criterion for the validity of consent to authorise military assistance,[168] it cannot be the only one.

Given this, therefore, the requesting state will be able to request military assistance if its government has effective control over its territory. However, even if the requesting state meets the requirement of democratic legitimacy in order to obtain military assistance, the requirement of effective control is still a subject of controversy since it is not clear to what extent control could be recognised as effective. For instance, even though Islamic State took control of significant part of Iraqi and Syrian territory from 2014 until November 2017, the US-led military intervention in Iraq, and the Russian and Iranian military intervention in Syria, has been justified because of requests by the legitimate and effective governments of Iraq and Syria. Eventually, it seems that the international community of states, while clarifying the concepts of effective control and democratic legitimacy, will need to take steps forward to strike a balance between these factual requirements of military assistance by request.

Apart from the factors mentioned above, military assistance by request will still be controversial in terms of validity, legality and enforceability, if the requesting state is engaged in a civil war. In principle, third-party states must legally refrain from interfering, assisting or participating in civil wars if the rebels or opposition groups have been granted recognition of insurgency or belligerency.[169] Therefore, in dealing with civil wars in which the control of a state is divided between warring factions, military intervention will be controversial, even if it is at the request of the territorial state's established government.[170]

As an exception, however, there is a well-accepted view indicating that military intervention by request in the internal armed conflict would be considered justified if there was a war against a violent ANSA or terrorist group committing atrocities against the state forces and civilians.[171] Under these circumstances, military intervention is acceptable only by the request of the government of the

[168] De Wet (2014), above n 166 at 206–207; Le Mon (2003), above n 165 at 745.

[169] *Case Concerning Military and Paramilitary Activities in and against Nicaragua* (27 June 1986), above n 4 at para 109. See also PC Szasz, 'Role of the United Nations in Internal Conflicts' (1983) 13 *Georgia Journal of International and Comparative Law* 345, 348; O Schachter, 'In Defence of International Rules on the Use of Force' (1986) 53 *The University of Chicago Law Review* 113, 137.

[170] Jennings and Watts (1996), above n 106 at 438. See also C Nowak, 'The Changing Law of Non-Intervention in Civil Wars – Assessing the Production of Legality in State Practice after 2011' (2018) 5 *Journal on the Use of Force and International Law* 40; Lumsden (2003), above n 43 at 795–838.

[171] The operations under 'such interventions may involve actual fighting by the foreign troops but [these operations] may also be limited to power projection or to other forms of active military support'. G Nolte, 'Intervention by Invitation' (2010) *Max Planck Encyclopaedias of International Law*, para 1, www.jura.uni-bonn.de/fileadmin/Fachbereich_Rechtswissenschaft/Einrichtungen/Lehrstuehle/Herdegen/de_Wet/WiSe_2017/Voelkerrecht_III__Collective_Security/Intervention_by_Invitation.pdf. See also L Visser, 'Intervention by Invitation and Collective Self-Defence: Two Sides of the Same Coin?' (2020) 7 *Journal on the Use of Force and International Law* 292, 296–98.

state in question and in support of the legitimacy of the government of the requesting state that is fighting terrorism and violent ANSAs.

Given that the primary objective of military assistance by request is suppressing the threat of terrorist groups or ANSAs against the requesting state, it is necessary to distinguish between military intervention by request within the territory of the requesting state and collective self-defence in support of a state which is the victim of an armed attack. The primary difference between these two categories of the use of force is about the location of the targets. In other words, military force used as part of military assistance by request is limited to the territory of the requesting state. If the requesting state is attacked on its territory by another state or by an ANSA, then the assisting state would only use force against the attacking state or the ANSA on the territory of the requesting state. By contrast, military force as part of collective self-defence can be used outside the requesting state's territory, that is, it can also be used within the territory of the state that attacked the requesting state in the first place.[172]

There exists no general rule in international law that provides that military intervention by request is an exception to the general prohibition on the use of force contained in Article 2(4) of the UN Charter. Conversely, military intervention in support of ANSAs or rebel groups is prohibited. Following the ICJ's jurisprudence once more, '... no such general right of intervention, in support of an opposition within another state, exists in contemporary international law'.[173] Moreover, any form of direct or indirect intervention in civil wars 'in violation of the [UN Charter], of the principles of non-intervention, of equal rights and self-determination of peoples and generally accepted standards of human rights and in particular when its object is to support an established government against its own population'[174] is prohibited.

Under no circumstances can the consent or request of a territorial state be used as a basis for committing human rights violations, such as assassinations, torture or any forms of inhumane treatment, or attacking civilians and civilian objects within the requesting state's territory. It is also widely held that military intervention by request in support of the requesting state which is engaged in a fight against a liberation movement struggling for its right to self-determination would constitute a violation of the general prohibition on the use of force, the political independence of the requesting state and the right to self-determination. In terms of Article 2(4) of the UN Charter, this would be defined as a use of force against the political independence of the requesting state engaged in a civil war.[175] Under these circumstances, the assisting state may be held responsible for the

[172] See in general, Visser (2019), above n 163 at 27–29.

[173] *Case Concerning Military and Paramilitary Activities in and against Nicaragua* (27 June 1986), above n 4 at para 209.

[174] See MG Hafner, 'Present Problems of the Use of Force in International Law: A Report of Sub-Group C on Military Assistance on Request' (2011) 49 *Archiv des Völkerrechts,* Article 3(1), 474.

[175] See O Schachter, 'The Right of States to Use Armed Force' (1984) 82 *Michigan Law Review* 1620, 1641; Wippman (1996), above n 166 at 212.

operations and wrongful conduct committed to repressing the legal demands of the people of the requesting state. According to Article 16 of the ILC's Draft Articles on the Responsibilities of States for Internationally Wrongful Acts (2001), a state which aids or assists another state in the commission of an internationally wrongful act by the latter is internationally responsible for doing so if: (a) that state does so with knowledge of the circumstances of the internationally wrongful act; and (b) the act would be internationally illegal if committed by that state.[176] In its commentary, the ILC states that 'such situations can arise when a state voluntarily assists or aids another state in carrying out conduct which violates the international obligations of the latter, for example, by knowingly providing an essential facility or financing the activity in question'.[177] However, it should be emphasised that aid or assistance by the assisting state should not be confused with the responsibility of the acting state. In such a case, the assisting state will only be responsible to the extent that its conduct has caused harm or has contributed to the internationally wrongful act; it is not responsible for the actions of the requesting state.[178]

Aside from the above, any type of operations by the assisting state must comply with the relevant provisions of international human rights law and *jus in bello*, as well as any conditions imposed by the requesting state. This is where the requesting state seeks assistance to defend its borders from external attacks, internal disturbances and isolated guerrilla or terrorist activities. Although the consent of the requesting state justifies the use of military force by the assisting state in its territory, there exists a general rule of international law, according to which all states are subject to the exercise of the applicable law, including *jus in bello*, during military operations, even within a foreign territory in support of the requesting state.

Upon evaluation of the capability and limitations on military intervention by request of the territorial state, the legality and impacts of the US-led coalition's military intervention in Iraq, and the Russian and Iranian military intervention in Syria in support of the requesting state, need to be assessed in the specific context of the war with Islamic State.

B. The Legality and Impact of Military Assistance in the War with Islamic State

Although the absolute preconditions of providing military assistance are either a request for assistance or the consent of the legitimate and effective government

[176] ILC, 'Draft Articles on Responsibility of States for Internationally Wrongful Acts' (Annex to the UNGA Resolution A/RES/56/83, 85th, 12 December 2001) (2001) 2 *Yearbook of the International Law Commission* 26.

[177] Ibid, Commentary to Article 16 at 66–67.

[178] Ibid. See also B Graefrath, 'Complicity in the Law of International Responsibility' (1996) 29 *Belgian Review of International Law* 371, 380.

of the requesting state, the absence of a consensus between the international community of states in this regard has long been a source of controversy and discrepancy in state practice.

While the US-led coalition intervened in the non-international armed conflict in Iraq against Islamic State at the request of the Iraqi central government, the US authorities did not receive consent or a request from the Syrian government to use force against Islamic State in Syria. However, Iran and Russia, as the Syrian government's strategic allies in the region, did intervene at the request of the Syrian government.

Rather than try to articulate all the parties' policies and perceptions surrounding military assistance, discussion in this section will consider the positions of the states in the US-led coalition, Russia and Iran in both Iraq and Syria as the assisting states in the war with Islamic State, and the legality and consequences of their military intervention and presence in these countries.

i. US Military Assistance to Iraq

Despite the lack of a consensus among the international community over a legal standard for when and under which conditions they can resort to extraterritorial armed force in self-defence against ANSAs, when there is no request or consent to intervention by the territorial state, the cogent argument is that international law allows states to request military assistance from other states to restore law and order within their territory.[179] Taken to its primary objective, the standard provides that the consent of the requesting state to intervene militarily in its territory – limited to the permissible scope of the consent – legitimises the military actions of the assisting state in support of the requesting state against ANSAs and terrorist groups. In this respect, the Iraqi central government's consent, and its request for external support to defeat Islamic State provided a legal basis for the formation of a global campaign against Islamic State on Iraqi territory. The Iraqi central government's 2014 appeals addressed to the UN resonated among the international community of states. Having remarked on its struggles against Islamic State, the Iraqi central government called on the UN member states to continue their alliance against the group. As a major constituent, the Iraqi central government notified the UN that it had previously requested the assistance of the international community. It stated that:

> While we are grateful for what has been done to date, it has not been enough. We, therefore, call on the United Nations and the international community to recognise the serious threat our country and the international order are facing. These international terrorist groups seek to eliminate borders, exacerbate violence, and fan the flames of civil war. On the other hand, the Iraqi Government is seeking to avoid

[179] See L Arimatsu and MN Schmitt, 'Attacking "Islamic State" and the Khorasan Group: Surveying the International Law Landscape' (2014) 53 *Columbia Journal of Transnational Law Bulletin* 1, 6.

> falling into a cycle of violence. To that end, we need your support in order to defeat [Islamic State] and protect our territory and people. In particular, we call on the Member States to assist us by providing military training, advanced technology and the weapons required to respond to the situation, with a view to denying terrorists staging areas and safe havens.[180]

What is clear is that the inability of the only partially effective government of Iraq to suppress the threat posed by Islamic State compelled the Iraqi authorities to make a request under the above-mentioned letters to the UN, which was the primary justification for the extraterritorial armed operations including the US-led coalition's airstrikes in northern Iraq.

More importantly, the explicit request of the Iraqi central government for military assistance in the war against Islamic State demonstrated that the government of a state does not lose the ability to request military assistance from external parties even if it is confronted by internal violence reaching the level of a non-international armed conflict.[181] Accordingly, given that one of the primary conditions of collective self-defence on behalf of Iraq was provided as a result of the request of the Iraqi central government as a victim state, it appears clear that the legitimacy of the US-led coalition's extraterritorial military operations against Islamic State in Iraqi territory is beyond dispute. Because of this, a large segment of the international community of states refrained from questioning the coalition's operations in Iraq.

Following the occupation of a significant portion of Iraqi territory in 2014, Islamic State attacked and killed thousands of civilians and captured hundreds of women and children as slaves in the northern towns populated by Yazidi minorities. In the aftermath of Islamic State's violent offensive, the US intervened in northern Iraq in 2014 with the justification that the US could not turn a blind eye when it had the unique capacity to avert a massacre. This humanitarian catastrophe compelled the Iraqi central government to request US support in the fight against Islamic State under 'Operation Inherent Resolve' in August 2014.[182]

Following the US's unilateral operations in Iraq, the US government formed a coalition to fight Islamic State. The coalition consisted of 79 countries and international institutions including the European Union (EU), NATO and the Arab League. As part of its operations, the US deployed its troops to advise the Iraqi army and also launched airstrikes against Islamic State for more than three

[180] Letter dated 25 June 2014 from the Permanent Representative of Iraq to the United Nations addressed to the Secretary-General, UN Doc S/2014/440 (25 June 2014). See also Letter dated 20 September 2014 from the Permanent Representative of Iraq to the United Nations addressed to the President of the Security Council, UN Doc S/2014/691 (22 September 2014); Letter dated 23 September 2014 from the Permanent Representative of the United States of America to the United Nations addressed to the Secretary-General, UN Doc S/2014/695 (23 September 2014).

[181] See 'The Fine Line Between Collective Self-Defense and Intervention by Invitation: Reflections on the Use of Force against "IS" in Syria', *Just Security* (17 February 2015), www.justsecurity.org/20118/claus-kreb-force-isilsyria/.

[182] See Scharf (2016), above n 18 at 8.

years on the Iraqi central government's written request. The Iraqi authorities also asked that it be provided with the ability to carry out drone strikes, and if the US was unwilling to do that, Iraq was prepared for the US to carry out the airstrikes itself.[183]

However, the coalition states launched airstrikes against Islamic State in a way that increased the humanitarian crisis on the ground.[184] The indiscriminate armed attacks, the attacks on legitimate targets and civilians that were launched by coalition drones without distinction, led to many civilian deaths and injuries and the destruction of homes, property and religious, cultural and historical sites. The coalition conducted 34,547 airstrikes between August 2014 and the end of June 2019. According to the report assessed by *Airwars*, at least 8,214–13,125 civilians were likely to have been killed by airstrikes since the beginning of Operation Inherent Resolve.[185]

Furthermore, despite the lack of transparency over the use of armed drones, it has been reported that drones were being used to some extent in airstrikes on Islamic State's oil installations. Although the role and exact impact of the use of drones in terms of potentially raising or reducing environmental risks to local populations in the mentioned operations is not clear, it is widely accepted that environmental impacts of the use of force in general, and the use of armed drones in particular, remain under-documented as a form of harm that is relevant to assessing the limits that might be placed on different weapons technologies.[186]

In summary, the US-led military intervention at the request of the Iraqi central government to fight Islamic State made a dire humanitarian crisis on the ground worse as a result of the disproportionate number of airstrikes. These adverse humanitarian consequences seem to support the idea that the consent or request of the host state is not enough to justify all forms of military force when supporting the requesting state against ANSAs, although the humanitarian

[183] See P Baker and E Schmitt, 'Many Missteps in Assessment of ISIS Threat', *New York Times* (29 September 2014), www.nytimes.com/2014/09/30/world/middleeast/obama-fault-is-shared-in-misjudging-of-isis-threat.html.

[184] See 'Syria and Iraq: ICRC Calls for Better Compliance with Humanitarian Law', *ICRC News* (26 September 2014), www.icrc.org/en/document/syria-and-iraq-icrc-calls-better-compliance-humanitarian-law.

[185] See 'US-led Coalition in Iraq and Syria', *Airwars* (November 2019), https://airwars.org/conflict/coalition-in-iraq-and-syria/; 'Death in the City: High Levels of Civilian Harm in Modern Urban Warfare Resulting from Significant Explosive Weapons Use', *Airwars* (May 2018), https://airwars.org/wp-content/uploads/2018/05/Airwars-Death-in-the-City-web.pdf; 'Civilian Deaths in the Anti-ISIS Bombing Campaigns 2014–2015', *Ceasefire Centre for Civilian Rights and Minority Rights Group International* (November 2015), www.minorityrights.org/wp-content/uploads/2015/11/CEASEFIRE-REPORT-Civilian-deaths-in-the-anti-ISIS-bombing-campaigns-2014-15.pdf; 'Annual Report on Civilian Casualties in Connection with United States Military Operations', *US Department of State* (2018), www.fas.org/man/eprint/civcas2018.pdf.

[186] Having said that, the lasting environmental impacts and long-term risks to human health from the use of force must, in turn, be curbed through more robust international rules. See D Weir and E Minor, 'Environmental Harm' in R Acheson et al (eds), *The Humanitarian Impact of Drones* (New York, Pace University, 2017) 32–34.

impacts of the extraterritorial use of force against Islamic State is a subject of *jus in bello*, which will be discussed in Chapter 3.

ii. Russian and Iranian Military Assistance to Syria

Among the external powers that intervened in the war with Islamic State, the Syrian regime's strategic allies, including Iran and Russia, have played a substantial role in support of the Syrian government to keep control of the capital containing the machinery of government, much of the western part of the country, and almost all of the coastal region. Both Iran and Russia have close ties with Bashar al-Assad's regime. Along with financial support, military advice and training, Iran has reportedly deployed 1,000 members of the Iranian Revolutionary Guard in support of the Syrian regime to fight Islamic State and opposition groups since 2011. Likewise, the Russian government played an active role in support of Assad's regime, having deployed approximately 4,000 personnel in Syria as of November 2015. It has also been reported that the Russian forces have included ground forces, naval units, combat aircraft and helicopters that have been used in airstrikes against Islamic State and other opposition groups since their arrival in the country in late August 2015.[187] The mere fact that Russia and Iran are in Syria shows that besides their own agendas, their primary and common objective has been aiding the Syrian government to retake control of the strategic territory it had lost to Islamic State.

During the eight-year Syrian civil war, which has driven instability in the Middle East, Iran has been one of the key regional powers that have intervened to support President Bashar al-Assad's regime. As discussed above, the consent and request of the host state engaged in a non-international armed conflict are the major justifications that constitute a legal basis for military intervention by third-party states in order to assist the host state in defending its integrity and independence. Clearly, military assistance at the request of the host state is also an exception to the principle of sovereign equality of states, which provides that the territorial integrity and political independence of states are inviolable.[188] In a sense, sovereign equality is based on the states' commitment to respect the personality, territorial integrity and political independence of other states. In that manner, military assistance by request indicates the consent of the legitimate government of a victim state (which is confronted with armed attacks) given to another state to use armed force against its enemies. In order to do this, the victim states may invite its allies to assist it in using military force in self-defence.

[187] TD Gill, 'Classifying the Conflict in Syria' (2016) 92 *International Law Studies* 355; M Hakimi, 'Defensive Force against Non-State Actors: The State of Play' (2015) 91 *International Law Studies* 1, 4, 24–25.

[188] Declaration on Principles of International Law Concerning Friendly Relations and Co-operation Among States in Accordance with the Charter of the United Nations, above n 42.

The permissibility of military assistance by request in civil wars like the one in Syria is still a subject of controversy among the international community.[189] However, there is evidence of state practice (that uses host state consent as a justification for military intervention in internal conflicts[190]) which is mostly based on the permissibility of military assistance by request of the territorial state.

The stronger view based on practice indicates the permissibility of the use of force in Syria, due to the fact that Bashar al-Assad's regime – as the internationally recognised legitimate government of Syria which has not been replaced by another political entity as a result of the ongoing war – has given consent. In other words, the consent and request of Bashar al-Assad as the official head of the Syrian government, who was elected in accordance with the Syrian Constitution, constitutes justification for third-party intervention in Syria.

This was also the Iranian authorities' justification for military intervention in Syria, assisting a large pro-government militia known as the National Defence Forces. They stated that their forces are present in Syria in response to the Syrian government's request to support Bashar al-Assad's legitimate government, and they will leave Syria if the Syrian government declares that their presence within Syrian territory is no longer necessary.[191] In other words, all their actions in supporting the Syrian regime, the key element of which is to safeguard the survival of Syria's embattled President Bashar al-Assad, have been taken in response to a request from the Syrian government, in compliance with the UN Charter, Article 2(4).

Apart from this, however, the Iranian position in Syria as a requested state is likely to be even more important when compared with the US-led coalition's intervention in Iraq, also by request. It appears that both Iran and Russia have been worried about the durability and survival of the Syrian regime because it is not only threatened by Islamic State but also by various domestic rebel groups

[189] Legal justification for unlawful intervention in civil wars is found in the 1975 Resolution of the Institute of International Law on The Principle of Non-Intervention in Civil Wars, in which civil wars are defined as internal or non-international armed conflicts between the government of a state and insurgent movements, whose aim is to overthrow the government or the political, economic or social order of the state, or to achieve secession or self-government for any part of the state; or non-international armed conflict between two or more groups contending for control of the state in the absence of an established government. See Justitia et Pace Institut de Droit International, 'The Principle of Non-Intervention in Civil Wars, Session of Wiesbaden' (14 August 1975), Article 1, www.idi-iil.org/app/uploads/2017/06/1975_wies_03_en.pdf.

[190] See 'The Legal Framework for the United States' Use of Military Force Since 9/11', A Speech Delivered by SW Preston in Annual Meeting of the American Society of International Law (Washington, DC, 10 April 2015), www.defense.gov/Newsroom/Speeches/Speech/Article/606662/.

[191] Gill (2016), above n 187 at 355–56. See also 'IRGC Official Hits Back at US's Pompeo Over Anti-Iran Remarks', *Tasnim News Agency* (25 May 2018), www.tasnimnews.com/en/news/2018/05/25/1734519/irgc-official-hits-back-at-us-s-pompeo-over-anti-iran-remarks; 'Iran Says to Maintain Military Presence in Syria Despite US Pressure', *Routers* (28 August 2018), www.reuters.com/article/us-mideast-crisis-syria-iran/iran-says-to-maintain-military-presence-in-syria-despite-u-s-pressure-idUSKCN1LD1JQ.

including the Syrian National Coalition, the Interim Government, the Turkish-backed Free Syrian Army, the Syrian Salvation Government, Hayat Tahrir al-Sham and the National Coordination Committee for Democratic Change, who are all opposing the Syrian government for very different reasons.[192] This can be observed more specifically where the Iranian forces fought against rebel groups in the defence of Bashar al-Assad's regime. At this stage, the legitimacy of the military assistance remains problematic since it has led to serious violations of *jus in bello*. It has been reported, for example, that the Syrian regime committed serious crimes amounting to war crimes in launching indiscriminate attacks on civilians, and deliberately attacking protected cultural objects.[193]

Thanks to Russian and Iranian support, Assad's regime has taken back control of much of western Syria. However, despite the Iranian and Russian positions being widely accepted as action in assistance at the request of the state, they still seem to be in violation of international law since it has already been explicitly identified in UN reports on many occasions that all states have an obligation to refrain from giving assistance in violation of international law through participation in war crimes and actions rising to the level of crimes against humanity.[194]

More precisely, the UNGA Resolution on the human rights situation in Syria has condemned the continued widespread and systematic gross violations of human rights and fundamental freedoms by the Syrian government, such as the use of heavy weapons and force against civilians, massacres, arbitrary executions, extrajudicial killings, the killing and persecution of protestors, human rights defenders and journalists, arbitrary detention, enforced disappearances, interference with access to medical treatment, torture, sexual violence and ill-treatment, including against children, as well as any human rights abuses by armed opposition groups.[195] The Resolution has also emphasised the need to

[192] For general information, see B Haddad and E Wind, 'The Fragmented State of the Syrian Opposition' in M Kamrava, *Beyond the Arab Spring: The Evolving Ruling Bargain in the Middle East* (Oxford, Oxford University Press, 2014) 397–436; D Byman, 'Six Bad Options for Syria' (2016) 38 *The Washington Quarterly* 171.

[193] See 'UN Commission of Inquiry on Syria: The Siege and Recapture of Eastern Ghouta Marked by War Crimes, Crimes against Humanity', *UN Human Rights Council* (20 June 2018), www.ohchr.org/EN/HRBodies/HRC/Pages/NewsDetail.aspx?NewsID=23226&LangID=E; 'Attacks on Syrian Civilians and Aid Workers in Aleppo Were War Crimes', *OHCHR* (3 March 2017), www.ohchr.org/EN/NewsEvents/Pages/WarCrimesInAleppo.aspx.

[194] See 'Human Rights Council Holds Urgent Debate on the Situation in Syria's Eastern Ghouta', *UN Human Rights Council – Commission Press Releases* (28 February 2012), www.ohchr.org/en/NewsEvents/Pages/DisplayNews.aspx?NewsID=22750&LangID=E; UNGA, 'Speakers Disagree Over Suitable Level of Intervention for Stopping Atrocity Crimes, as General Assembly Concludes Debate on Responsibility to Protect', UN Doc GA/12038 (2 July 2018), www.un.org/press/en/2018/ga12038.doc.htm; *Case Concerning Military and Paramilitary Activities in and against Nicaragua* (27 June 1986), above n 4 at para 46; *Application of the Convention on the Prevention and Punishment of the Crime of Genocide (Bosnia and Herzegovina v Serbia and Montenegro)*, Judgment, ICJ Reports (26 February 2007), para 166.

[195] UNGA, Situation of Human Rights in the Syrian Arab Republic, Resolution A/HRC/21/L.32 (24 September 2012), para 4.

conduct an international, transparent, independent and prompt investigation into abuses and violations of international law, with a view to holding to account those responsible for violations and abuses, which will include those that may amount to crimes against humanity and war crimes.[196]

In terms of responsibility for serious violations within the host state's territory, the third parties intervening in the Syrian civil war, even at the request of the Syrian government, are committed to respecting the fundamental rules of *jus in bello* and the implementation of the obligations as contained in Common Article 1 of the 1949 Geneva Conventions and in Article 1(1) of Additional Protocols I and III.[197] Ever since the adoption of the UN Charter and with international law regulating *jus ad bellum* and *jus in bello*, it has generally been accepted that under no circumstances, even in support of the requesting state, can any state involved in any form of armed conflict be excused of human rights violations such as assassination, torture or other kinds of inhumane treatment, or attacking civilians and civilian targets within the host state's territory. Given this, continuing to assist the Syrian regime when there is significant evidence that the government is committing serious crimes inside its borders, entails the involved states' international responsibility for supporting and closing their eyes to the violations of *jus in bello* by using excessive, indiscriminate and disproportionate force against opposition groups in the course of the 'war on terrorism'.

Russia's military intervention in Syria serves as another example of military assistance at the request of the Syrian government. The presence of the Russian military within Syrian territory had become a common sight during the war with Islamic State. In terms of the legality of the use of force in a foreign territory, the Russian militarily operations in Syria do not require much commentary since the operations had been undertaken at the request of the Syrian government. According to the Russian authorities, 'on 30 September 2015, following a request of the Syrian leadership, the President of Russia asked for and received the consent of the Federation Council to use the armed forces of the Russian Federation in the Syrian Arab Republic'.[198] In this sense, thus, Russian military intervention in Syria is more similar to the US-led coalition's intervention in Iraq, whereas the states participating in the airstrikes against Islamic State, in legally justifying their actions, have largely relied on a general assertion that military action on a state's territory with the consent of its government is legal.

[196] Ibid, at para 10.

[197] See in general, U Palwankar, 'Measures Available to States for Fulfilling Their Obligation to Ensure Respect for International Humanitarian Law' (1994) 34 *International Review of the Red Cross* 9.

[198] Letter dated 1 September 2015 from the Permanent Representative of the Russian Federation to the United Nations addressed to the Secretary-General (S/2015/678), UN Doc S/2014/695 (30 September 2015) 4, 30. See also M Bodner, 'Russia Begins Airstrikes in Syria', *The Moscow Times* (30 September 2015), www.themoscowtimes.com/2015/09/30/russia-begins-air-strikes-in-syria-a49973.

In contrast, the US authorities stated that:

> … we believe that any actions we would take, to include airstrikes, would be consistent with international law, as we have a request from the Government of Iraq. So we [have] essentially been asked and invited to take these actions by the Government of Iraq, and that provides the international legal basis.[199]

For the same reason, Russia joined in the pre-existing non-international armed conflict between Syria and Islamic State and therefore became a party to the conflict alongside the Syrian government. However, the problem which arises in this case is that the Russian operations also deliberately targeted other groups that opposed the Syrian regime.[200] It has been reported that the majority of its operations have targeted areas under the control of rebel groups and civilians where none of Islamic State's fighters were located. In other words, Russia's military operations at the request of the Syrian government had little impact on Islamic State and more impact on the civilians and opposition groups, particularly those who backed the Western powers.[201]

Even so, both Russia and Iran, which have frequently justified their military intervention in Syria as being with the consent and request of the Syrian government, condemned the US-led coalition's military operations in Syria, assuming that all states have a right to territorial integrity and that, therefore, the use of force in another state without its consent is the same as conducting operations against that state.[202]

Nevertheless, Russia and Iran's military assistance to the Syrian government has been controversial in itself with regard to the host state's power to make a request. Given Bashar al-Assad's re-election in 2014, it is difficult to challenge the legitimacy of his authority since the majority of the international community of states still consider him the legitimate president of Syria. In addition, the UN, which supported the aspirations of the Syrian people for a peaceful, democratic and pluralistic society in several resolutions, has not ruled on the illegality or illegitimacy of Bashar al-Assad's regime.[203]

However, the legality and legitimacy of military intervention/assistance at the request of a territorial state which has lost control of part of its territory can be challenged in some ways. As previously discussed, effective control and

[199] See 'Background Briefing by Senior Administration Officials on Iraq', *The White House Office of the Press Secretary* (8 August 2014), https://obamawhitehouse.archives.gov/the-press-office/2014/08/08/background-briefing-senior-administration-officials-iraq.

[200] V Koutroulis, 'The Fight against the Islamic State and Jus in Bello' (2016) 29 *Leiden Journal of International Law* 827, 836; J Borger, 'Russia Committed War Crimes in Syria, Finds UN Report', *The Guardian* (2 March 2020), www.theguardian.com/world/2020/mar/02/russia-committed-war-crimes-in-syria-finds-un-report.

[201] See M Czuperski et al, *Distract, Deceive, Destroy: Putin at War in Syria* (Washington, DC, Atlantic Council, 2016) 11–12, 20; Borger (2 March 2020), above n 200.

[202] Hakimi (2015), above n 187 at 4, 24–25.

[203] D Dam-de Jong, *International Law and Governance of Natural Resources in Conflict and Post-Conflict Situations* (Cambridge, Cambridge University Press, 2015) 55.

democratic legitimacy are the primary requirements for the validity and effectiveness of military assistance by request. The cogent arguments indicate that a state that has lost control of its territory, either partially or fully, cannot be recognised as being effective. In other words, the validity of any granting of consent or request for assistance will be scrutinised closely if the government of the requesting state has lost effective control over its territory. From this particular perspective, Iran and Russia's military assistance to Syria is controversial, even though it is by the request of the Syrian government. This is because it is unclear whether even a partially ineffective government has the power to consent to or request military assistance.[204] What is clear is that the Syrian government requested military assistance to recapture its lost territory. However, while the Syrian government's request for military assistance from Iran and Russia can be challenged by other states, Iran and Russia insist on the legality and legitimacy of their assistance because it is at the request of the legitimate and effective government of Syria.

Therefore, because states have not coalesced around a particular standard for effective control, and it is unclear to what extent control over territory makes a government effective, the international community will be able to plausibly invoke the consent and request of the requesting state's legitimate government even if has partially lost control of its territory. In essence, the lack of transparency and consensus over the particular criteria in defining the requirement of effective control will obscure the most important practical procedures in international law, which can open the doors to a wide variety of different practices by the states due to their own assessment of the situation. These ambiguities could lead the international community to adopt a double standard in applying military assistance by request.

For instance, the UNSC's approach to the Arab coalition's military assistance to Yemen at the request of an ineffective government has resulted in a humanitarian catastrophe in Yemen. The Council kept its silence on military assistance to Yemen at the request of the former Yemeni President Mansour Hadi, whose government lost effective control over Yemeni territory, while it has verbally condemned the overthrow of the government by the Houthis.[205] In the same way, the effectiveness of the Malian government, which invited France to support it in fighting against terrorists after losing control of more than half of its territory between 2013 and 2014, has not been challenged by the UNSC.[206]

[204] See in general, E Lieblich, 'Intervention and Consent: Consensual Forcible Interventions in Internal Armed Conflicts as International Agreements' (2011) 29 *Boston University International Law Journal* 337, 339–42.

[205] UNSC, Resolution 2201, UN Doc S/RES/2201 (15 February 2015); K Beckerle, 'Where Does the UN Security Council Stand on Yemen?', *Amnesty International* (8 November 2018), www.hrw.org/news/2018/11/08/where-does-un-security-council-stand-yemen.

[206] For general information, see K Bannelier and T Christakis, 'Under the UN Security Council's Watchful Eyes: Military Intervention by Invitation in the Malian Conflict' (2013) 26 *Leiden Journal of International Law* 855.

Considering state practice in the absence of normative criteria to clarify the extent of actual and effective control of states over their territory, some key guidelines might be distilled from the following relevant precedents. The Iraqi and Syrian governments' requests for military assistance, having lost control of some parts of their territories to Islamic State, indicate that those governments have not been able to maintain their authority without the assistance and protection of external powers. Furthermore, the majority of the international community of states apathetically tolerated unlawful operations under military assistance as part of a much more extensive range of conditions justified by the legitimate government's consent and request.

Over and above these precedents, regardless of whatever the assisting states assert as the legal basis for military intervention in Iraq and Syria – military assistance at the request of effective or ineffective governments – the humanitarian impacts of such interventions must be the primary concern of the international community. No international or regional treaty/convention regulates guidelines that justify the targeting of civilians with the purpose of fighting ANSAs or any violent groups which attack civilians discriminately. Having dealt with the humanitarian consequences of the US, Russian and Iranian military interventions within both Iraq and Syria, it appears clear that military operations at the request of the partially effective governments of Iraq and Syria have exceeded their primary objective of defending the requesting state's borders from outside attacks, internal disturbances and isolated guerrilla or terrorist activities.[207] Even taking the request of the Iraqi and Syrian governments into consideration, the important question is still whether the main objective of the military assistance was to aid the territorial state to protect its people from terrorist actions and to minimise civilian casualties, given the increased number of civilian casualties and the targeting of civilian property and natural resources in the wake of extraterritorial use of force. Particularly in Syria, this has led to additional challenges regarding violations of *jus in bello*.

IV. CONCLUDING REMARKS

In order to address the legality of using force against Islamic State both in Iraq and Syria, Chapter 2 has evaluated the use of force by the US-led coalition states in fighting Islamic State, which they justified with the fact that both Iraq and Syria had been unwilling or unable to suppress the threat of Islamic State, and

[207] Although more than two states engaged in the war with Islamic State, this did not internationalise the non-international armed conflict between Iraq and Islamic State. Instead, the military operations of the intervening states are integrated into the pre-existing non-international armed conflict and are regulated by *jus in bello* since no state has argued the inapplicability of this law to the initial phase of external military operations. For more detailed discussion, see Koutroulis (2016), above n 200 at 832.

the use of military force in Syria by Iran and Russia, which was at the Syrian government's request.

Having shown that the 'unwilling or unable theory' is a controversial concept in international law, Chapter 2 has also considered the problematic dimensions of the military force used by the US-led coalition states under the right of self-defence against Islamic State. Given the necessity and proportionality conditions outlined in *jus ad bellum* in the exercise of the right of self-defence, and the military legitimacy of selected targets, it has been argued that the US's actions are still disputed due to the excessiveness of the force used in Syria and its humanitarian impacts on non-military targets including civilian populations and property and natural resources.

In exploring the external powers' justifications in using force against Islamic State without the consent of the territorial state, this chapter has also examined the treaty-based interventions of the Turkish authorities under the current *jus ad bellum* and general international law provisions. In doing so, Chapter 2 has argued that although Turkey has been frequently targeted by Islamic State's cross-border terrorist activities, neither the 1998 Adana Security Agreement nor the 2010 Joint Cooperation Agreement authorise Turkish military intervention in Syrian territory. While both treaties require the contracting parties to take 'necessary measures' to combat all forms of terrorism, this chapter has argued that inferring military intervention from the provisions of the treaties is almost impossible, and therefore, Turkey's cross-border operations in northern Syria, which are justified under the bilateral treaties signed between the two sides, is an approach which stems from a self-interested interpretation of the key provisions of the treaties where both Turkey and Syria consent to take 'necessary measures' for certain purposes. Moreover, it has been argued that even the treaty-based use of force does not allow the intervening state to take advantage of the treaty to justify its political and territorial tendencies within the territory of the state in question.

By finding an overlap between *jus ad bellum* and *jus in bello*, this chapter has demonstrated that Iran and Russia, as intervening states in the Syrian civil war – even at the request of the Syrian government– are committed to ensuring respect for the fundamental rules of *jus in bello* and the implementation of the obligations as contained in Common Article 1 of the 1949 Geneva Conventions and Article 1(1) of Additional Protocols I and III. It finds that under no circumstances, even in support of the requesting state, can any state involved in any form of armed conflict be excused of human rights violations such as assassination, torture or other kinds of inhumane treatment, or attacking civilians and civilian targets within the host state's territory. Chapter 2 has concluded, therefore, that continuing to assist the Syrian regime when there is significant evidence that the government is committing serious crimes inside its borders, entails the involved states' (Russia and Iran) international responsibility for supporting or turning of a blind eye to the violations of *jus in bello* by using excessive, indiscriminate and disproportionate force against opposition groups in the course of the 'war on terrorism'.

3

The Legality of the Attacks on Energy Resources Occupied by Islamic State as a Matter of Jus in Bello

'There will be associated political reasons for armed conflict, but the purpose of targeting is to achieve the submission of the opposing party to the conflict and, having done so and quite possibly as a result of having done so, to cause the adverse party to do or refrain from doing some act or acts as dictated by the 'victorious' party'.[1]

I. INTRODUCTION

IT IS UNIVERSALLY agreed that principles and entitlements under *jus in bello*, and the general rules of *jus in bello*, including the distinction between civilian and military objectives, proportionality and necessity, should generally apply whatever the cause of armed conflict. On that basis, this chapter analyses the applicability of *jus in bello* to armed attacks on energy resources and *jus in bello* obligations by which the perpetrators are bound.

Chapter 3 is structured as follows. It begins by considering the concept of occupation and exploitation of energy resources in the occupied territories and reviewing the international legal framework under which the occupying power has no legal right to seize and confiscate the resources of the occupied territory in its own interests. It then explores the general rules of *jus in bello* applicable to the military operations of foreign states against Islamic State. It also provides a general overview of the link between the prohibition on armed attacks on energy resources as installations containing dangerous forces and the prohibition on unnecessary destruction of the natural environment during armed conflicts. In particular, Chapter 3 explores states' obligation to protect the civilian population during self-defence actions under the 1949 Geneva

[1] WH Boothby, *The Law of Targeting* (Oxford, Oxford University Press, 2012) 4.

Conventions and its 1977 Additional Protocol II as the basis for *jus in bello*. Chapter 3 aims to understand how violations of the customary rules of *jus in bello* through environmental destruction as a result of unnecessary and disproportionate military actions against Islamic State have been justified by the actors involved through recourse to the right of self-defence.

Finding the war with Islamic State as a piece of substantial evidence, the last chapter of the book considers what *jus in bello* can tell us about the destruction of the natural environment during armed conflicts as being related to the objectives that contribute to the 'war-sustaining capability' of the enemy. When evaluating this issue, Chapter 3 draws significantly upon the conclusion that destroying or seizing the enemy's property without imperative necessity is a direct violation of *jus in bello* under the rules surrounding the protection of 'state property'.

II. THE OCCUPATION AND EXPLOITATION OF ENERGY RESOURCES IN THE OCCUPIED TERRITORIES

A. Introductory Remarks

The military occupation of territory is considered to be an act of aggression and a violation of the general prohibition on the use of force in international law.[2] The protection of civilians and their rights, and respect for the sovereign rights of the ousted government are the obligations of an occupier that are embodied in the international law of occupation and are a core component of *jus in bello*. However, occupying powers frequently use armed force against groups opposing occupation in order to maintain order within their occupied territory. Similarly, armed groups belonging to the ousted government or groups opposed to occupation often use force against the occupier to bring an end to the occupation. Occupation is defined as the establishment of a hostile, foreign authority over a portion of foreign territory and is a fact that is relevant to the international legal order as it triggers the applicability of a variety of international rules, including international human rights law, the law of occupation and *jus in bello*. A particular problem arises, however, when the occupier is an ANSA such as a terrorist group.

According to Common Article 2, the four 1949 Geneva Conventions apply to any occupied territory during international hostilities. They also apply in situations where the occupation of state territory meets with no armed resistance. In a sense, although there are no regulations for armed resistance against an occupier in the law of occupation, and it has not been recognised by international

[2] UNGA, Resolution 3314, Definition of Aggression, UN Doc 3314 (XXIX) (14 December 1974), Art 3.

law, *jus in bello* will be applied in cases of use of force against an occupier as the main source of legitimising resistance against the occupying power.[3] Having looked at state practice under *jus in bello*, it can be argued that the people of an occupied territory have the right to resist an occupying power when that occupier refuses to negotiate and where it maintains territory under occupation for an extended period.[4]

Furthermore, the rights and obligations of the occupying power are spelled out primarily in the IV Hague Convention Respecting the Laws and Customs of War on Land[5] (Articles 42–56), the IV Geneva Convention Relative to the Protection of Civilian Persons in Time of War (Articles 27–34 and 47–78), in certain provisions of Additional Protocols I and II and in the customary rules of *jus in bello*.[6] What is clear, however, is that the mentioned regulations apply only to situations where the occupying power is a state – such as Israel's occupation of the West Bank and Gaza (since 1967), the occupation of the north-eastern Democratic Republic of Congo by Uganda (1998–2003), and the occupation of Iraq (2003–2005).[7] The question remains, therefore, whether the military occupation of Syrian and Iraqi territory and their energy resources are subject to *jus in bello*. In other words, the issue is whether ANSAs are bound by *jus in bello* as regulated by the Geneva Conventions. What is certain is that the drafters of the Geneva Conventions were united, after long discussions, in the view that *jus in bello* as a matter of 'treaty law' could bind ANSAs. Therefore, since the rules stated in Common Article 3 to the Geneva Conventions have been characterised as 'elementary considerations of humanity',[8] this makes the ANSAs' position explicit by imposing obligations on 'each Party to non-international armed conflicts' – the states and ANSAs – which cannot be violated during international or non-international armed conflicts.[9]

[3] M Longobardo, *The Use of Armed Force in Occupied Territory* (Cambridge, Cambridge University Press, 2018) 135–49; R Giladi, 'The Jus Ad Bellum/Jus in Bello Distinction and the Law of Occupation' (2018) 41 *Israel Law Review* 246, 251–52.

[4] Longobardo (2018), above n 3 at 163.

[5] Convention (IV) Respecting the Laws and Customs of War on Land and Its Annex: Regulations Concerning the Laws and Customs of War on Land (The Hague, 18 October 1907).

[6] See 'Occupation and International Humanitarian Law: Questions and Answers', *ICRC* (4 April 2004), www.icrc.org/en/doc/resources/documents/misc/634kfc.htm.

[7] For further discussion, see E Benvenisti, *The International Law of Occupation* (Oxford, Oxford University Press, 2012) 167–275; D Mandsager et al, 'Jus in Bello: Occupation Law and the War in Iraq' (2004) 98 *Proceedings of the Annual Meeting (American Society of International Law)* 117; V Koutroulis, 'Of Occupation, Jus ad Bellum and Jus in Bello: A Reply to Solon Solomon's "The Great Oxymoron: Jus in Bello Violations as Legitimate Non-Forcible Measures of Self-Defense: The Post-Disengagement Israeli Measures towards Gaza as a Case Study"' (2011) 10 *Chinese Journal of International Law* 897; Longobardo (2018), above n 3 at 1–19.

[8] *Case Concerning Military and Paramilitary Activities in and against Nicaragua (Nicaragua v United States of America)*, Judgment, ICJ Reports (27 June 1986), para 218.

[9] K Fortin, *The Accountability of Armed Groups under Human Rights Law* (Oxford, Oxford University Press, 2017) 180–82; T Meron, *The Humanization of International Law* (Leiden & Boston, Martinus Nijhoff, 2006) 21.

Even though the applicability of *jus in bello* to ANSAs is still controversial, it is widely accepted that such actors are bound by customary international law, including the principles of distinction between civilian objects and military objectives, proportionality in attacks, precautions in attacks, and the prohibition of indiscriminate attacks.[10] The idea is that although ANSAs have not signed or agreed to any international treaties, and have no involvement in the law-making process of treaties, or customary international law, they are still bound by *jus in bello*.[11] Regardless of the fact that violent ANSAs like Islamic State simply ignore the principles by attacking civilians, it is widely accepted that customary international humanitarian law is applicable to ANSAs, as it has been supported by the Declaration of Common Article 3 of the 1949 Geneva Conventions.[12] In the same way, an armed group possessing a higher level of organisation and effective control over a territory will be bound by the norms in Additional Protocol II, which are deemed to be customary rules of international law.[13] The problem which remains in this respect is the lack of efficient enforcement in international law of *jus in bello* rules as they apply to ANSAs, and the failure to prosecute *jus in bello* violations, which paves the way for the laws to simply be ignored.

B. The Measures Taken by Islamic State in the Use, Exploitation and Arbitrary Destruction of Local Resources as an Occupier

i. Legal Review

A discussed in Chapter 1, Islamic State is an ANSA that has fought against the Syrian and Iraqi central governments. The conflicts between them have been characterised as non-international armed conflicts under Common Article 3 of the 1949 Geneva Conventions, Additional Protocol II, and the customary rules of *jus in bello*. More importantly, the primary conditions for ANSAs to be considered a party to a non-international armed conflict have been met by Islamic State under Article 1 of the Annex to the IV Hague Convention. These

[10] For general information, see J-M Henckaerts and L Doswald-Beck, *Customary International Humanitarian Law – Vol I: Rules* (Cambridge, Cambridge University Press, 2005) 3–67; A Cassese, *International Law* (Oxford, Oxford University Press, 2005) 415–20.

[11] A Roberts and S Sivakumaran, 'Lawmaking by Nonstate Actors: Engaging Armed Groups in the Creation of International Humanitarian Law' (2012) 37 *Yale Journal of International Law* 107, 108; APV Rogers, *Law on the Battlefield* (Manchester, Manchester University Press, 2004) 221. See also *Case Concerning Military and Paramilitary Activities in and against Nicaragua* (27 June 1986), above n 8 at paras 118–20.

[12] See A Bellal et al, 'International Law and Armed Non-State Actors in Afghanistan' (2011) 93 *International Review of the Red Cross* 47, 62–63; J Somer, 'Jungle Justice: Passing Sentence on the Equality of Belligerents in Non-International Armed Conflict' (2007) 89 *International Review of Red Cross* 655.

[13] Fortin (2017), above n 9 at 206.

provisions specify that the laws, rights, and duties of war apply not only to armies but also to militia and volunteer corps fulfilling the following conditions:

(1) to be commanded by a person responsible for his subordinates;
(2) to have a fixed distinctive emblem recognisable at a distance;
(3) to carry arms openly; and
(4) to conduct their operations in accordance with the laws and customs of war.

In countries where militia or volunteer corps constitute the army or form any part of it, they are included under the denomination of 'army'.[14]

In the same way, Article 1 of Additional Protocol II to the Geneva Conventions provides that it:

> … shall apply to all armed conflicts which are not covered by Article 1 of Protocol I. It shall also apply to all conflicts which take place in the territory of a High Contracting Party between its armed forces and dissident armed forces or other organised armed groups that exercise such control over a part of its territory as to enable them to carry out sustained and concerted military operations and to implement this Protocol.

Given this, it can be said that Islamic State, as a party to the non-international armed conflicts in Iraq and Syria, must properly respect *jus in bello* regulated by the above-mentioned conventions and the customary rules of *jus in bello*. As evidence of this, the UNSC's resolutions on Islamic State have characterised the conflicts in Syria and Iraq as non-international armed conflicts where the Council has recalled the need for all parties to respect the relevant provisions of *jus in bello* and the UN guiding principles of emergency humanitarian assistance.[15] However, a related argument is that perhaps the UNSC itself has placed these obligations on all parties and that the wording of the resolutions indicates that Islamic State is bound to comply with the laws regulated by the Geneva and the Hague Conventions, and the customary *jus in bello*.

Thus, in view of the above, there is ample evidence that ANSAs are subject to *jus in bello* and must comply with treaty law and customary international law that regulates non-international armed conflicts. Bearing in mind that the rights and obligations of occupying powers are subject to *jus in bello*, the major rules applicable to military occupation – including the IV Hague Convention, the IV Geneva Convention and its Additional Protocols I and II – will also apply to military occupation by ANSAs. In this respect, one of the most significant

[14] For more details, see JR Baker and HG Crocker, *The Laws of Land Warfare: Concerning the Rights and Duties of Belligerents as Existing on August 1, 1914* (Washington, DC, Government Printing Office, 1919) 9–10; D Schindler and J Toman (eds), *The Laws of Armed Conflicts: A Collection of Conventions, Resolutions, and Other Documents* (Dordrecht, Martin Nijhoff, 1998) 75; US War Department, *Rules of Land Warfare 1914* (Washington, DC, Government Printing Office, 1914) 21.

[15] See UNSC, Resolution 2170, UN Doc S/RES/2170 (15 August 2014); UNSC Resolution 2178, UN Doc S/RES/2178 (24 September 2014); UNSC, Resolution 2191, UN Doc S/RES/2191 (17 December 2014); UNSC, Resolution 2249, UN Doc S/RES/2249 (20 November 2015); UNSC, Resolution 2253, UN Doc S/RES/2253 (17 December 2015).

issues that arises is the legal status of public, private, movable and immovable properties, including the energy resources within the occupied territory.

The most important question, however, is whether and to what extent the occupying power can capture and use the territory's resources in the aftermath of taking effective control. In this respect, previous chapters have discussed how Islamic State strengthened its military capabilities by taking control of major oil facilities in Iraq and Syria immediately after occupying those territories.

The legal status of the properties in occupied territory and the rights and obligations of the occupying power are primarily subject to the IV Hague Convention, which provides a cogent regulation on this subject in Article 55:

> The occupying state shall be regarded only as administrator and usufructuary of public buildings, real estate, forests, and agricultural estates belonging to the hostile state, and situated in the occupied country. It must safeguard the capital of these properties and administer them in accordance with the rules of usufruct.

Yoram Dinstein has argued that the rules of a usufruct are: that the occupying power may use, lease, consume or sell resources insofar as capital is not depleted. However, it does not mean that the occupying power can claim ownership over immovable public property and sell or transfer them.[16]

Further to this, it might be argued at first sight that this particular regulation does not cover energy resources in the occupied state, including oil facilities. However, given that the law of occupation (as part of *jus in bello*) does not transfer any authority to the occupying power, and the occupying power is bound to administer the territory on a temporary basis and respect the laws of the occupied state, it can be claimed that natural wealth, including energy resources, falls within the categories of property protected by the IV Hague Convention. In such a legal framework, therefore, the exploitation of the resources of the occupied territory is subject to limitations, and the occupying power may only use, consume or sell them, and has no legal right to seize and confiscate.[17] This means that the ownership of the immovable properties of the occupied state is not transferrable to the occupying power and the occupying power is not allowed to seize or confiscate them in its interests. Principally, granting occupying powers (including ANSAs) the right of usufruct gives them an incentive to protect law and order in the occupied territory and respect *jus in bello*.[18] Also, the concept of usufruct does not entail an unlimited right for the occupier to use the proceeds from the exploitation of energy resources to

[16] Y Dinstein, *The International Law of Belligerent Occupation* (Cambridge, Cambridge University Press, 2009) 214.

[17] See M Pertile, 'The Changing Environment and Emerging Resource Conflicts' in M Weller (ed), *The Oxford Handbook of the Use of Force in International Law* (Oxford, Oxford University Press, 2015) 1085–86.

[18] See R Kolb and R Hyde, *An Introduction to the International Law of Armed Conflicts* (Oxford, Hart Publishing, 2008) 232–33; Dinstein (2009), above n 16 at xi.

enhance their military capabilities; it merely grants the occupier a right to set up and maintain a civilian administration on behalf of the population.[19]

What is clear, however, is that the occupying power's right to use, lease or consume the resources of an occupied territory has its limits. Regardless of the silence of Article 55 of the IV Hague Convention about the exact extent of the occupying power's right to exploit and use natural wealth – including energy resources – in the occupied territory, precedent indicates that the occupier is not allowed to waste or destroy the occupied territory's resources for its benefit.[20] In that sense, destruction, improper exploitation or use of the resources are incompatible with Article 55 of the IV Hague Convention. In fact, such a practice might be considered an explicit example of a violation of international law that may also amount to the crime of pillage, prohibited as a norm of customary international law and applicable to both international and non-international armed conflicts.[21]

Indeed, the most widely discussed example – the illegal practices of Israel regarding its exploitation of Palestine's natural wealth and resources – may be illustrative in highlighting the limitations of the occupying power's right to use the resources of occupied territories. The UN's approach to the natural resources of occupied Palestinian territory sheds further light on the exploitation and use of the energy resources of an occupied state, mentioning that Israel's exploitation of Palestine's natural resources 'for its own use' is a direct violation of its legal responsibilities as an occupying power.

Consistent with this, UNGA Resolution 3175 (1973) considers that all measures undertaken by Israel to exploit the human and natural resources of the occupied Palestinian territories are illegal. Furthermore, the right of occupied states to restitution and full compensation for the exploitation, looting, and damages to natural resources, as well as the exploitation of the occupied territories has been affirmed by the UNGA.[22] It appears that Resolution 3175 (1973) reinforces the right of peoples and nations to permanent sovereignty over their means of subsistence, including natural wealth and resources, as a branch of the right to self-determination. Accordingly, the plundering and exploitation of the natural wealth and resources of an occupied state by the occupying power is a violation of *jus in bello*.[23]

[19] See D Dam-de Jong, *International Law and Governance of Natural Resources in Conflict and Post-Conflict Situations* (Cambridge, Cambridge University Press, 2015) 423.

[20] UNGA, Resolution 66/225, Permanent Sovereignty of the Palestinian People in the Occupied Palestinian Territory, Including East Jerusalem, and of the Arab Population in the Occupied Syrian Golan Over Their Natural Resources, UN Doc A/RES/66/225 (13 January 2012). See also 'Israel's Exploitation of Palestinian Resources is Human Rights Violation, Says UN Special Rapporteur for the Situation of Human Rights in the OPT', *UN Press Release* (18 March 2019), www.un.org/unispal/document/israels-exploitation-of-palestinian-resources-is-human-rights-violation-says-un-special-rapporteur-for-the-situation-of-human-rights-in-the-opt-press-release/.

[21] Henckaerts and Doswald-Beck (2005), above n 10, Rule 52 at 182.

[22] UNGA, Resolution 3175, UN Doc A/RES/3175 (17 December 1973), paras 2–3.

[23] *Case Concerning Armed Activities on the Territory of the Congo (Democratic Republic of the Congo v Uganda)*, Judgment, ICJ Reports (19 December 2005), paras 44–45. See also A Cassese,

More generally, it is important to underline that, in principle, the occupying power must not use its authority to exploit the population or resources of the occupied territory for its own benefit and must refrain from encroaching upon the lives of the local inhabitants. In international law, property can be defined as including movable and immovable objects, and as long as natural resources, including crude oil, are not extracted, they are part of the environment and therefore qualify as immovable property.[24] To highlight this with an actual example from case law and practice, it is worth looking at the 1956 judgment of the Court of Appeal of Singapore in the *Singapore Oil Stocks* case, in which the Court established that immovable resources also include subterranean oil reserves, but that these resources would be categorised as movable, once extracted.[25] The extracted resources would then fall under Article 53(1) of the IV Hague Convention, which deals with the occupied state's movable property.

Although Article 55 of the IV Hague Convention deals with an occupied state's immovable property – including public buildings, real estate, forests, and agricultural estates – it is silent on the use of other resources such as oil. However, it is widely accepted that immovable resources, including oil, cannot be removed for the benefit of the occupying power. Instead, the occupying power is obliged to maintain oil wells and other such facilities.[26] In this way, the occupying power cannot exploit the oil wells in a wasteful way that can lead to a depletion in the reserves: it is permitted to exploit resources only to the extent necessary to manage the occupied territory during the occupation.

Clearly, the occupying power cannot legally seize revenues from the natural resources of occupied territories given that it is only considered to be an administrator of the resources. The resolution adopted by a meeting of international jurists during the 1943 London International Law Conference is significant evidence for this, as it indicates that the occupying power must use the revenues of the occupied territory's immovable resources for the occupation, and that '[t]he rights of the occupant do not include any rights to dispose of property, rights or interests for purposes other than the maintenance of public order and

Self-Determination of Peoples: A Legal Reappraisal (Cambridge, Cambridge University Press, 1994) 171–72; MN Shaw, *Title to Territory* (Oxford, Oxford University Press, 1986) 91; D Cambou and S Smis, 'Permanent Sovereignty Over Natural Resources from a Human Rights Perspective: Natural Resources Exploitation and Indigenous Peoples' Rights in the Arctic' (2013) 22 *Michigan State International Law Review* 347, 361–67; UNGA, Resolution 1803, Permanent Sovereignty Over Natural Resources, UN Doc A/RES/1803 (XVII) (14 December 1962), para 1.

[24] Dam-de Jong (2015), above n 19 at 217. See also BM Claggett and OT Johnson Jr, 'May Israel as a Belligerent Occupant Lawfully Exploit Previously Unexploited Oil Resources of the Gulf of Suez' (1978) 72 *American Journal of International Law* 558, 562–63.

[25] See *NV De Bataafsche Petroleum Maatschappli & Others v The War Damage Commission*, Judgment of the Court of Appeal of Singapore (13 April 1956), (1956) 5 *International and Comparative Law Quarterly* 84.

[26] See 'The War in Iraq and International Humanitarian Law: Frequently Asked Questions on Occupation (FAQ)', *Human Rights Watch* (16 May 2003), www.hrw.org/legacy/campaigns/iraq/ihlfaqoccupation.htm.

safety in the occupied territory'.[27] Having said this, the precedent has been established based upon the inalienable rights of the population of the occupied territories over their natural resources, including land, water and energy. With that in mind, the exploitation and export of the energy resources of occupied territories will, therefore, be in direct violation of Article 55 of the IV Hague Convention.

Moreover, precedent and doctrine have already shown that an occupying power must cease the exploitation, damage, cause of loss or depletion and endangerment of natural resources in occupied territory.[28] From this particular perspective, therefore, we need to bear in mind that the occupying power has no right to enrich itself with the local resources of the occupied territory. This means that the occupying power's authority does not entitle it to exploit immovable resources, including energy resources, for its own purposes.[29]

In addition to the above-mentioned regulations prohibiting the occupying power's illegal actions concerning natural resources, the occupying power is also obliged to be diligent in protecting the resources of the occupied territory. According to Article 23(g) of the IV Hague Convention, the occupying power is forbidden 'to destroy or seize the enemy's property, unless such destruction or seizure be imperatively demanded by the necessities of war'. This has also been stated by Article 53 of the IV Geneva Conventions:

> Any destruction by the occupying power of real or personal property belonging individually or collectively to private persons, or to the state, or to other public authorities, or to social or co-operative organisations, is prohibited, except where such destruction is rendered absolutely necessary by military operations.

What is particularly significant is that both regulations provide that the destruction of, or tangible damage to property as an act of violence,[30] will be lawful if it is a legitimate military objective. The main challenge that remains, however, is that the destruction of natural resources of the occupied territory, which may

[27] See R Dobie Langenkamp and RJ Zedalis, 'What Happens to the Iraqi Oil? Thoughts on Some Significant, Unexamined International Legal Questions Regarding Occupation of Oil Fields' (2003) 14 *European Journal of International Law* 417, 431. See also UNGA, 'Implications, Under International Law, of the United Nations Resolutions on Permanent Sovereignty Over Natural Resources, on the Occupied Palestinian and Other Arab Territories and on the Obligations of Israel Concerning Its Conduct in These Territories – Report of the Secretary-General', UN Doc A/38/265-E/1983/85 (21 June 1983), Annex, https://unispal.un.org/DPA/DPR/unispal.nsf/0/6D55C7F840E6DA06052567C9004B75DE.

[28] For general information, see Benvenisti (2012), above n 7 at 81–82; UNGA, 'Permanent Sovereignty of the Palestinian People in the Occupied Palestinian Territory, Including East Jerusalem, and of the Arab Population in the Occupied Syrian Golan Heights Over their Natural Resources', UN Doc A/C.2/74/L.45 (24 October 2019), www.undocs.org/A/C.2/74/L.45.

[29] This is an approach that has been reaffirmed in different cases, such as Israel's use of Egyptian oil resources during their occupation of the Sinai Peninsula (1967–1982) and the exploitation of the Iraqi oil resources during the occupation in 2003. Benvenisti (2012), above n 7 at 82.

[30] See Y Dinstein, *The Conduct of Hostilities under the Law of International Armed Conflict* (Cambridge, Cambridge University Press, 2016) 2.

be necessary from the occupying power's perspective as a legitimate military objective, might be considered unnecessary, illegal and an act of violence by the occupied state and other states. As might be expected, this can be regarded as grounds for the international community of states, particularly the occupied states, to seek new rules or revisions to the relevant Geneva and Hague regulations which are greatly needed in order to curb the occupying powers' illegal actions in occupied territory.

ii. Responsibility for the Illegal Use, Exploitation and Destruction of Local Resources

In literal terms, the occupying power is bound to comply with the regulations of Additional Protocol II to the Geneva Conventions and the customary rules of *jus in bello*. In this regard, both states and ANSAs are also bound to comply with *jus in bello* and have responsibility for any crimes committed during conflicts and military occupation. More specifically, ANSAs violating the law of occupation in particular, and *jus in bello* in general, are subject to both domestic law and Article 8 of the Rome Statute of the ICC concerning war crimes.

Having categorised war crimes as the result of violations of *jus in bello* applicable both in international and non-international armed conflicts, Article 8(2)(a)(iv) has considered that, in general, 'extensive destruction and appropriation of property, not justified by military necessity and carried out unlawfully and wantonly' can be regarded as a war crime. It seems that, in general terms, this regulation covers both international and non-international armed conflicts.

As Islamic State's war in Iraq and Syria has already been characterised as a non-international armed conflict, it appears that the group's illegal measures during its armed occupation of Iraqi and Syrian territory must be analysed under Article 8(2)(e)(xii). This provides that serious violations of the laws and customs applicable in armed conflicts not of an international character within the established framework of international law, namely the destruction or seizing of the property of an adversary, unless such destruction or seizure be imperatively demanded by the necessities of the conflict, are considered to be war crimes and the perpetrators are criminally responsible for their actions.

It must also be noted that ANSAs cannot evade criminal responsibility for the destruction of property that is not justified by necessity merely because of their status as non-parties to the Rome Statute. Pursuant to Article 23(g) the IV Hague Convention, destroying or seizing 'the enemy's property, unless such destruction or seizure be imperatively demanded by the necessities of war' is specifically prohibited. This is the primary feature of the Hague Conventions binding all states and, where relevant, all parties to the conflict, without the need for formal adherence since they are considered as embodying the rule of customary international law and are binding on states which are not formally parties to them.[31] Under these circumstances, the international community of states is entitled to try, and prosecute, members of ANSAs being accused of named crimes during conflicts and military occupation. This is a matter of treaty-based jurisdiction, which is also contained in Article 146 of the IV Geneva Convention, and provides:

> Each High Contracting Party shall be under the obligation to search for persons alleged to have committed, or to have ordered to be committed, such grave breaches, and shall bring such persons, regardless of their nationality, before its own courts. It may also, if it prefers, and in accordance with the provisions of its own legislation, hand such persons over for trial to another High Contracting Party concerned, provided such High Contracting Party has made out a 'prima facie' case.

In this respect, the UNSC's counterterrorism regulations shed further light on the legal framework against members of ANSAs being accused of war crimes, and violations of *jus in bello*. The UNSC's relevant resolutions have explicitly expressed the need for regional and international cooperation against terrorism. Alongside Resolution 2249 (2015), in which the UNSC urged all states to take necessary measures in compliance with international law, the UN Charter, international human rights, refugee law and *jus in bello* to prevent and suppress terrorist acts of Islamic State in Iraq and Syria, the UNSC has emphasised in Resolution 2170 (2014) that it needs to 'ensure that [Islamic State], ANF and all other individuals, groups, undertakings and entities associated with Al-Qaida are held accountable for abuses of human rights and violations of [*jus in bello*]'[32] in Iraq and Syria. In addition, it also needs to ensure that states:

> Co-operate in efforts to find and bring to justice individuals, groups, undertakings and entities associated with Al-Qaida including [Islamic State] and [Al-Nusrah Front (ANF)] who perpetrate, organise and sponsor terrorist acts and in this regard underline the importance of regional cooperation.[33]

Aside from the UNSC resolutions, the UNGA unanimously affirmed the Principles of International Law Recognized in the Charter of the Nürnberg Tribunal and the Judgment of the Tribunal on 11 December 1946. The Nürnberg principles were then adopted by the ILC in 1950,[34] thereby 'codifying the jurisdictional right of all states to prosecute the offences addressed by the International Military Tribunal (IMT) at Nuremberg, namely war crimes, crimes against

[31] H-G Dederer, 'Enemy Property' in F Lachenmann and R Wolfrum (eds), *The Law of Armed Conflict and the Use of Force: The Max Planck Encyclopedia of Public International Law* (Oxford, Oxford University Press, 2016) 361–62; TD Gill et al (eds), 'Final Report ILA Study Group on the Conduct of Hostilities' (2016) 19 *Yearbook of International Humanitarian Law* 287, 306.

[32] UNSC, Resolution 2170, UN Doc S/RES/2170 (15 August 2014).

[33] Ibid.

[34] See ILC, 'Principles of International Law Recognized in the Charter of the Nürnberg Tribunal and in the Judgment of the Tribunal' (1950) 2 *Yearbook of the International Law Commission* 374, 374.

humanity and aggression'.[35] It is clear, therefore, that the mentioned crimes covered by universal jurisdictions have been established by both international treaties and customary international law.[36]

In such a case, therefore, no limitations or amnesty may be applied in order to bar the prosecution of such crimes, even if the perpetrators are nationals of a non-party state to the treaties that established the mentioned crimes, given that customary international law and the customary rules of the international treaties bind even non-party states. This is the primary objective of the use of universal jurisdiction as a legal tool, as it ensures that the worst human rights crimes, war crimes and crimes against humanity will not remain unpunished.

Whatever the reasons that may explain Islamic State's illegal use, exploitation and destruction of energy resources in its occupied territories, it is difficult to justify them under the necessity principle. Following the occupation of 90,800 km^2 of territory in Iraq and Syria,[37] Islamic State took over all the oil fields there and used the revenues to help fund its sprawling operations. Throughout 2014, Islamic State took over more than 60 per cent of oil production in Syria and almost 10 per cent of Iraqi oil production. As a result, they had a total production capacity of 80,000–120,000 barrels of oil per day. US estimates claim that Islamic State's oil transactions from this period generated between $2 million and $4 million daily, which meant an annual profit of $73–$146 million for Islamic State from oil sales alone.[38] However, in response to the US-led coalition airstrikes and the military operations of the American-backed SDF, Islamic State's forces destroyed much of the oil infrastructure. From the outset, Islamic State fighters targeted oil and gas fields, pipelines and energy facilities in order to seize control of them. After taking control of the resources, they then attacked energy targets with the aim of weakening the occupied territories' energy industry in order to stop the supply of oil and gas to Western countries and to start oil or gas fires to create a smokescreen to cover their retreat.[39]

Altogether, given that the ANSAs are obliged to comply with the Geneva Conventions, the Hague Regulations and the customary rules of *jus in bello*, it appears that the illegal measures taken by Islamic State, the occupying power, in using, exploiting, damaging and destroying the oil resources of Iraq and Syria, have been in direct violation of *jus in bello*. Even though Islamic State occupied a significant portion of Iraqi and Syrian territory for the purpose of establishing an Islamic Caliphate, the group also destroyed the major oil wells following its

[35] MP Scharf, 'Application of Treaty-Based Universal Jurisdiction to Nationals of Non-Party States' (2001) 35 *New England Law Review* 363, 371.

[36] Ibid, at 363.

[37] See L Tichý l, 'The Islamic State Oil and Gas Strategy in North Africa' (2019) 24 *Energy Strategy Reviews* 254, 255.

[38] M Martin and H Solomon, 'Islamic State: Understanding the Nature of the Beast and Its Funding' (2017) 4 *Contemporary Review of the Middle East* 18; Tichý l (2019), above n 37 at 255.

[39] Ibid, at 256. See also M Carlisle, 'Trump Keeps Talking About Syria's Oil Fields: Here's What's Going on with Them', *Time* (26 October 2016), www.time.com/5710576/trump-oil-syria/.

defeat in Iraq and Syria while using the major energy resources of both countries in order to improve its economic and military capabilities.

However, it is not surprising that occupying powers are often reluctant to implement *jus ad bellum* and *jus in bello*, mainly based on the principles of distinction and necessity, as they usually target civilians and civilian objects and destroy natural resources in their occupied territory because they do not want to acknowledge their position as an occupier.[40] In addition, the customary and treaty law regulating the rights and obligations of the occupying powers are not sufficiently clear or comprehensive in terms of protection of the natural resources of an occupied territory. The IV Geneva Convention and the IV Hague Convention, as the primarily applicable laws in situations of occupation, are not sufficiently clear regarding the major problems in administering an occupied territory and its immovable resources, which may include oil. Moreover, the mentioned conventions do not clarify the extent of the rights and obligations of the occupying power in managing the local resources. This lack of transparency can allow any occupying power to interpret the regulations in line with its political aspirations.

A legal objection that could be raised against the formation of the grounds for such an interpretation and implementation of the laws regulating military occupation could be that the relevant international treaties and conventions must be required to meet certain regulations regarding the extent of the rights and obligations of the occupying power, and the protection of the occupied states' resources. The UNSC, when it acts within its competence on discerning a threat against international peace and security, will become the primary authority that can impose unconditional obligations on states and ANSAs.

In this sense, the decisions of the UNSC, properly taken in the exercise of its competence, cannot be summarily reopened because of the pre-eminence of the resolutions. This is, in fact, the major function of the UNSC, as it acts beyond the scope of international treaties by creating legally binding obligations. Furthermore, as required by Article 103 of the UN Charter, in the event of a conflict between the obligations under the UN Charter and the obligations under any other international agreement, the obligations under the Charter, including UNSC resolutions, shall prevail. However, in order to ensure prompt and effective action by the UNSC, the permanent members of the Council must keep the stability, international peace and security beyond their political objectives. It is clear, therefore, that the lack of such action allowed Islamic State to conduct large-scale illegal actions by using, exploiting and destroying energy resources within its occupied territories in Iraq and Syria, which compelled the external powers to use force against it in both countries.

[40] Longobardo (2018), above n 3 at 270–75.

III. THE DESTRUCTION OF ENERGY RESOURCES DURING ARMED CONFLICT

A. Introductory Remarks

As discussed earlier, destroying natural resources that are part of the natural environment – which can not only affect economic activity but also affect the survival of our species – during armed conflicts is a matter for *jus in bello*, which permits it only under specific circumstances. Therefore, depending on the circumstances, states have to assess the extent of the risk to the environment that may arise from the destruction of natural resources. Prevention of environmental damage, however, is one of the primary principles of customary international law that could continue to apply irrespective of the applicability of the treaty in which it is incorporated.[41]

The US Military Commissions Act of 2009, as part of US domestic law, characterises the destruction of the natural environment during hostilities as related to the objectives that contribute to the 'war-fighting' or 'war-sustaining capability' of the enemies,[42] and states that the US cannot be considered responsible for environmental destruction during armed conflicts.

It should be noted from the outset that the Iraqi and Syrian oil refineries and installations occupied by Islamic State were targeted by both the US-led coalition and Russian forces in their roles as major external powers using extraterritorial armed force against Islamic State.[43] However, because of the controversial approach of the US authorities to the war-sustaining capability of the enemy as a justification for destroying Islamic State's oil refineries and installations, the US-led coalition's airstrikes on the Iraqi and Syrian energy resources occupied by Islamic State, and their lawfulness under *jus in bello*, is the focal point of this part of the book.

As a subject of international law, attacks on works and installations containing dangerous forces 'namely dams, dykes and nuclear electrical generating stations, and other installations located at or in their vicinity',[44] and against military objectives located in their vicinity is prohibited by *jus in bello*. Rule 42 of the ICRC's Customary International Humanitarian Law Study and the ICRC's Commentary to Article 56 of Additional Protocol I to the Geneva

[41] Dam-de Jong (2015), above n 19 at 191.

[42] The US Military Commissions Act of 2009 (HR-6166) (17 October 2006), para 950v, www.gpo.gov/fdsys/pkg/BILLS-109s3930enr/pdf/BILLS-109s3930enr.pdf.

[43] See J Emery, 'The Convoluted Coalition against ISIS', *Small Wars Journal* (19 January 2016), www.smallwarsjournal.com/jrnl/art/the-convoluted-coalition-against-isis; D Stupples, 'To Defeat Islamic State We Must Sever Its Oil Lifeline – Here's How', *The Conversation* (3 December 2015), www.theconversation.com/to-defeat-islamic-state-we-must-sever-its-oil-lifeline-heres-how-51751; 'Fire and Oil: The Collateral Environmental Damage from Airstrikes on ISIS Oil Facilities', *Conflict and Environment Observatory* (13 January 2016), www.ceobs.org/fire-and-oil-the-collateral-environmental-damage-from-airstrikes-on-isis-oil-facilities/.

[44] Henckaerts and Doswald-Beck (2005), above n 10 at 139–142.

Conventions state that works and installations containing dangerous forces are those that, if attacked, 'may cause the release of dangerous forces and consequent severe losses among the civilian population'.[45] The prohibition of armed attacks on such objectives means that particular care must be taken if works and installations containing dangerous forces are attacked, in order to avoid the release of dangerous forces and severe losses among the civilian population.[46] Furthermore, Additional Protocol I to the 1949 Geneva Conventions in Article 56 and Additional Protocol II in Article 15 deal with the prohibition of armed attacks on works and installations containing dangerous forces. However, the regulations mentioned limit the prohibition to dams, dykes and nuclear electrical generating stations while they provide that works or installations containing dangerous forces, namely dams, dykes and nuclear electrical generating stations, shall not be made the object of attack, even where these objects are military objectives, if such attack may cause the release of dangerous forces and consequent severe losses among the civilian population.

Other military objectives located at or in the vicinity of these works or installations shall not be made the object of attack if such an attack may cause the release of dangerous forces from the works or installations and consequent severe losses among the civilian population.

One might argue that these specific rules have not become part of customary international law. However, practice shows that states are conscious of the high risk of severe incidental losses which can result from attacks on such works and installations when they constitute military objectives. Consequently, they recognise that in any armed conflict, particular care must be taken in case of an attack to avoid the release of dangerous forces and consequent severe losses among the civilian population. This requirement was found to be part of customary international law and is applicable in both international and non-international armed conflicts.[47]

However, has been agreed that oil rigs, oil storage facilities, and oil refineries are not objects containing dangerous forces within the meaning of Article 15 of Additional Protocol I and Article 56 of Additional Protocol II and that, if these objects are to be given any special protection by the Protocols, it should be done by another article, perhaps by a special article for that purpose.[48] This also underlies the US authorities' approach, which mentions that energy resources, which are mainly oil installations, are military objectives that effectively contribute to the enemy's capacity to wage war. Consequently, their total or partial

[45] Y Sandoz et al, *Commentary on the Additional Protocols to the Geneva Conventions* (Geneva, Martinus Nijhoff, 1987) 665.

[46] Henckaerts and Doswald-Beck (2005), above n 10 at 139–42.

[47] J-M Henckaerts, 'Study on Customary International Humanitarian Law: A Contribution to the Understanding and Respect for the Rule of Law in Armed Conflict' (2005) 87 *International Review of the Red Cross* 175, 191.

[48] Sandoz et al (1987), above n 45 at 668.

destruction, capture, or neutralisation would constitute a definite military advantage to the attacker at the time of the armed attack.[49] This categorisation is based on the US Military Commissions Act of 2009 of the US jurisdiction, which states that the term 'military objective' means combatants and those objects during hostilities which, by their nature, location, purpose, or use, effectively contribute to the war-fighting or war-sustaining capability of an opposing force and whose total or partial destruction, capture, or neutralisation would constitute a definite military advantage to the attacker under the circumstances at the time of an attack.[50]

Characterising Islamic State's oil refineries as military objectives under this jurisdiction stems from the US interpretation of the law, regulated in Article 52(2) of Additional Protocol I to the 1949 Geneva Conventions, which provides that:

1. Civilian objects shall not be the object of attack or of reprisals. Civilian objects are all objects which are not military objectives as defined in paragraph 2.
2. Attacks shall be limited strictly to military objectives. In so far as objects are concerned, military objectives are limited to those objects which by their nature, location, purpose or use make an effective contribution to military action and whose total or partial destruction, capture or neutralization, in the circumstances ruling at the time, offers a definite military advantage.
3. In case of doubt, whether an object which is normally dedicated to civilian purposes, such as a place of worship, a house or other dwelling or a school, is being used to make an effective contribution to military action, it shall be presumed not to be so used.

Article 52 only specifies military objectives in the second paragraph. According to the ICRC, as provided in paragraph 2, an objective must meet two criteria to be a military objective.

(a) The object, by its nature, location, purpose, or use, has to contribute effectively to the military action of the enemy. The object's 'nature' refers to its intrinsic character. This category comprises all objects directly used by the armed forces: weapons, equipment, transport, fortifications, depots, buildings occupied by the armed forces, staff headquarters, communications centres, etc.[51] 'Location' admits that there are some objects that, by their nature, have no military function but which, by their location, make an effective contribution to military action. Therefore, an object may be a military objective simply because it is situated in an area that is a legitimate target. From this point of view, a specific area of land may be a military objective if its total or partial destruction, capture or neutralisation in the circumstances at the time offers a definite military advantage. The object's 'purpose' refers to the enemy's intended future use of it, based on reasonable

[49] J-M Henckaerts and L Doswald-Beck, *Customary International Humanitarian Law – Vol II: Practice* (Cambridge, Cambridge University Press, 2005) 184.
[50] The US Military Commissions Act of 2009 (HR-6166), above n 42 at para 950 p(a)(1).
[51] Sandoz et al (1987), above n 45 at 636.

belief. And the object's 'use' is about the current function of the object. For example, there is a consensus that weapons factories and even extraction industries providing raw materials for such factories are military objectives, because they serve the military, albeit indirectly.[52]

(b) The object's destruction, capture or neutralisation has to offer a definite military advantage to the attacker. Following from the requirement of a definite military advantage, it is not lawful to launch an attack that offers only a potential or indeterminate advantage. Therefore, those ordering or executing such an attack must have sufficient intelligence available to take this requirement into account. If there is any doubt about whether an object which is normally used for civilian purposes is being used to make an effective contribution to military action, presume that it is not being so used.[53]

Although this rule has limited the list of works or installations that can release dangerous forces in the case of attack, it does not mean that other energy installations are not dangerous. There are many other types of energy resources – mainly oil production installations and oil storage facilities – that are excluded from the scope of Articles 15 and 56 of Additional Protocols to the Geneva Conventions. This has been analysed in the context of environmental damage, in light of the customary principles of 'necessity' and 'proportionality'. Even when targeting admittedly legitimate military objectives, there is a need to avoid excessive long-term damage to the economic infrastructure and natural environment which would have an adverse effect on the civilian population. Indeed, military objectives should not be targeted if the attack is likely to cause collateral damage to the environment, which would be excessive in relation to the direct military advantage that the attack would be expected to confer.[54] Evidently, the First Gulf War proved that oil refineries and production installations are too much of a natural military objective in many situations, and would need special protection because of their significant potentially harmful and long-term environmental impact and risk to human health.[55] Targeting oil refineries and installations by air and sea results in air pollution, grave damage to the industrial sector, and the risk of the release of hazardous waste. In a sense, the natural environment, which cannot be separated from human life, is the 'silent victim'[56] of armed conflicts and must be protected from attack.

[52] Ibid.

[53] Ibid, at 637. See also ICRC, *The Law of Armed Conflict: Conduct of Operations – Part A* (Geneva; ICRC Press, 2002) 4–5.

[54] APV Rogers, 'Zero-Casualty Warfare' (2000) 82 *International Review of the Red Cross* 165, 177–78.

[55] UNEP, *Desk Study on the Environment in Iraq* (Nairobi, UNEP Publications, 2003) 65–68.

[56] R Rayfuse, 'Rethinking International Law and the Protection of the Environment' in R Rayfuse (ed), *War and the Environment: New Approaches to Protecting the Environment in Relation to Armed Conflict* (Leiden, Brill Nijhoff, 2014) 1; DC Aini and DR Banjarani, 'Environmental Protection in Armed Conflict According to International Humanitarian Law' (2018) 3 *Tadulako Law Review* 12, 13–14. See also 'On International Day, UN Urges Protection of Environment from Ravages of

With regard to this issue, which is the primary subject of this part of the book, the US-led coalition forces' attacks[57] on Iraqi and Syrian oil facilities occupied by Islamic State as military objectives have been subject to controversy. Specifying the scope of the illegality of targeting an installation that is part of the natural environment, but which contains dangerous forces, can be done through an evaluation in the context of the standards of *jus in bello*.

B. The Protection of Natural Resources through the Obligation to Protect the Natural Environment

i. Legal Review

According to Article 52(2) of Additional Protocol I to the 1949 Geneva Conventions, it is accepted that oil facilities are legitimate military targets. Article 52(2) states:

> Attacks shall be limited strictly to military objectives. In so far as objects are concerned, military objectives are limited to those objects which by their nature, location, purpose or use make an effective contribution to military action and whose total or partial destruction, capture or neutralization, in the circumstances ruling at the time, offers a definite military advantage.

Within this context, the acceptability of targeting oil facilities as legitimate military targets during armed conflict is highly contentious because of the environmental impact of their destruction. The Iran-Iraq War is one of the notable instances in which the UNSC condemned violations of *jus in bello* – in particular, the provisions of the 1949 Geneva Conventions in all their aspects – and called for the immediate cessation of military operations against civilian targets. According to the Council, both parties were to refrain from any action that might have endangered peace and security as well as marine life in the Persian Gulf.[58]

Fires at oilfields, installations and oil storage facilities can last a long time and can release clouds of pollution over wide areas. The destruction of oil facilities might give rise to toxic air pollution, or oil might seep into the ground and poison water supplies. More importantly, if the oilfields and installations

War: The UN Secretary General Message for the International Day for Preventing the Exploitation of the Environment in War and Armed Conflict', *UN News* (6 November 2014), https://news.un.org/en/story/2014/11/482922-international-day-un-urges-protection-environment-ravages-war.

[57] After Islamic State advanced into Iraq from Syria in June 2014, US President Barack Obama authorised targeted airstrikes against Islamic State militants in Iraq and Syria in August 2014. The US then formed an international coalition to counter Islamic State. Over 60 nations and partner organisations agreed to participate, contributing either military forces or resources (or both) to the campaign. See 'Keynote Address by General John Allen, Special Presidential Envoy for the Global Coalition to Counter-ISIL', *Brooking Institution* (3 June 2015), www.brookings.edu/wp-content/uploads/2015/04/060315BROOKINGSDOHA.pdf.

[58] UNSC, Resolution 540, UN Doc S/RES/540 (31 October 1983).

are located in a coastal state, oil spills can inflict huge environmental damage on coastal marshlands and fishing grounds and may be devastating to marine life,[59] such as that which occurred during the First Gulf War. In its resolution regarding the First Gulf War, the UNGA expressed its deep concern regarding environmental damage and the depletion of natural resources, including the destruction of oil-well heads and the release of crude oil into the sea. In the same way, the UNGA stated that the wanton destruction of the natural environment was contrary to international law, and existing provisions prohibited such acts.[60] It is also worth noting that although the UNGA's resolutions are non-binding, they can provide important evidence for establishing the existence of a rule or *opinio juris*, since the formulation and expression of state practice in matters pertaining to international law is manifested through the UNGA resolutions.[61]

Above all, the question is whether or not targeting the oil facilities can be a necessary and proportionate military action during armed conflict. What is clear is that oil resources, and oil installations in general, are protected by the general principle of 'prohibition of armed attacks on the natural environment' under Article 55(1) of Additional Protocol I to the 1949 Geneva Conventions.

According to Article 55(1) of Additional Protocol I:

> Care shall be taken in warfare to protect the natural environment against widespread, long-term and severe damage. This protection includes a prohibition of the use of methods or means of warfare which are intended or may be expected to cause such damage to the natural environment and thereby to prejudice the health or survival of the population.

In its substance, Article 55(1) prohibits widespread, long-term and severe damage to the environment, which reiterates the regulation contained in Article 22 of the 1899 and 1907 Hague Conventions providing that the right of belligerents to adopt means of injuring the enemy is not unlimited (prohibited methods of warfare), and Article 55(1) draws a connection between damage to the natural environment and its effects on civilians (civilian protection). In essence, the provisions contained in Article 55(1) do not duplicate each other. However, although both provisions afford protection to the natural environment from damaging weapons and methods of warfare, it is perhaps enough to note that the thrust of the protection is clear from the four years of negotiations on Additional Protocol I and is firmly rooted in the protection of 'people'.[62]

[59] Y Dinstein, 'Protection of Environment in International Armed Conflicts' (2001) 5 *Max Planck Yearbook of United Nations Law* 523, 523–24.

[60] UNGA, Resolution 47/37, UN Doc A/RES/47/37 (25 November 1992).

[61] Legality of the Threat or Use of Nuclear Weapons, Advisory Opinion, ICJ Reports (8 July 1996), para 70; SP Ng'ambi, 'Permanent Sovereignty Over Natural Resources and the Sanctity of Contracts, from the Angle of Lucrum Cessans' (2015) 12 *Loyola University Chicago International Law Review* 153, 157–58.

[62] See K Hulme, *War Torn Environment: Interpreting the Legal Threshold* (Leiden, Martinus Nijhoff, 2004) 11; Sandoz et al (1987), above n 45 at 410.

The problem which arises at this point is the Additional Protocol's lack of a precise definition of the term 'widespread, long-term and severe damage' as the key elements of its environmental regulations in Article 55(1). In connection with this, the Annex of the non-binding Environmental Modification Convention (1976) (ENMOD),[63] which was adopted several months before Additional Protocol I, has interpreted the above-mentioned terms as follows: (a) 'widespread': encompassing an area on the scale of several hundred square kilometres; (b) 'long-term': lasting for a period of months, or approximately a season; and (c) 'severe': involving serious or significant disruption or harm to human life, natural and economic resources or other assets.[64]

According to the ICRC Commentary, the natural environment refers to the system of inextricable interrelations between living organisms and their inanimate environment, whereas effects on the human environment are understood as effects on 'external conditions and influences which affect the life, development and survival of the civilian population and other living organisms'.[65] The environment in this sense may be indirectly damaged by the targeting of oil resources and facilities as legitimate military objectives. In such a case, the affected elements of the natural environment constitute civilian objects, and damage to these elements would then be 'collateral damage', which is only permissible to the extent that it is not 'excessive' in relation to the concrete and direct military advantage anticipated as a result of the attack.[66] This means that, if an element of the natural environment is lawfully attacked because it constitutes a military objective, there may be long-term environmental damage beyond the actual destruction.[67]

However, it should be noted that despite the possibility of clarifying the relevant facts regarding the damage, assessment of the extent of environmental damage and its widespread, long-term and severe impact can be quite difficult when the damage occurs outside of military objectives, such as the subsequent oil spills and air pollution caused by an attack against an oil installation or refinery.

This is due to the restrictive and unclear definition of the term 'widespread, long-term and severe' as the threshold of impermissible environmental damage defined by Additional Protocol I, which may be identified as a major gap in the existing international legal framework of *jus in bello* regarding the practical

[63] Convention on the Prohibition of Military or Any Other Hostile Use of Environmental Modification Techniques (ENMOD Convention) (adopted by Resolution 31/72 of the UNGA on 10 December 1976).

[64] Annex to the ENMOD Convention (adopted by Resolution 31/72 of the UNGA on 10 December 1976). See also UNEP, *Protecting the Environment During Armed Conflict: An Inventory and Analysis of International Law* (Nairobi, UNEP Publications, 2009) 52.

[65] Sandoz et al (1987), above n 45 at para 1451.

[66] M Bothe et al., 'International Law Protecting the Environment During Armed Conflict: Gaps and Opportunities' (2010) 92 *International Review of the Red Cross* 569, 577.

[67] Ibid, at 578.

issues of proportionality, where environmental damage is seen as collateral damage caused by armed attacks on military objectives.[68]

Following Additional Protocol I, Rule 43 of the ICRC Customary International Humanitarian Law Study states that 'launching an attack against a military objective which may be expected to cause incidental damage to the environment, which would be excessive in relation to the concrete and direct military advantage anticipated, is prohibited'.[69] Such an attack is not in conformity with the principle of 'necessity', which implies that the use of military force is only justified to the extent that it is necessary for achieving a defined military objective. In literal terms, 'military necessity, as understood by modern civilised nations, consists of the necessity of those measures which are indispensable for securing the ends of the war, and which are lawful according to the modern law and usages of war'.[70] In other words, military actions that do not serve any evident military purpose are forbidden.[71] However, the outline of Article 55(1) refers to a general prohibition, according to which an attack on the natural environment that causes or may cause widespread, long-term and severe damage to the natural environment is prohibited, irrespective of necessity and proportionality. In other words, taking into consideration that the natural environment itself is an object of legal protection in times of armed conflict, it implies that traditional perceptions of proportionality and necessity have become obsolete.[72]

In view of this, therefore, even if it is accepted that 'oil facilities' are military objectives, there is no valid reason to exclude them from serving as installations whose destruction in times of armed conflict might lead to extensive environmental damage, such as that mentioned in Article 55(1), as a conventional rule which embodies a general obligation to protect the natural environment against widespread, long-term and severe environmental damage. Besides which, given that this regulation is also contained in Article 56 of Additional Protocol II,[73] it might be argued that oil resources and facilities are indirectly protected during both international and non-international armed conflicts.

[68] Ibid, at 570, 578.

[69] Henckaerts and Doswald-Beck (2005), above n 10 at 143. For a discussion, see N Hayashi, 'Requirements of Military Necessity in International Humanitarian Law and International Criminal Law' (2010) 28 *Boston University International Law Journal* 39.

[70] F Lieber, 'Instructions for the Government of Armies of the United States in the Field', Promulgated as No 100 (The Lieber Code) by President Lincoln (24 April 1863), Art 14, https://ihl-databases.icrc.org/ihl/INTRO/110.

[71] UNEP (2009), above n 64 at 11; Dinstein (2016), above n 30 at 89–90.

[72] C Droge and M-L Tougas, 'The Protection of the Natural Environment in Armed Conflict – Existing Rules and Need for Further Legal Protection' (2013) 82 *Nordic Journal of International Law* 21, 27; AO Adede, 'Protection of the Environment in Times of Armed Conflict: Reflections on the Existing and Future Treaty Law' (1994) 1 *Annual Survey of International & Comparative Law* 161, 170.

[73] Art 56 of Additional Protocol II states: 'even where these objects are military objectives, if such an attack may cause the release of dangerous forces and consequent severe losses among the civilian population'.

Moreover, although the regions containing civilian populations and energy resources occupied by Islamic State in Iraq and Syria have not been under the control of the territorial state, the military intervention by the US-led coalition states adversely impacted on both civilians and energy resources. As Terry D Gill has argued, any attack on an ANSA which might affect civilians or civilian objects would be subject to virtually the same degree of protection from the effects of hostilities under the legal regime applicable to non-international armed conflicts as they enjoy under the regime on international armed conflicts.[74] Destroying oil wells under the control of an ANSA, therefore, might violate the rule that warring states must protect the natural environment. In a sense, even though Additional Protocol I applies only to international armed conflicts, the parties to a non-international armed conflict are encouraged to apply the same rules that protect the environment during international armed conflict. Environmental damage in armed conflicts can take many forms and therefore non-international armed conflicts must also be considered. Accordingly, states are urged to incorporate such rules into their military manuals and instructions on *jus in bello* in a way that does not discriminate based on how a conflict is characterised.[75]

Given that the US is not a state party to Additional Protocol I, and that the US does not accept Article 55(1) of Additional Protocol I as customary international law,[76] it is still extremely controversial to allege that the explicit obligations contained in Article 55(1) have not achieved the required near-universal adherence because of opposition by the US. In support of this argument, the ICRC Customary International Humanitarian Law Study includes a simplified version of Article 55(1) of Additional Protocol I in Rule 45 to constitute customary international law, stating that:

> The use of methods and means of warfare that are intended or may be expected, to cause widespread, long-term, and severe damage to the natural environment is prohibited. Destruction of the natural environment may not be used as a weapon.[77]

Notwithstanding, what has been served as the widespread, long-term and severe standard under Article 55(1) can be less strict than the traditional rules of necessity and proportionality under certain circumstances. In a sense, Article 55(1) excludes minor and short-term damage to the natural environment.

[74] TD Gill, 'Classifying the Conflict in Syria' (2016) 92 *International Law Studies* 355, 369.

[75] See Henckaerts and Doswald-Beck (2005), above n 49 at 845; A Roberts, 'Environmental Issues in International Armed Conflict: The Experience of the 1991 Gulf War' (1996) 69 *International Law Studies* 222, 257.

[76] JE Bond et al, 'Determining Customary International Law Relative to the Conduct of Hostilities in Non-International Armed Conflicts' (1987) 2 *American University Journal of International Law and Policy* 415, 424. See also JR Crook, 'United States Responds to ICRC Study on Customary International Law' (2007) 101 *American Journal of International Law* 639, 639–41.

[77] P Sands, *Principles of International Environmental Law* (Cambridge, Cambridge University Press, 2003) 314; Henckaerts and Doswald-Beck (2005), above n 10 at 151; Bothe et al (2010), above n 66 at 574.

Accordingly, it can be argued that the protection of the natural environment under Article 55(1) of Additional Protocol I is not sufficient, since it does not afford adequate protection during times of armed conflict and it appears that such protection must therefore be strengthened.[78]

As regards the destruction and armed attacks on oil refineries and oil storage facilities, it is hardly necessary to stress the grave danger to the natural environment that might follow for the civilian population as a matter of Article 55(1).[79] This means that even though oil installations can be considered military objectives, state practice considers the environment to be a prima facie civilian object. It is not considered to be a military objective under Rule 10 of the ICRC Customary International Humanitarian Law Study, which provides that 'civilian objects are protected against attack, unless and for such time as they are military objectives'. Therefore, alleged attacks on such objects have generally been condemned.[80]

In that regard, oil resources, just like the natural environment, must be considered civilian objects that need to be protected under the customary rule of 'distinction between civilian objects and military objectives' contained in Article 52 (2) of Additional Protocol I to the 1949 Geneva Conventions.

Although the ICJ has refrained from accepting the protective nature of Article 55(1) as customary international law and has identified it only as 'additional protections for the environment',[81] the ICRC considered these regulations to be customary international law. According to the ICRC, the right of the warring parties to choose methods or means of warfare is not unlimited and now there is sufficient state practice to support the idea that this prohibition is considered as a rule of customary international law, which is applicable in both international and non-international armed conflicts.[82] In addition, the Committee Established to Review the NATO Bombing Campaign against the Federal Republic of Yugoslavia opined that Article 55(1) may reflect the current customary international law.[83]

Overall, the US's unilateral position might be considered to be a major challenge for the prevention of environmental damage in time of armed conflict,

[78] See L Lijnzaad and GJ Tanja, 'Protection of the Environment in Times of Armed Conflict: The Iraq-Kuwait War' (1993) 40 *Netherlands International Law Review* 169, 182.

[79] Sandoz et al (eds) (1987), above n 45 at 668.

[80] Henckaerts and Doswald-Beck (2005), above n 10 at 34.

[81] Legality of the Threat or Use of Nuclear Weapons (8 July 1996), above n 61 at para 242. For a discussion on the disputable nature of Art 55(1) of Additional Protocol I, see K Hulme, 'Natural Environment' in E Wilmshurst and S Breau (eds), *Perspectives on the ICRC Study on Customary International Humanitarian Law* (Cambridge, Cambridge University Press, 2007) 204–37.

[82] Henckaerts and Doswald-Beck (2005), above n 10 at 151. See also PJ Richards and MN Schmitt, 'Mars Meets Mother Nature: Protecting the Environment during Armed Conflict' (1999) 28 *Stetson Law Review* 1047, 1075; WA Solf, 'Protection of Civilians against the Effects of Hostilities Under Customary International Law and Under Protocol I' (1986) 1 *American University International Law Review* 117, 134.

[83] Dinstein (2001), above n 59 at 534–35.

which stems from the lack of clarity and precision in Additional Protocol I regarding widespread, long-term and severe damage and the exact threshold of the damage contained in Article 55(1).

ii. Identification of Environmental Destruction

According to the ICRC Commentary on the 1977 Additional Protocols to the 1949 Geneva Conventions, the natural environment covers the environment in which people are living. As discussed earlier, Article 55(1) of Additional Protocol I contains a general rule for the protection of the natural environment, which provides that all states shall take care in warfare to protect the natural environment against widespread, long-term and severe damage. Article 55(1) includes a prohibition of the intentional use of methods, means of warfare or any kind of use of force which may be expected to cause such damage to the natural environment that it will prejudice the health or survival of the local population. Despite the uncertainty of the term widespread, long-term and severe, however, it seems that Article 55(1) implies a connection between the environment and humankind.[84] This particular meaning stems from the Commentary to Additional Protocols which makes it clear that 'natural environment' should be interpreted in general terms, meaning that the natural environment does not only consist of objects that are indispensable to the survival of a civilian population, such as foodstuffs, agricultural areas for the production of foodstuffs, crops, livestock, drinking water supplies and irrigation works. It also includes forests and other vegetation, as well as fauna and other biological or climatic elements.[85]

The wording of Article 55(1) indicates that it prohibits damage to this general concept of the natural environment, whose destruction will be severely detrimental to human life since it endangers civilian lives in the first place. In addition, even if the surrounding natural environment is damaged or destroyed in the course of a legitimate military operation, a positive effort must be made to restrict the range of damage.[86] Article 55(1) has serious implications for the environmental impacts of the destruction of natural resources in times of armed conflict. Notwithstanding, the problem which remains is the scope of widespread, long-term and severe damage regulated by Article 55(1) as a protection requirement. Although the Protocol does not define the mentioned terms, it seems that it establishes an excessive threshold for environmental damage, since the ICRC Commentary considers the meaning of 'long-term' refers to 'decades' rather than months or seasons. This is, in any case, due to the weakness and insufficiency of Additional Protocol I, which may exclude a lot of

[84] Roberts (1996), above n 75 at 233.

[85] Sandoz et al (1987), above n 45 at para 2126; Hulme (2004), above n 62 at 12–13.

[86] M Walzer, *Just and Unjust Wars: A Moral Argument with Historical Illustrations* (New York, Harper Collins, 1977) 151.

forms of environmental damage that will allow warring parties to target natural resources as part of the natural environment.[87]

Alongside Additional Protocol I, there are a variety of international instruments and treaties that cover international norms governing the protection of the environment, including the UNGA resolutions, the Declaration of the UN Conference on the Human Environment (the non-binding Stockholm Declaration of 1972),[88] the Report of the UN Conference on Environment and Development (the non-binding Rio Declaration of 1992)[89] and the 1949 Geneva Conventions. Although the Rio Declaration and Stockholm Declaration are both non-binding instruments, 'the prevention of environmental damage' is the most significant common provision that is contained in the second part of both Stockholm Principle 21 and Rio Principle 2, which establishes a state's responsibility to ensure that activities within their control do not cause damage to the environment of other states or areas beyond national jurisdiction or control. While some countries still question the customary legal nature of Stockholm Principle 21, there is no doubt that this obligation (a no damage principle) has become part of general international law, and has also expressly been endorsed by the ICJ as a rule of customary international law.[90]

However, only Additional Protocol I (including a couple of relative provisions) and the non-binding 1976 ENMOD Convention mention the protection of the aforementioned objects as parts of the natural environment 'in times of armed conflict'. Within this context, what should be borne in mind in relation to the ENMOD Convention is that it is essentially not applicable to environmental destruction during armed conflicts. As used by Article II, the term 'environmental modification techniques' in the title refers to any technique for changing – through the deliberate manipulation of natural processes – the dynamics, composition or structure of the Earth, including its biota, lithosphere, hydrosphere and atmosphere, or of outer space. It protects the natural environment through the prohibition of the use of environmental modification techniques that have severe, widespread or long-lasting impacts in the form of destruction, damage or injury to any other state party. Further to this, the ENMOD

[87] Roberts (1996), above n 75 at 233.

[88] Declaration of the United Nations Conference on the Human Environment (Stockholm, 5–16 June 1972), UN Doc A/CONF.48/14/Rev.1, www.un-documents.net/aconf48-14r1.pdf.

[89] Rio Declaration on Environment and Development (Annex I of the Report of the United Nations Conference on Environment and Development), UN Doc A/CONF.151/26 (Vol I) (Rio de Janeiro, 3–14 June 1992), www.un.org/en/development/desa/population/migration/generalassembly/docs/globalcompact/A_CONF.151_26_Vol.I_Declaration.pdf.

[90] G Handl, 'Declaration of the United Nations Conference on the Human Environment (Stockholm Declaration), 1972 and the Rio Declaration on Environment and Development, 1992' (2012) *UN Audiovisual Library of International Law* 1, 4, https://legal.un.org/avl/pdf/ha/dunche/dunche_e.pdf; Pulp Mills on the River Uruguay (Argentina v Uruguay), Judgment, ICJ Reports (20 April 2010), para 101; Legality of the Threat or Use of Nuclear Weapons (8 July 1996), above n 61 at para 29; T Koivurova, 'Due Diligence' (2013) *Max Planck Encyclopaedia of Public International Law* 1, www.arcticcentre.org/loader.aspx?id=78182718-d0c9-4833-97b3-b69299e2f127.

Convention does not set out sanctions for any state party that violates the Convention.[91]

Additional Protocol I is one of the major provisions of *jus in bello* that governs the protection of the natural environment in armed conflicts. However, mention should also be made of the fact that the provisions of Additional Protocol I are only applicable to international armed conflicts; they do not cover environmental destruction during non-international armed conflicts. In other words, the specific provisions in Additional Protocol I purport to regulate the degree of environmental damage that can be caused in an international armed conflict, but interestingly, there are no such restrictions applicable to non-international armed conflicts and they are not regulated by either the Geneva Conventions and its Additional Protocols or the Hague Regulations. It appears, therefore, that only the 'prohibition of attacks upon works and installations containing dangerous forces' contained in Article 15 of Additional Protocol II could be (indirectly) relevant to the protection of the natural environment during non-international armed conflicts.[92] Further to this, the drafters of the ICRC Customary International Humanitarian Law Study have entirely expanded this regulation to incorporate the prohibition of attacks upon works and installations containing dangerous forces in both international and non-international armed conflicts in Rule 43. The Rule is entitled 'Application of General Principles on the Conduct of Hostilities to the Natural Environment' and state practice establishes it as a norm of customary international law. Even though some states have not ratified Protocol I and II, the customary rules of *jus in bello* bind all states regardless of whether they are parties to the Geneva Conventions and the Additional Protocols.

More importantly, the ILC's new Draft Principles on the Protection of the Environment in Relation to Armed Conflict, adopted on 8 July 2019, indicates that the international community of states should positively contribute to international efforts to protect the natural environment and natural resources during international and non-international armed conflicts where they recognise the importance and relevance of existing rules and call for them to be implemented and respected in armed conflicts. Eventually, the parties to a non-international armed conflict will be encouraged to apply the same rules that protect the environment in international armed conflict.[93]

[91] See for more details, O Das, *Environmental Protection, Security and Armed Conflict: A Sustainable Development Perspective* (Cheltenham, Edward Elgar Publishing, 2013) 131–32.

[92] WD Verwey, 'Protection of the Environment in Times of Armed Conflict: In Search of a New Legal Perspective' (1995) 8 *Leiden Journal of International Law* 7, 29–30; Bond et al (1987), above n 76 at 486.

[93] For general information, see T Smith, 'Critical Perspectives on Environmental Protection in Non-International Armed Conflict: Developing the Principles of Distinction, Proportionality and Necessity' (2019) 32 *Leiden Journal of International Law* 759; H-P Gasser, 'For Better Protection of the Natural Environment in Armed Conflict: A Proposal for Action' (1995) 89 *American Journal of International Law* 637.

A large number of the ILC members and the states in the Sixth Committee of the UNGA agreed to address non-international armed conflicts as subject to the Draft Principles. According to the commentary on the Draft Principle 1, no distinction is made between international armed conflicts and non-international armed conflicts in terms of protection of the natural environment.[94]

Evaluation of the environmental damage that has resulted from the targeting of Islamic State's oilfields and installations in Syria and Iraq, and identifying the extent and level of the destruction of the oilfields and the impact on the environment, on people and on wildlife, requires particular expertise. However, there is no doubt that environmental destruction is inevitable when natural resources are targeted. It is partly for this reason that the UNGA, in its Resolution adopted in 1992 'urges states to take all measures to ensure compliance with the existing international law applicable to the protection of the environment in times of armed conflict'.[95]

Most of the Syrian oilfields occupied by Islamic State that were destroyed by the US-led coalition forces held underground reserves of crude oil, meaning that the damage to the natural environment as a result of explosions and fires would be widespread and severe. Accordingly, any justification for the destruction of the natural environment based upon the necessity principle, under the customary Rule 44 of the ICRC Customary International Humanitarian Law Study and Article 55(1) of Additional Protocol I, depends on the 'threshold level of the destruction/damage'. The threshold of the destruction should be identified in line with Article 55(1) of Additional Protocol I, which prohibits widespread, long-term and severe damage to the natural environment. In particular, it could be argued that this is a triple cumulative standard that is almost impossible to achieve because of the imprecise definitions of the term widespread, long-term and severe. In other words, proving that a violation occurred is bound by three imprecise conditions. Instead, the three conditions attached to the prohibition of Article 55(1) of Additional Protocol I are excessively restrictive, making prohibition much too narrow from an environmental point of view. Therefore, the exact scope of what is prohibited remains uncertain and is thus difficult to implement or enforce. This is one of the most important gaps in the existing framework of *jus in bello*, which will need to be rectified.[96]

Consequently, the issue remains regarding the determination of the threshold of damage to the natural environment in a region of conflict. Based on the information currently available, it cannot be definitively stated that the US-led coalition's airstrikes against the Islamic State's oilfields led to significant

[94] See The Draft Principles on Protection of the Environment in Relation to Armed Conflicts – Report of the ILC (adopted by the Commission on First Reading in seventy-first session), UN Doc A/74/10 (8 July 2019), 216. See also 'Why Legal Principles on War and Environment Matter', *UNEP* (20 August 2019), www.unenvironment.org/news-and-stories/story/why-legal-principles-war-and-environment-matter.

[95] UNGA, Resolution 47/37, UN Doc A/RES/47/37 (25 November 1992), para 1.

[96] Bothe et al (2010), above n 66 at 576.

environmental damages as a result of oil spills or fires. What is indisputable is that the present and long-term impacts of the destruction of Islamic State's oil refineries are not known at present, as measuring those impacts will be difficult, if not impossible. Therefore, determining pollution levels, and assessing the risks to the civilian population and their environment in Syria or Iraq depends on detailed studies as well as the monitoring and evaluation of air, water and soil.

In the case of Islamic State, the information available is based on the fact that the coalition forces were launching airstrikes against Islamic State's refineries. Although the US authorities have claimed that the White House had been reluctant to bomb oil wells held by Islamic State, reports indicate that the US-led coalition forces regularly bombed oil wells and refineries that had been captured by Islamic State, causing localised pollution.[97] This policy, which aimed to stop oil revenues, had little effect on demand and caused the civilian population and armed groups to turn to informal oil-refining methods – a highly polluting process which adversely affected communities and the environment across Syria's oil-producing areas. As a result, the massive displacement of parts of the Syrian population created environmental stresses in neighbouring countries.[98] Even worse, the US-led coalition appeared to be unconcerned about the environmental damage their attacks caused. As the Pentagon's Press Secretary, John Kirby, pointed out, the direct and indirect impact of environmental destruction resulting from targeting the Islamic State's oilfields was not foremost in the minds of the US-led coalition. In the press briefing of 8 June 2015, Kirby stated that:

> I'm not an environmental expert. I cannot dispel the fact that in some of these targets there may still be some fires burning as a result of what was hit. … The crude had to get trucked into these refineries to then get refined and then to be sold on the black market. So, you know, it is possible that at some of them there was not any. I just do not know. We are still working our way through that. But I cannot completely ignore the possibility that there might still be some oil fires burning because of this.[99]

This statement is directly related to the 'definite military advantage' expressed in Article 52 (2) of Additional Protocol I to the 1949 Geneva Conventions as a permissive factor for military forces in the conduct of military operations.

[97] W Zwijnenburg and A Waleij, 'Fire and Oil: The Collateral Environmental Damage of Airstrikes on ISIS Oil Facilities', *New Security Beat* (13 January 2016), www.newsecuritybeat.org/2016/01/fire-oil-collateral-damage-airstrikes-isis-oil-facilities/; DC Harary 'Environmental Decisions in the Context of War: Bombing ISIL's Oil' (2016) 2 *Centre for Development and Strategy*, www.envirosagainstwar.org/2017/07/27/environmental-decisions-in-the-context-of-war-bombing-isils-oil/.

[98] See 'Country Brief: Syria', *Conflict and Environment Observatory* (26 March 2018), www.ceobs.org/country-brief-syria/; 'Report Highlights Health and Environmental Impact of Makeshift Oil Refineries in Syria', *Conflict and Environment Observatory* (5 September 2016), www.ceobs.org/report-highlights-health-and-environmental-impact-of-makeshift-oil-refineries-in-syria/.

[99] See 'Department of Defence Press Briefing by Rear Admiral Kirby in the Pentagon Briefing Room', *US Department of Defence* (25 September 2014), www.defense.gov/News/Transcripts/Transcript-View/Article/606932/department-of-defense-press-briefing-by-rear-adm-kirby-in-the-pentagon-briefing/.

Military advantage refers to the advantage anticipated from the attack when considered as a whole and not just from isolated or particular parts of the attack.[100] It is widely accepted that an assessment of military advantage can be made in light of an attack as a whole, as distinct from specific parts of the attack. Furthermore, an attack as a whole is a finite event, not to be confused with the entire war.[101] However, the US-led coalition forces' attacks on Islamic State's oil refineries were not the main priority for the coalition, and they targeted[102] Islamic State's refined oil and crude without considering the possible scale of the environmental damage as a result of their airstrikes. The airstrikes were carried out without knowing whether the attacks might cause long-term and widespread damage to the natural environment or be a threat to the civilian population. This means that the destruction of Islamic State's oil refineries did not, in practice, confer a definite military advantage for the US and coalition states.

What must be kept in mind is that even if a particular object satisfies the criteria of Article 52(2) and qualifies as a military objective, it is not always necessary to attack it. The attacking commander must ensure that any collateral damage is not disproportionate to the military advantage anticipated.[103] In summing up, as an objective, it is only an objective that is estimated to carry the lowest collateral damage that can be selected if all of the military objectives in question produce a similar military advantage.[104] Clearly, even if the determination of a threshold for environmental damage as a result of the destruction of an enemy's energy resources is almost impossible, a definite military advantage must be identified. Otherwise, the targeting of oil facilities and installations, especially crude oil which is still in the ground and is immovable, would violate the principle of necessity because it will cause unnecessary damage to the environment.

iii. Environmental Destruction as a War Crime: The Prevention Means of the 1998 Rome Statute

Despite the fact that states are responsible for protecting the natural environment against widespread, long-term and severe damage, and that armed attacks on the natural environment by way of reprisals which have been regulated by

[100] UK Ministry of Defence, *The Manual of the Law of Armed Conflict* (Oxford, Oxford University Press, 2005), 87.

[101] See Y Dinstein, 'Legitimate Military Objectives Under the Current Jus in Bello' (2002) 78 *International Law Studies* 139, 144–45.

[102] The US-led coalition's airstrikes on 8 June 2015 hit two crude oil collection points of Islamic State near Dayr Az Zawr in Syria. See 'Airstrikes Destroy ISIL Oil Infrastructure, Tactical Vehicles', *US Department of Defence* (8 June 2015), www.defense.gov/News/Article/Article/604791/.

[103] See Cassese (2005), above n 10 at 417.

[104] D Turns, 'Military Objectives' in R Liivoja and T McCormack (eds), *Routledge Handbook of the Law of Armed Conflict* (London, Routledge, 2016) 151–52.

the 1949 Geneva Conventions and its 1977 Additional Protocol I have been prohibited, a large number of armed attacks have taken place around the world that have caused environmental damage as a result of targeting energy facilities, mainly oil facilities and refineries. These are probably the most significant examples of violations of Additional Protocol I and the Rome Statute regulations protecting the environment.

In order to strengthen the protection of the environment during armed conflicts, the destruction of the natural environment without necessity has now been identified as a criminal offence within the context of international law. The first support for this argument is the Draft Code of Crimes against the Peace and Security of Mankind[105] drafted by the ILC in 1996.

According to Article 20(g) of the Draft Code:

> In the case of armed conflict, using methods or means of warfare not justified by military necessity with the intent to cause widespread, long-term and severe damage to the natural environment and thereby gravely prejudice the health or survival of the population and such damage occurs.

This not only constitutes a war crime but also a crime against the peace and security of mankind when committed in a systematic manner or on a large scale. The Draft Code was later superseded by the 1998 Rome Statute as the first international treaty that has expanded the scope of environmental crime. The Draft Code's approach to environmental crime was supported by Article 8(2)(b)(iv) of the Rome Statute, which stated that intentionally launching an attack in the knowledge that such an attack will cause incidental loss of life or injury to civilians, damage to civilian objects, or widespread, long-term and severe damage to the natural environment, which would clearly be excessive in relation to the concrete and direct overall military advantage anticipated, will be a serious violation of the laws and customs applicable in international armed conflict within the established framework of international law.

The primary difference between the two categories of the Rome Statute and the Draft Code of the ILC is that Article 20(g) of the Draft Code of the ILC considered that intentional conduct of widespread, long-term and severe damage to the natural environment without necessity could constitute a war crime when committed during both an international or a non-international armed conflict. In other words, Article 20(2) applies in the case of both international and non-international armed conflict, in contrast to the more limited

[105] ILC, 'Draft Code of Crimes against the Peace and Security of Mankind 1996' (1996) 2 *Yearbook of the International Law Commission* 17, 53–54. For discussion, see M Cherif Bassiouni, 'The History of the Draft Code of Crimes against the Peace and Security of Mankind' (1993) 27 *Israel Law Review* 247; R Rayfuse, 'The Draft Code of Crimes against the Peace and Security of Mankind: Eating Disorders at the International Law Commission' (1997) 8 *Criminal Law Forum* 43; L Barrionuevo Arevalo, 'The Work of the International Law Commission in the Field of International Environmental Law' (2005) 32 *Boston College Environmental Affairs Law Review* 493, 501–506.

scope of applications that cover war crimes that have their basis in Article 55(1) of Additional Protocol I.[106]

As a rule, in cases of long-term and widespread damage to the natural environment, environmental destruction without military necessity will make the attackers responsible (individual criminal responsibility) for their actions during armed conflicts. However, presuming that international criminal law contains secondary norms, this does not mean that individuals will be personally criminally responsible for environmental crimes. A narrow criminal provision on environmental damage during armed conflict may alter the underlying primary obligation of states to prevent a broader range of environmental damage.[107] Additionally, all states, as discussed above, have an obligation to prevent environmental damage during armed conflicts under the customary *jus in bello*.

Similarly, Article 8(2)(b)(iv) of the Rome Statute requires that the damage must be widespread, long-term and severe in order for prosecutions to be made. However, expanding the scope of unacceptable damage to the natural environment and the ambitious language used in the text has come under severe criticism. With regard to the prohibited conduct regulated in this article, the requirement of proscribed armed attack as an attack which would be 'excessive' in relation to the concrete and direct overall military advantage anticipated, constitutes a major obstacle to the application of this provision. In terms of Article 8(2)(b)(iv), the intentions and thought behind the widespread, long-term and severe environmental damage must be the 'attack' and the 'knowledge' that the environmental damage is disproportionate to the 'overall military advantage anticipated'. In this sense, prosecution of the commander of the attack will depend on detailed knowledge of the alleged perpetrator based on his/her 'foreseeable' perceptions at the time, and the knowledge of what widespread, long-term and severe damage means. In other words, will the attack cause such a level of damage, and will the damage probably be disproportionate to the anticipated advantage of the military operation?[108] Nevertheless, the question remains, of whether a commander of the state involved in an armed conflict can be expected to be able to identify potential widespread, long-term and severe damage as a result of his/her attacks. What is clear is that the assessment of military advantage depends on extremely complex conditions, given that it not only requires knowledge of the technical aspects of *jus in bello* but also the operational context within which that law is applied. In other words,

[106] ILC (1996), above n 105 at 56.

[107] Speaking in a broad sense, international criminal law presupposes a primary norm prohibiting behaviour that constitutes a crime, while many primary obligations do not trigger criminal sanctions. See Bothe et al (2010), above n 66 at 574.

[108] R Gilman, 'Expanding Environmental Justice after War: The Need for Universal Jurisdiction Over Environmental War Crimes' (2011) 22 *Colorado Journal of International Environmental Law and Policy* 447, 455; SR Freeland, *Addressing the Intentional Destruction of the Environment During Warfare Under the Rome Statute of the International Criminal Court* (Cambridge, Intersentia Publishers, 2015) 210.

understanding how wars are fought, and in particular, the impact of the levels of war on how hostilities are conducted, is critical to assessing military advantage in contemporary conflicts.[109]

Regarding 'concrete and direct overall military advantage', the Preparatory Commission for the ICC has already mentioned that this expression refers to a military advantage that is 'foreseeable by the perpetrator' at the relevant time of the armed conflict, and it may or may not be temporally or geographically related to the object of the attack. It reflects the proportionality requirement inherent in determining the legality of any military activity undertaken in the context of armed conflict.[110]

Nevertheless, in cases of environmental crimes committed as part of a plan or policy, such as the previously planned mass bombardment of the enemy's energy resources – which was essentially intentional in the case of the US-led coalition's military attacks on Islamic State's oil facilities and refineries – it is, therefore, quite difficult to claim that the perpetrator was not able to foresee and make a value judgement and to conclude that damage would be excessive. The support for this argument is the US official John Kirby's statement mentioning that conduct regarding environmental destruction during the war with Islamic State has been exercised under governmental authority.[111]

In such cases, it is surmised that the perpetrator of attacks is knowledgeable and can foresee a concrete and direct overall military advantage. Likewise, it cannot be claimed that the perpetrator of attacks would have no prior knowledge about the extent of potential injury or damage to civilian objects and the natural environment, which would be excessive in relation to the concrete and direct overall military advantage anticipated. This is subject to 'military proportionality', according to which even if a target is a legitimate military objective, it should not be attacked if such an attack 'may be expected to cause incidental loss of civilian life, injury to civilians, damage to civilian objects, or a combination thereof, which would be excessive in relation to the concrete and direct military advantage anticipated' (Article 51(5)(b) of Additional Protocol I). According to the ICRC Commentary to the 1977 Additional Protocols, military advantage can only consist of ground gained or in annihilating or weakening the enemy armed forces. Of course, the words 'concrete and direct' impose stricter conditions on the attacker than those implied by the criteria defining military objectives in Article 52(2) of Additional Protocol I (general protection of civilian objects). In all, military proportionality is aimed at establishing an equitable balance between humanitarian requirements and the unfortunate necessities of

[109] See K Watkin, 'Military Advantage: A Matter of "Value", Strategy, and Tactics' (2014) 17 *Yearbook of International Humanitarian Law* 277, 282.

[110] See K Dörmann, 'Preparatory Commission for the International Criminal Court: The Elements of War Crimes – Part II: Other Serious Violations of the Laws and Customs Applicable in International and Non-International Armed Conflicts' (2001) 83 *International Review of the Red Cross* 461, 471.

[111] US Department of Defence (25 September 2014), above n 99.

war. It is by no means as clear as it might have been, but under the circumstances, it seems a reasonable compromise between conflicting interests, and a praiseworthy attempt to impose some restrictions in a domain where arbitrary behaviour has existed too often.[112]

Further to this, when there is a choice of methods and means of warfare, a commander should choose those which are most likely to reduce or minimise incidental civilian casualties and damage (Article 57(2)(a)(ii) of Additional Protocol I) and the perpetrator needs to refrain from launching any attacks that may be expected to violate the proportionality principle (Rules 17 and 18 of the ICRC Customary International Humanitarian Law Study).[113] There is a broad consensus among the states and the ICRC commentators in support of the idea that the destruction of objectives such as oil-refining facilities, which simultaneously serve civilian and military purposes,[114] puts an end to their use by civilians, and the reverberating effects of such damage form part of the incidental damage that must be taken into account under the proportionality principle.[115] This means that they must be able to assess and avoid the expected collateral civilian damage and casualties, which have been defined as 'the foreseeable reverberating effects of an armed attack',[116] or 'loss of life of, or injury to civilians or other protected persons, and damage to or the destruction of the natural environment or objects that are not in themselves military objectives'[117] arising from the targeting of energy facilities, mainly oil refineries. In general, an armed operation is proportionate when it does not cause incidental damage and civilian casualties which are excessive in relation to the value of the expected result of the whole military operation.[118]

Viewed from this perspective, it is necessary to determine the extent of the knowledge possessed by the US-led coalition forces as to the targeting of Islamic State's oil facilities as military objectives, the extent to which the attacks could have been reasonably anticipated to cause environmental damage, and whether the coalition could reasonably have resorted to other less harmful methods for achieving its military objectives of disabling Islamic State's oilfields and installations. Notwithstanding, it is more difficult to conclude whether or not the

[112] Sandoz et al (1987), above n 45 at paras 2218–19.

[113] CJ Greenwood, 'Current Issues in the Law of Armed Conflict: Weapons, Targets and International Criminal Liability' (1997) 1 *Singapore Journal of International & Comparative Law* 441, 461–62. See also H Shue and D Wippman, 'Limiting Attacks on Dual-Use Facilities Performing Indispensable Civilian Functions' (2002) 35 *Cornell International Law Journal* 559.

[114] Shue and Wippman (2002), above n 113 at 562.

[115] L Gisel, 'Relevant Incidental Harm for the Proportionality Principle' (2015) *Proceedings of the 16th Bruges Colloquium: Urban Warfare* 118, 123; Shue and Wippman (2002), above n 113 at 111.

[116] Shue and Wippman (2002), above n 113 at 112.

[117] San Rome Manual on International Law Applicable to Armed Conflicts at Sea (12 June 1994), Art 13(c), https://ihl-databases.icrc.org/ihl/INTRO/560. For further discussion, see L Doswald-Beck, 'The San Remo Manual on International Law Applicable to Armed Conflicts at Sea' (1995) 89 *American Journal of International Law* 192; L Doswald-Beck (ed), *San Remo Manual on International Law Applicable to Armed Conflicts at Sea* (Cambridge, Cambridge University Press, 1995) 119–21.

[118] Henckaerts and Doswald-Beck (2005), above n 49 at 323.

perpetrator at the time launched an attack with 'knowledge' about the concrete and direct military advantage anticipated and its potential impacts on civilian objects, including the natural environment.

Aside from the proportionality criterion, the principle of distinction is a fundamental step taken towards humanitarian objectives, assuming that the protection of civilians and civilian objects, sparing them during an armed conflict to limit the pain and suffering caused by warfare, are the main objectives of *jus in bello*. The principle of distinction, which is established as customary international law and is applicable in both international and non-international armed conflicts, requires that 'the parties to the conflict must at all times distinguish between civilian and military objectives and attacks may only be directed against military objectives. In other words, attacks must not be directed against civilian objects'.[119] The core component of this principle, which was regulated in Articles 48, 51(2) and 52(2) of Additional Protocol I without reservations, is that the only legitimate objective that states should endeavour to accomplish during armed conflict is to weaken the military forces of the enemy. In this sense, it can be argued that using '*and*' between the terms 'widespread, long-lasting *and* severe' in Article 8(2)(b)(iv) of the Rome Statute, inspired by Article 55(1) of Additional Protocol I, moves away from the main objective of *jus in bello* by expanding the scope for illegal damage to the natural environment.

On this subject, it seems that the ENMOD Convention was successful in promoting the effective protection of the natural environment and civilian objects from the effects of conflict since it requires a much lower threshold of environmental damage, with the triple cumulative standard being replaced by an alternative one. In other words, the ENMOD Convention has narrowed the scope of the prohibited conduct of damage to the natural environment by using '*or*' instead of '*and*', changing the term to 'widespread, long-lasting *or* severe'. Besides which, the ENMOD defines the term 'long-lasting' as lasting for 'a period of months or approximately a season', while Additional Protocol I specifies the term 'long-term' as a matter of 'decades'.[120] In essence, one might argue that this is a success for ENMOD since no large-scale 'environmental modification tactics'[121] have been reported in the 50 years since its adoption in 1976.[122] Some scholars in the literature have highlighted that no large-scale environmental modification tactics have been reported because this threshold

[119] Freeland (2015), above n 108 at 143; Henckaerts and Doswald-Beck (2005), above n 10, Rule 1 at 3.

[120] Sandoz et al (1987), above n 45, paras 1454–55 at 416–18. For more details, see B Boothby, 'The Law of Weaponry – Is It Adequate?' in MN Schmitt and J Pejic (eds), *International Law and Armed Conflict: Exploring the Faultlines* (Leiden, Martinus Nijhoff, 2017) 305–306; Solf (1986), above n 82 at 134.

[121] According to Art 2 of the ENMOD Convention, the term 'environmental modification techniques' refers to any technique for changing, through the deliberate manipulation of natural processes, the dynamics, composition or structure of the Earth, including its biota, lithosphere, hydrosphere and atmosphere, or of outer space. See ENMOD Convention, above n 63.

[122] UNEP (2009), above n 64 at 12.

has never been reached so far, not even by the Vietnam War or the First Gulf War in the 1990s, and the prevailing opinion in doctrine and state practice denied any violation of Additional Protocol I during the First Gulf War.[123] However, the UNSC Resolution 687 (1991) determined that the targeting of Kuwaiti oil facilities by the Iraqis was an obvious violation of existing international law.[124] The UNSC and the US were convinced that *jus in bello* constituted a sufficiently solid basis for the protection of the natural environment in times of armed conflict. After all, although the US and Iraq were not contracting parties to Additional Protocol I, and the UNSC is not clear about the exact principles and rules of *jus in bello*, the question of the legality or illegality of the Iraqi military operations vis-à-vis the natural environment can be addressed from two angles: (a) damage resulting from attacks on the environment as such; and (b) damage arising from the use of the environment as a method or instrument of warfare.[125]

In light of all the reasons discussed above, it seems that Article 8(2)(b)(iv) of the Rome Statute restricted the scope and effectiveness of environmental war crimes with a less effective provision, which seems to simply be a reflection of the ICC's policy of compromise regarding environmental war crimes. This is the reason why no-one has been prosecuted, and no charges have ever been filed under Article 8(2)(b)(iv) for environmental crimes: it is simply more difficult for a defendant to know what widespread, long-term and severe damage means, as there is no legal consensus as to its meaning. A commander will be able to plead a defence based upon a misunderstanding of the scope of widespread, long-term and severe damage. As the Policy Paper of the ICC Office of the Prosecutor (OTP) emphasised, the impact of such crimes may be assessed in light of, inter alia, the increased vulnerability of victims and the environmental damage inflicted on the affected communities. Given this, the Office will give particular consideration to prosecuting Rome Statute crimes that are committed by means of, or that result in, inter alia, the destruction of the environment, the illegal exploitation of natural resources, or the illegal dispossession of land.[126]

In practice, the Rome Statute has taken a crucial step forward by characterising environmental destruction during armed conflicts as a war crime. However, assuming the lacunae in Article 8(2)(b)(iv) of the Rome Statute and its ineffective provision, it seems likely that the ICC will be unable to make an

[123] S Oeter, 'Methods and Means of Combat' in D Fleck and M Bothe (eds), *The Handbook of International Humanitarian Law* (Oxford, Oxford University Press, 2013) 119; Dinstein (2016), above n 30 at 520–30.

[124] UNSC, Resolution 687, UN Doc S/RES/687 (3 April 1991), para 16. For more details, see Lijnzaad and Tanja (1993), above n 78 at 169.

[125] Lijnzaad and Tanja (1993), above n 78 at 169. For further discussion, see AM Al-Damkhi, 'Kuwait's Oil Well Fires, 1991: Environmental Crime and War' (2007) 64 *International Journal of Environmental Studies* 31.

[126] ICC/OTP, Policy Paper on Case Selection and Priotisation (15 September 2016), para 41, www.icc-cpi.int/itemsDocuments/20160915_OTP-Policy_Case-Selection_Eng.pdf; Gilman (2011), above n 108 at 455.

effective judgement of whether an environmental war crime has been committed by punishing wartime environmental damage. Where environmental destruction during conflicts takes place through the targeting of energy facilities – mainly oil installations and crude oil reserves that are still underground – it can be concluded that environmental destruction during armed conflicts happens with regularity. Closing this gap might be achieved if Article 8(2)(b)(iv) sets forth attainable definitions for the terms widespread, long-term, and severe damage in order to derive a narrow scope of the prohibited conduct of damage to the natural environment during armed conflicts. At present, it is not clear whether the three terms should be interpreted as they are in Additional Protocol I (which requires a higher threshold of environmental damage) or in the ENMOD Convention (which requires a much lower threshold).

In summary, interpretation of the language in a way that requires a higher threshold is problematic since it might be used by warring states as military justification to target natural resources during armed conflicts in the direction of their political objectives. At this point, the extraterritorial use of force against Islamic State and destruction of the energy resources under its effective control in Iraq and Syria as military objectives continues to be a controversial subject.

Regardless of the insufficiency of the Rome Statute in establishing individual responsibility for environmental war crimes, the responsibility of the states involved in the war with Islamic State for environmental damage and its potential impact over time, including its effect on human health, is the other crucial point to be taken into consideration and discussed separately. No international regulations allow the destruction of a territorial state's energy resources which are occupied by an ANSA, given that occupation is a temporary situation and the local resources are the property of the territorial state at all times and must be protected under *jus in bello*. However, it appears that the lack of consensus on the customary legal nature of the relevant rules of *jus in bello*, with regard to the protection of the natural environment in times of armed conflict, has paved the way for states to interpret the primary principles of *jus in bello*, including necessity in a broader sense, as a way of justifying their actions from a military standpoint.

C. The Protection of Natural Resources as State Property

As a general practice, as recognised by the ICJ, the natural resources of a territorial state are the property of that state and they have 'permanent sovereignty over their natural resources' as a principle of customary international law. The rights and duties emanating from this principle remain in effect at all times, including during armed conflict and occupation.[127] This is because the occupying power

[127] *Case Concerning Armed Activities on the Territory of the Congo* (19 December 2005), above n 23 at para 229, 244; UNGA, 'Permanent Sovereignty of the Palestinian People in the Occupied

does not acquire sovereignty over occupied territory and its control of an occupied territory's natural resources is only a temporary situation.[128] In such cases, the states involved in armed conflict against the occupying ANSAs cannot resort to any particular armed actions that may damage the natural resources that are part of the environment for any reason, because such actions would touch upon the essential interests of other states, particularly the territorial state.[129]

Even though attacks on state property during armed conflicts have been one of the most controversial issues in the context of *jus in bello*, the unnecessary destruction of property, even if that property is under the effective control of an occupying power – either states or ANSAs – is a violation of *jus in bello*.[130] Contrary to the provision contained in Article 55(1) of the Additional Protocol, which generally prohibits the destruction of the natural environment irrespective of necessity and proportionality during armed conflicts, destruction or seizure of the property of an adversary is allowed by imperative 'necessity'. In this regard, Article 147 of the IV Geneva Convention has advanced this rule by providing that '… extensive destruction and appropriation of property, not justified by military necessity and carried out unlawfully and wantonly' are grave breaches of the Geneva Conventions which form the core of *jus in bello*. As discussed above, the property could be part of the territorial state's natural resources, including energy resources that are part of the natural environment. The targeting a territorial state's property not justified by military necessity has also been prohibited by Rule 50 of the ICRC Customary International Humanitarian Law Study. The rule has identified the prohibition of the 'destruction or seizure of the property of an adversary unless required by imperative necessity' as a norm of customary international law which is already recognised in the Lieber Code (Articles 15 and 16) and by the IV Hague Convention (Article 23(g)).[131]

In the same way, the prohibition of the destruction of the natural environment, when it is not justified by necessity and is carried out wantonly, is an accurate reflection of customary international law which is also reiterated in the non-binding San Remo Manual (1995).[132] Further to this, the extensive

Palestinian Territory, Including East Jerusalem, and of the Arab Population in the Occupied Syrian Golan Over Their Natural Resources', UN Doc A/RES/66/225 (13 January 2012). See also Ng'ambi (2015), above n 61 at 158–59; KN Gess, 'Permanent Sovereignty Over Natural Resources: An Analytical Review of the United Nations Declaration and Its Genesis' (1964) 13 *International and Comparative Law Quarterly* 398.

[128] T Ruys and S Verhoeven, 'DRC v Uganda: The Applicability of International Humanitarian Law and Human Rights Law in Occupied Territory' in R Arnold and N Quenivet (eds), *International Humanitarian Law and Human Rights Law: Towards a New Merger in International Law* (Leiden, Martinus Nijhoff, 2008) 161.

[129] See Dam-de Jong (2015), above n 19 at 191.

[130] See Gill (2016), above n 74 at 369.

[131] Henckaerts and Doswald-Beck (2005), above n 10 at 175–177.

[132] Doswald-Beck (1995), above n 117 at para 44; Dinstein (2016), above n 30 at 193; Solf (1986), above n 82 at 128.

destruction and appropriation of an enemy's private and public property in international and non-international armed conflicts, when unjustified by necessity and carried out unlawfully and wantonly, is considered to be a war crime under the 1998 Article 8(2) of the Rome Statute. More precisely, the Rome Statute has considered 'destroying or seizing the property of an adversary unless such destruction or seizure be imperatively demanded by the necessities of the conflict' as a war crime in non-international armed conflicts. Importantly, no official contrary practice was found that related to either international or non-international armed conflicts.[133]

Moreover, the destruction and seizure of property, when not demanded by the necessities of war, has been prohibited by Article 23(g) of the regulations annexed to the IV Hague Convention, which states that:

> The right of belligerents to adopt a means of injuring the enemy is not unlimited … to destroy or seize the enemy's property unless such destruction or seizure be imperatively demanded by the necessities of war.

The main controversy surrounding the prohibition of the destruction of state property is due to the interpretation of the notion of 'effective contribution of the property to military actions' foreseen in Article 52(2) of Additional Protocol I to the 1949 Geneva Conventions. Therefore, we need to comprehend, first of all, how a particular object makes an effective contribution to military action, and we also need to determine what exactly is meant by effective contribution.

Keeping in mind that energy resources, facilities and refineries are state property, the protection of sites and installations containing dangerous forces is established as a norm of customary international law[134] that is applicable in both international and non-international armed conflicts. However, the matter is still controversial because of the different comments and interpretations made by states. The most contentious issue is that energy resources, when used by states or ANSAs to sustain their capacity to wage war and to survive, could be targeted under *jus in bello* as a necessity of the conflict. In this regard, the actions of the US, particularly regarding Islamic State's oil facilities, were significant. According to the US, energy resources that have been occupied by Islamic State and are necessary to its survival as its main revenue source could be legitimately targeted as 'war-sustaining objects'.[135] The US does not accept that prohibiting attacks on works and installations containing dangerous forces can be sustained absolutely if, under the circumstances at the time, they are lawful military objectives. Generally, the US's general practice is based on the legality of armed attacks on economic targets that indirectly but effectively support the enemy's operations to gain a definite military advantage.

[133] Henckaerts and Doswald-Beck (2005), above n 10 at 177.

[134] S Sivakumaran, *The Law of Non-International Armed Conflict* (Oxford, Oxford University Press, 2012) 69; Henckaerts (2005), above n 47 at 191.

[135] For more details, see R Goodman, 'The Obama Administration and Targeting "War-Sustaining" Objects in Non-International Armed Conflict' (2016) 110 *American Journal of International Law* 663.

More precisely, the US has tried to justify the coalition's airstrikes on Islamic State's oil refineries in Syria in the absence of the Syrian government's request and consent. According to the US, the destruction of such installations must not cause excessive injury to civilians or civilian objects. However, under some circumstances, attacks on objects such as dams, dykes and nuclear electrical generating stations may result in distinct and substantial military advantages, depending on the military use of such objects.[136] In fact, the US has interpreted the concept of military objectives under Article 52 of Additional Protocol I in very broad terms and has considered war-supporting economic facilities to be military objectives. However, the US's basis for targeting Islamic State's oil resources is highly controversial; the legality of attacks on war-sustaining or purely economic targets as legitimate military objectives has not been accepted in practice by other states or by military doctrine and it cannot be demonstrated that such objects make an effective contribution to military actions and that their destruction confers a definite military advantage to the coalition.[137]

In this sense, therefore, the US's approach seems problematic because, first of all, oil resources were not the only revenue source of Islamic State; the group was able to generate income from many other sources. Moreover, the permanent members of the UNSC had already deplored the violation of *jus in bello* and expressed their deepening concern over the widening of the conflict through the escalation of armed attacks on purely civilian targets, and on the oil installations of littoral states such as Iraq.[138]

Furthermore, it is difficult to justify targeting energy resources as state property under 'necessity'. As pointed out by the ICJ, states must take environmental considerations into account when assessing what is necessary and proportionate in the pursuit of legitimate military objectives. Respect for the environment is one of the elements that goes into assessing whether an action conforms with the principles of [military] necessity and proportionality.[139]

Oil was not Islamic State's only revenue source. According to a study of the Centre for the Analysis of Terrorism, apart from the revenues from natural resources including oil, natural gas, phosphates, cement and agriculture, Islamic State was generating billions of dollars of income from criminal activities, including extortion, kidnap and ransom, foreign donations, and the trafficking of antiquities.[140] Islamic State's most significant sources of revenue were closely tied to its territory as it took control of large areas of Syria and Iraq and made

[136] Henckaerts and Doswald-Beck (2005), above n 49 at 824.

[137] Ibid, at 188; Turns (2016), above n 104 at 154.

[138] UNSC, Statement by the President, UN Doc S/PV.2730 (22 December 1986) 3.

[139] Legality of the Threat or Use of Nuclear Weapons (8 July 1996), above n 61 at para 30.

[140] L Bindner and G Poirot, *ISIS Financing in 2015* (Paris, CAT, 2016) 9–20; H Banai, 'International and Regional Responses: An Appraisal' in F al-Istrabadi and S Ganguly (eds), *The Future of ISIS: Regional and International Implications* (Washington, DC, Brookings Institution Press, 2018) 154; A Basit, 'Foreign Fighters in Iraq and Syria – Why So Many?' (2014) 6 *Counter Terrorist Trends and Analyses* 4, 7.

sure that people and businesses paid taxes directly to them. Collecting taxes from the population under its control, charging fees for certain services, and raising levies on trade passing through its territory were the other major sources of Islamic State's income.[141] However, by November 2016, Islamic State had lost 62 per cent of its mid-2014 'peak' territory in Iraq, and 30 per cent in Syria, meaning that there were fewer people and businesses to tax.[142]

The IV Geneva Convention (Article 147) and Additional Protocol I (Articles 52 and 55) are the main provisions creating a legal basis for environmental protection during armed conflicts. The focal point of these regulations is the consideration of natural resources as civilian property which should be protected during armed conflicts. Destroying natural resources without this being a necessity is, therefore, a violation of Article 147 of the IV Geneva Convention, as detailed below.

> Grave breaches to which the preceding Article relates shall be those involving any of the following acts if committed against persons or property protected by the present Convention: … extensive destruction and appropriation of property, not justified by military necessity and carried out unlawfully and wantonly.

In the case of Islamic State, the destruction of the oilfields and installations occupied by Islamic State by the US-led coalition's airstrikes need to be justified by 'necessity'. The main point here is the nature and activities of the oil facilities and installations. In other words, it has to be clear whether or not Islamic State's oil facilities had a military nature and contributed effectively to their military campaigns, given that the Geneva Conventions and Additional Protocols do not cover installations when they are used in regular and direct support of military operations.[143]

Accordingly, it should also be clarified whether Islamic State used the oil facilities for military purposes. In this respect, a distinction has to be made between refined oil, which is contained in silos, and crude oil, which is still situated in the ground and cannot be moved. Crude oil cannot be used for military purposes and therefore cannot make an effective contribution to military action since it is not suitable for transport.[144] In contrast, refined oil, which is derived from crude oil, can be transported.

[141] See P Blannin, 'Islamic State's Financing: Sources, Methods and Utilisation' (2017) 9 *Counter Terrorist Trends and Analyses* 13; J Hansen-Lewis and JN Shapiro, 'Understanding the Daesh Economy' (2015) 9 *Perspectives on Terrorism* 142; A Levallois, 'The Financing of the "Islamic State" in Iraq and Syria (ISIS)' (2017) *Directorate- General for External Policies of the European Union* 1, 16. See also 'For ISIS, Losing Territory Means Losing Revenue', *The Wall Street Journal* (18 October 2017), www.wsj.com/articles/for-isis-losing-territory-means-losing-revenue-1508355115.

[142] S Heißner et al, *Caliphate in Decline: An Estimate of Islamic State's Financial Fortunes* (London, The International Centre for the Study of Radicalisation and Political Violence, 2017) 3, 7.

[143] Solf (1986), above n 82 at 134.

[144] For more details, see Hulme (2004), above n 62 at 198–200.

From this point of view, even if it is accepted that the US's practice of targeting oil refineries as legitimate military objectives is justifiable under necessity, it must be clarified that the US's practice refers only to the refined oil products of Islamic State as part of its revenue. This type of energy is transportable, and the environmental damage as a result of military attacks might not be widespread or long-term. However, this is not the case for crude oil, since it is situated in the ground; targeting such an energy source would cause 'long-term and widespread damage'. According to UNEP, burning crude oil releases a wide range of pollutants, including soot and gases that can cause skin irritation and shortness of breath. UNEP reported that during the war with Islamic State in Iraq, fumes from burning stockpiles of sulphur dioxide and oil wells that were set ablaze led to further suffering for civilians in Iraqi Kurdistan.[145] Hence, only some of the US-led coalition's airstrikes against Islamic State's oil facilities are justifiable under necessity, since most of their targets were Islamic State's crude oil collection points.[146]

Although Islamic State has made millions of dollars from its oil revenues, it is not reasonable to assume that its survival was based only on its captured oil resources. In other words, targeting Islamic State's oil installations in order to damage its military capabilities did not serve any obvious military purpose, and had not been successful. Engaging in non-military activities, including energy trading, smuggling and collecting taxes from the regions under their effective control are the most important factors ensuring the survival of ANSAs.[147] Importantly, increasing revenue in different ways will ultimately make the ANSAs powerful enough to engage in armed conflict. It is important, therefore, to distinguish between their revenue sources. In other words, targeting only one of the revenue sources of violent ANSAs – citing it as a war-sustaining capability in terms of the attacking state's unilateral assessment – would be extremely difficult to justify under the necessity ground. What is certain is that the military activities, cross-border terrorist actions and the growing financial strength of Islamic State were not halted by the coalition's airstrikes on its captured oilfields and installations. More precisely, it is even accepted that any revenue

[145] See 'ISIL's 'Scorched Earth Policy' Creating Environmental and Health Havoc in Mosul, Warns UN', *UN News Centre* (27 October 2016), www.un.org/apps/news/story.asp?NewsID=55411#.WgV8B2hSzIU.

[146] For example, on 5 January 2015, the coalition forces conducted 14 airstrikes in Syria, hitting five of Islamic State's crude oil collection points. The coalition aircraft, in six airstrikes, struck five of Islamic State's crude oil collection points and a crude oil pipeline near Dayr az Zawr. See 'Combined Joint Task Force Continues Airstrikes against ISIL', *US Department of Defence* (5 January 2015), www.defense.gov/News/Article/Article/603879/; 'Airstrikes Destroy ISIL Infrastructure in Syria, Iraq', *US Department of State* (11 August 2015), https://archive.defense.gov/news/newsarticle.aspx?id=129448.

[147] See M Eleftheriadou, 'Elements of "Armed Non-State Actors" Power: The Case of Al-Qaeda in Yemen' (2014) 25 *Small Wars & Insurgencies* 404; T Eaton et al (eds), *Conflict Economies in the Middle East and North Africa. Chatham House Report* (London, Chatham House, 2019) 13.

source belonging to ANSAs can be targeted as a legitimate military objective, targeting the civilian population working at Islamic State's oil installations, or all of the population paying taxes to Islamic State, might also be justified as being legitimate military objectives, since civilians make a considerable contribution to the development of Islamic State's economic base. However, there is a consensus among the international community of states that distinguishing between civilians and combatants during armed conflict is a customary rule of *jus in bello* since civilians cannot constitute a military advantage for any attacker under any circumstances.

Given this, targeting Iraqi and Syrian crude oil fields under the effective control of Islamic State as the sources of its revenues based on the 'legitimate military objectives' justification would appear problematic. In this regard, the First Gulf War was one of the most notorious cases since the war caused long-term and widespread environmental damage. The 752 Kuwaiti oil wells that were set on fire burned for more than nine months – thick smoke blocked out the sun, temperatures dropped locally, and the fallout of oil, soot, sulphur and acid rain affected many areas. In addition, air quality was severely impaired over the short term by the plumes of smoke, which stretched at one point for over 100 km. Additionally, land, ground and surface water were contaminated by the release of oil compounds to the detriment of vegetation, animals and the local population.[148]

Consequently, in order to avoid damaging the natural environment, it seems likely that improving cooperation between states to monitor the trade or smuggling in oil and other oil products by Islamic State instead of targeting its oil facilities could have been more effective in reducing its economic and eventually its military capabilities. There is a consensus among the majority of scholars that targeting oil facilities and refineries is only permissible if the enemy is using the facilities for military purposes. While the connection between the revenue generated by Islamic State's oil exports and its military actions is too remote to be made, the targeting of oil facilities and refineries to stop refined oil from being supplied to Islamic State's military groups fits logically within the scope of fighting a war. However, if such attacks are intended to stop the sale of smuggled oil, the proceeds of which would finance Islamic State's activities, only part of which includes military action, the determination of such attacks as military objectives is potentially much more controversial.[149]

As noted earlier, the US-led coalition forces targeted Islamic State's refineries, pump sites, oil installations and tanker trucks, which led to inevitable

[148] M DuBarry Huston, 'Wartime Environmental Damages: Financing the Cleanup' (2002) 3 *University of Pennsylvania Journal of International Law* 899, 909–10. See also CC Joyner and JT Kirkhope, 'The Persian Gulf War Oil Spill: Reassessing the Law of Environmental Protection and the Law of Armed Conflict' (1992) 24 *Case Western Reserve Journal of International Law* 29.

[149] K Watkin, 'Targeting "Islamic State" Oil Facilities' (2014) 90 *International Law Studies* 499, 504–505.

environmental damage as a result of spills and fires. Considering the prospective environmental damage to be a result of targeting the Syrian and Iraqi oil resources occupied by Islamic State, the legality of the US-led coalition's reactions when fighting the militants remains controversial.

In any event, overall responsibility for environmental destruction is still disputed. This is due to the contested nature of the general prohibition of widespread, long-term and severe damage to the natural environment, the controversies surrounding its customary legal nature in Additional Protocol I and the ENMOD Convention in the protection of the natural environment in times of armed conflict, and the fact that the US is not a party to Additional Protocol I. Nonetheless, as discussed above, there is a consensus among the international community of states that destroying or seizing the enemy's property without imperative necessity in international and non-international armed conflicts is a direct violation of *jus in bello*. As noted above, the Rome Statute considers these acts to also constitute serious violations of the laws and customs applicable both in international and non-international armed conflicts, and therefore regarded as war crimes.

The requirement that environmental damage must be 'long-term' if it continues to be measured in decades will limit the utility of the environmental provisions of Additional Protocol I. While in many situations, other provisions including those protecting civilian objects and the state property and their customary legal nature are not considered to be controversial as they probably have more relevance to the protection of the natural environment. In that respect, Article 147 of the IV Geneva Convention, Article 23(g) of the IV Hague Convention, Article 56 of Additional Protocol I and Article 15 of Additional Protocol II to the Geneva Conventions are the major applicable regulations in the protection of natural resources as part of the environment and also indirect protection of state property in times of armed conflict as the general regulations that state practice establishes them as norms of customary international law both in international and non-international armed conflicts. The application of the aforementioned regulations in the absence of particular provisions protecting the environment in times of armed conflict would significantly restrain military activities that may cause or are intended to cause significant environmental damage during armed conflicts. Under these circumstances, it would not be surprising to suggest that the terms 'widespread, long-term and severe' in Additional Protocol I belong to earlier concepts of what constitutes environmental protection and will need to be re-interpreted or revised, since they clearly do not bestow protection on the natural environment in times of armed conflict.[150]

[150] Roberts (1996), above n 75 at 266–67.

IV. RESPONSIBILITY FOR THE ENVIRONMENTAL IMPACTS FOLLOWING THE DESTRUCTION OF ENERGY RESOURCES DURING ARMED CONFLICTS

A. Contextual Background

The 'obligation to protect the environment' is an accepted customary rule of *jus in bello* concerning the conduct of hostilities both in international and non-international armed conflicts. As discussed earlier, military operations that cause damage to the natural environment are in violation of this principle, which is only laid down in Additional Protocol I to the Geneva Conventions (Article 55(1)). However, the ambiguity of the various interpretations has created grounds for controversy on the scope of environmental crimes under the 1998 Rome Statute, which is likely to be enough to justify military operations against energy resources that will lead to environmental damage. Although Common Article 3 of the Geneva Conventions and Additional Protocol II, which is dedicated to non-international armed conflicts, contains no provision on war crimes and does not recognise criminal responsibility for serious breaches, the Rome Statute is apparently following a compromise policy by expanding the scope of what constitutes environmental crimes, which seems to preserve the military policies of the states involved in the conflicts.[151]

Assuming that the protection of civilians as a cornerstone of *jus in bello* takes priority over a state's interests, expanding the conditions for the identification of environmental war crimes could be inconsistent with the rationality of *jus in bello*. In this case, it can be referred to Article 51(5)(b) of Additional Protocol I, which requires that 'an attack which may be expected to cause incidental loss of civilian life, injury to civilians, damage to civilian objects, or a combination thereof, which would be excessive in relation to the concrete and direct military advantage anticipated' is to be considered an indiscriminate attack. In essence, these kinds of military operations are evidently in violation of the customary 'principle of distinction' between civilian and military objectives. As noted earlier, despite the impossibility of identification of the 'long-term, widespread and severe' impact of such operations in the future, the serious damage inflicted on the natural environment and the indirect impact on human health and wildlife is undeniable.

The US authorities have justified their attacks ('operations in the absence of an invitation or consent of the Syrian government') on Syrian oil resources

[151] See in general, C Byron, *War Crimes and Crimes against Humanity in the Rome Statute of the International Criminal Court* (Manchester, Manchester University Press, 2009); WA Schabas, *The International Criminal Court: A Commentary on the Rome Statute* (Oxford, Oxford University Press, 2016); Freeland (2015), above n 108.

occupied by Islamic State by characterising them as war-sustaining capabilities since these refineries were economic assets supporting Islamic State's operations by providing fuel to run the Islamic State's military operations and financing its continued attacks throughout Iraq and Syria.[152] However, it appears that turning a blind eye to the potential and unprecedented impact of such operations on both the natural environment and the human population of the region stems from the restrictive and unclear meaning of the terms 'widespread, long-term and severe' in both Additional Protocol I and the Rome Statute. These three conditions are considered to be the threshold of unacceptable environmental damage caused by attacks on energy resources, contrary to the proportionality issues, which constitute grounds for self-serving interpretations of both military objectives and military advantage.

It seems likely that the current situation has forced the UNEP Assembly to adopt a Draft Resolution on Pollution Mitigation and Control in Areas Affected by Armed Conflict or Terrorism,[153] which addresses the loss of environmental governance as well as the coping strategies that communities affected by pollution are often forced into by armed conflicts. In accordance with the Draft Resolution, the long-term socio-economic consequences of the degradation of the environment and natural resources resulting from pollution caused by armed conflict or terrorism, which include, inter alia, the loss of biodiversity, the loss of crops or livestock, and the lack of access to clean water and agricultural land, the negative and sometimes irreversible impacts on ecosystem services and their impact on sustainable recovery, contributing to further forced displacement related to environmental factors. In terms of the statements used by the Draft Resolution, including 'irreversible impacts on ecosystem services', the coalition's airstrikes and military operations on refined and crude oil resources in Iraq and Syria, which are considered part of the natural environment, might be characterised as internationally wrongful acts that need to be evaluated within the context of the current legal framework.

More precisely, pollution resulting from the attacks on energy resources has an indirect impact on human health and therefore poses particular risks for the people in vulnerable situations in violation of the environmental norms of *jus in bello*. In that regard, Article 55(1) of Additional Protocol I of the Geneva Conventions is the key instrument of *jus in bello*, which prohibits operations that are intended or may be expected to cause damage to the natural environment and to human health.[154] As has already been evidenced by the aftermath of the First Gulf War, the resulting pollution and environmental damage from burning oil wells threatens human health and livelihoods. In other words, air,

[152] US Department of Defence (25 September 2014), above n 99.

[153] See Draft Resolution on Pollution Mitigation and Control in Areas Affected by Armed Conflict or Terrorism (UN Doc UNEP/EA.3/L.5) (Nairobi, 4–6 December 2017).

[154] For more details, see P-M Dupuy and JE Viñuales, *International Environmental Law* (Cambridge, Cambridge University Press, 2018) 413–17.

soil, and maritime pollution from oil spillages and fires are the main environmental consequences stemming from the destruction of natural resources that are part of the natural environment.[155]

As reaffirmed in the Report by the UN Conference on Environment and Development, the so-called Rio Declaration on Environment and Development, 'human beings are at the centre of concerns for sustainable development [and] they are entitled to a healthy and productive life in harmony with nature'.[156] This is, in fact, a reflection of the principle of the protection of human life and health by limiting the impact of armed conflict as the primary objective of *jus in bello*. By contrast, the compatibility of such operations with the principle of proportionality requires the perpetrator to consider all options when making targeting decisions, including verifying the target, the timing of the strike (eg is there a time when fewer civilians will be around?), the weapons used, and warnings and evacuations for the civilian population in the area. Therefore, there has to be a balance between necessity and proportionality, which could also mean refraining from launching an attack which may be expected to cause incidental loss of civilian life, injury to civilians, damage to civilian objects, or a combination thereof, which would be considered excessive over the concrete and direct military advantage anticipated. In other words, any harm to the civilian population has to be balanced against military advantage. This has been reflected in Article 51(5)(b) of Additional Protocol I, according to which, any attacks that are expected to cause 'excessive' loss of civilian life, injury to civilians, and/or damage to civilian objects, concerning the concrete and direct military advantage anticipated, can be considered to be indiscriminate. The term 'excessive' in Additional Protocol I calls for a balance to be struck between military advantage and potential harm to the civilian population.[157]

Having undertaken such an assessment by taking into account that targeting energy resources during armed conflicts may ultimately lead to severe environmental damage, it is worth looking at how criminal responsibility for natural resource destruction could be applied during the war with Islamic State.

B. The Application of International Criminal Responsibility for Natural Resource Destruction during the War with Islamic State

Establishing a link between the object being attacked and its connection to military activity and identifying the military advantage for the US-led coalition forces to carry out airstrikes against Islamic State's oil refineries and production

[155] See International Law and Policy Institute, *Protection of the Natural Environment in Armed Conflict: An Empirical Study* (Oslo, ILPI, 2014) p 14; UNEP (2003), above n 55 at 56–57.

[156] Rio Declaration on Environment and Development, above n 89, Principle 1.

[157] See Greenwood (1997), above n 113 at 461–62; Henckaerts and Doswald-Beck (2005), above n 10, Rule 1 at 14.

facilities is quite challenging. Justifying environmental destruction or the killing of civilians working at Islamic State's oil installations is extremely controversial because potential collateral casualties and the effects of the destruction of oil facilities as a result of airstrikes are unavoidable. Correspondingly, the war-sustaining criteria that the US uses as justification for destroying energy resources remain open to criticism as it consciously disregards the potential risk of incidental damage to the natural environment and to human health. It also raises the question of why the perpetrating states which justify armed attacks on any kind of target (especially economic targets) turn a blind eye to the indirect and potentially deadly impact of such operations on the health of both civilians and the natural environment.

Because of the greater probability of legal challenges to the identification of war-sustaining or economic targets that can be characterised as legitimate military objectives, the US forces' war-sustaining criteria has not been accepted either in military doctrine or in the practice of states where disagreements exist regarding the range of targets that can be legitimately attacked.[158] In this sense, it can be argued that environmental destruction as a result of attacks on energy resources, even under necessity, cannot be considered as grounds for the perpetrating states to breach their primary obligation of protecting the natural environment and the safety of civilians during conflicts. Otherwise, they might be held responsible for their internationally wrongful acts of environmental destruction, causing direct or indirect damage to human health, regardless of whether there is a higher or lower threshold level being applied regarding environmental destruction. The responsibility of states for their internationally wrongful act of environmental destruction is a matter for the law of state responsibility and *jus in bello*, and it is necessary to evaluate under what conditions an international obligation is breached by states that have the right to invoke the consequences of such a breach, and how they breach it.

As addressed by the Draft Articles on Responsibility of States for Internationally Wrongful Acts (2001)[159] adopted by the ILC, the characterisation of an internationally wrongful act is governed by international law, and such a characterisation is unaffected by the characterisation of the same act as lawful by domestic law.[160] Returning to the US's statement about the destruction of Islamic State's energy resources being justified under the war-sustaining approach, therefore, it is important to note that the US's responsibility for the internationally wrongful acts of environmental destruction authorised by the US government[161] would be the case under international law.

[158] Watkin (2014), above n 149 at 503.

[159] ILC, 'Draft Articles on Responsibility of States for Internationally Wrongful Acts' (Annex to the UNGA Resolution A/RES/56/83, 85th, 12 December 2001) (2001) 2 *Yearbook of the International Law Commission* 26, 26–143.

[160] Ibid, Art 3 at 36.

[161] For more details, see US Department of Defence (25 September 2014), above n 99.

An obvious example relevant to the topic is the First Gulf War, when US forces were not internationally considered responsible for any large-scale environmental destruction, as there was no evidence that the US forces intended large-scale destruction because specific directions were not issued to the troops. In this way, they could not be held responsible for any environmental destruction during or after the war.[162] As the ICC/OTP has emphasised, the manner of commission of the crimes may be assessed in light of, inter alia, the extent to which the crimes were systematic or stemmed from a 'plan or organised policy' resulting from the abuse of power.[163]

According to Article 42 of the ILC's Draft Articles (2001):

> [A] state is entitled, as an injured state, to invoke the responsibility of another state if the obligation breached is owed to (a) That State individually; or (b) A group of states including that state, or the international community as a whole, and the breach of the obligation: (i) Specifically affects that state; or (ii) Is of such a character as radically to change the position of all the other states to which the obligation is owed with respect to the further performance of the obligation.

The wording of Article 42 has designated two categories of states that have a right to invoke international responsibility for wrongful acts. The first category is individual states that can invoke responsibility in cases where there is a violation of an obligation regulated by a bilateral treaty owed particularly to that state. The second category is a group of states, or the international community as a whole, which can invoke responsibility in cases where there is a violation of an obligation regulated by a multilateral treaty that can affect all the other states.

It seems that the second category concerns the violation of the international customary rules of international law as accepted by the international community of states. In this respect, the ICJ's jurisprudence is not only based on states' responsibility for their internationally wrongful acts against the injured state but also for the wrongful acts towards any other state or the international community as a whole. The ICJ has pointed out that an essential distinction should be drawn between the obligations of a state towards the international community as a whole, and those arising vis-à-vis another state in the field of diplomatic protection. By their very nature, the former is the concern of all states. In view of the importance of the rights involved, all states can be held to have a legal interest in their protection; they are obligations *erga omnes*.[164]

In terms of the ICJ's jurisprudence, therefore, the obligation of a state to protect the natural environment during armed conflicts is an *erga omnes* obligation, which any state can complain about if there is a breach. The states' failure to comply with the obligation to protect the natural environment during armed

[162] For general information, see JE Seacor, 'Environmental Terrorism: Lessons from the Oil Fires of Kuwait' (1996) 10 *American University International Law Review* 481; Roberts (1996), above n 75 at 268.

[163] See ICC/OTP (15 September 2016), above n 126 at para 41.

[164] See *Case Concerning Barcelona Traction, Light and Power Company, Limited (Belgium v Spain)*, Judgment, ICJ Reports (5 February 1970), para 33.

conflicts is related to the international community as a whole. Consequently, any breach will justify invoking the international responsibility of the perpetrator for environmental destruction, which can be done by individual states or the international community as a whole. In other words, all states may have a legal interest in invoking a state's responsibility for wrongful acts, even if none of them is individually affected by the internationally wrongful acts of that state.[165]

This concept is handled by Article 48 of the Draft Articles (2001), which states that:

> 1. Any state other than an injured state is entitled to invoke the responsibility of another state in accordance with Paragraph 2 if: (a) The obligation breached is owed to a group of states including that state and is established for the protection of a collective interest of the group; or (b) The obligation breached is owed to the international community as a whole.

Nevertheless, neither Article 42 nor Article 48 have determined what kind of 'injury' (direct or indirect) allows a state to be held responsible for its internationally wrongful acts. This is based on the corollary of the international law of state responsibility, which prevents states from avoiding responsibility for the indirect impact of damages to natural resources by characterising them as legitimate military targets. This approach was taken based on the treaty interpretation rules of the 1969 Vienna Convention on the Law of Treaties which requires that 'a treaty shall be interpreted in good faith in accordance with the ordinary meaning to be given to the terms of the treaty in their context and in the light of its object and purpose' (Article 31) and should be in line with the 'supplementary means of interpretation' (Article 32). In other words, a state's responsibility hinges on an interpretation of the material rules of international law that are applicable in relation to environmental damage during armed conflicts. From this point of view, it might be recognised that Articles 42 and 48 cover both direct and indirect damage to the natural environment.

Following this approach, 'prohibition of targeting the natural environment' and indirect protection of the natural environment under Article 55(1) of Additional Protocol I might be recognised as the general principles of *jus in bello* within the context of the Geneva Law, the primary object of which is the protection of civilian objects during armed conflicts. Support for this argument is the long-standing rule of customary international law, outlined in Article 3 of the IV Hague Convention and Article 91 of Additional Protocol I. It is also repeated in Rule 149 of the ICRC Customary International Humanitarian Law Study, which provides that:

> A Party to the conflict which violates the provisions of the Conventions or of this Protocol shall, if the case demands, be responsible to pay compensation. It shall be responsible for all acts committed by persons forming part of its armed forces.

[165] Ibid.

According to the ICRC, state practice establishes the above rule as a norm of customary international law, which is applicable to violations committed in both international and non-international armed conflicts.[166]

Altogether, this is based on the state responsibility for violations of *jus in bello* committed by members of the state's armed forces as part of customary international law, and thus applicable to the violations of all rules of *jus in bello*. The responsibility for such wrongful acts will be determined even if the servicemen in question were acting wholly outside the scope of their official duties and this was obvious to all concerned. Therefore, if fleeing soldiers from an army in which all discipline had collapsed set fire to oil installations in the course of looting, and thus caused damage to the environment, this act would engage the responsibility of their state under the customary rule of 'responsibility of states for all acts committed by persons forming part of its armed forces', even if the state would not have been held responsible under the normal principles set out in the ILC's 2001 Draft Articles.[167] Nonetheless, due to the ambiguity in the threshold requirements including widespread, long-term and severe terms, which have caused significant controversy, the evaluation of a state's responsibility for the destruction of natural resources (where an indirect impact on the environment, human health and wildlife is inevitable) based upon these conditions would be difficult under the law of state responsibility.

Regarding the issue of responsibility for environmental damage caused during armed conflict, the indirect protection of the natural environment might also be challenged within the context of property rights, including clean air as a natural environmental property. At this point, natural resources, which can be owned by individuals, associations or governments, can also be thought of as environmental properties. The destruction of energy resources may then lead to the displacement[168] of the indigenous population who are generally the primary victims of the direct and indirect environmental impacts brought about by the destruction of energy resources.[169] This is about state responsibility for the internationally wrongful act of violating environmental property rights during armed conflicts. In this sense, as reported to the ILC in 2014, any use of force which causes damage to civilian objects, including the natural environment and human life, is disproportionate to the direct military advantage anticipated (collateral environmental damage) and is therefore prohibited, even if it is directed against military objectives and is necessary to achieve a defined

[166] See Henckaerts and Doswald-Beck (2005), above n 10 at 530.

[167] Ibid.

[168] See UNSDN, Indigenous Peoples: Conflict, Peace and Resolution (15th session of UNPFII, 17 May 2016).

[169] Preliminary Report on the Protection of the Environment in Relation to Armed Conflicts, submitted by Special Rapporteur Marie G Jacobsson to the International Law Commission, UN Doc A/CN.4/674 (Geneva, 5 May–6 June and 7 July–8 August 2014) paras 164–66, www.un-documents.net/a25r2625.htm.

military object.[170] This means that necessity alone cannot render proportionality effective, even in terms of the US's own war-sustaining criteria.[171]

In general terms, although the use of force may be justified under the necessity criteria, it can also make the attacker's state responsible for any violations of *jus in bello* because of the disproportionality of the attacks in the sense of their foreseeable impacts on civilian objects. It can be argued that despite the US war-sustaining criteria, which has generally been used to justify its airstrikes on Islamic State's oil resources, the operations on 'refined' and 'crude oil' were disproportionate in practice, even though they were accepted as legitimate military targets. Furthermore, Syria faced serious environmental challenges as a result of pollution, creating serious human health problems and potentially turning northern and eastern Syria into an environmental wasteland thanks to the coalition's airstrikes against numerous makeshift refineries in the north and east of the country. According to the US military, the coalition forces attacked and destroyed hundreds of oil installations and fuel trucks under Islamic State's control in both Iraq and Syria between October 2014 and December 2016.[172]

The Rome Statute regards as a war crime the launching of an attack in the *knowledge* that such an attack will cause incidental loss of life or injury to civilians or damage to civilian objects or to the natural environment. In this regard, the Pentagon Press Secretary, retired Rear Admiral John Kirby, supported this argument when he stated on 25 September 2014 that possible environmental damage from the coalition's airstrikes against oil installations controlled by Islamic State in northern and eastern Syria was not high on the list of concerns of those planning the attacks.[173] This is the practical basis for the claim that the coalition forces were targeting Islamic State's oilfields and facilities, knowing that their strikes could impact upon the natural environment and human health. Therefore, they must be held responsible at an international level.

Notwithstanding its significance to the natural environment and human health in general, some of the most intractable problems may arise regarding the criminal responsibility of the external powers involved in environmental crimes during the war with Islamic State. First, the Rome Statute's provision on 'intentionally launching an attack' can lead to the criminal prosecution of 'individuals' by the ICC, but it does not extend the possibility for the ICC to exercise jurisdiction when it comes to 'criminal state responsibility' in front of the ICC. Second, no clarification is provided in Article 8(2)(b)(iv) of the Rome Statute as to what is envisaged by each of the terms 'widespread, long-term

[170] Henckaerts and Doswald-Beck (2005), above n 10 at 46, 143.

[171] J Dill, *Applying the Principle of Proportionality in Combat Operations* (Oxford, Oxford Institute for Ethics, Law and Armed Conflict, 2010) 2.

[172] W Zwijnenburg and K Te Pas, *Amidst the Debris: A Desktop Study on the Environmental and Public Health Impact of Syria's Conflict* (Utrecht, Pax for Peace Organization, 2015) 24. See also 'Operation Inherent Resolve Targeted Operations to Defeat ISIS', *US Department of Defence* (31 December 2016), www.dod.defense.gov/OIR/Airstrikes/.

[173] US Department of Defence (25 September 2014), above n 99.

and severe damage' as they appear in that provision.[174] Therefore, the requirement of 'intentionally launching an attack in the knowledge that such attack will cause widespread, long-term and severe damage to the natural environment which would be clearly excessive in relation to the concrete and direct overall military advantage anticipated' (Article 8(2)(b)(iv)), constitutes a major obstacle to the application of this provision. Overall, clarification of the proscribed environmental damage as widespread, long-term, and severe damage, which is still not clear enough, is a reflection of the ambitious language used by the Rome Statute that paves the way for excluding the destruction of natural resources from the scope of war crimes contained within the Rome Statute that are subject to 'universal jurisdiction'. However, this should not be considered as giving permission to the states that are not parties to the ICC and the Rome Statute to ignore the provisions of the Geneva Conventions protecting the natural environment, civilian objects and state property during armed conflicts. Rather, states that are not parties to the ICC and the Rome Statute are obliged to co-operate with the ICC under the provisions in the Geneva Conventions whereby states must 'respect and ensure respect' for *jus in bello* as a universal responsibility contained in Common Article 1 of the 1949 Geneva Conventions and in Common Article 1(1) of Additional Protocols I and III.[175]

More importantly, the ICC and the Rome Statute have been very significant, even if major players at the international level, including the US, China, Russia and India, are not parties to the ICC and the Rome Statute. However, the contradictory provisions regulated under Article 8 of the Rome Statute regarding the international and non-international armed conflicts in terms of the punishment of war crimes is a step backwards, while there is a tendency in international law to eradicate such a legal division and margin, and to establish a uniform law applicable to armed conflicts in all forms. This is because armed conflicts acquired international, non-international or internationalised characteristics during the second half of the twentieth century. Accordingly, the nature of conflicts is irrelevant when humanitarian issues come into question. However, while state practices have indicated that even the applicable laws regulated by the Geneva Conventions have become ineffective, the ICC is still expected to take the lead by considering non-international armed conflicts to be a common problem that must be tackled by the international community in the same way as international conflicts.

Above all, valuing 'necessity' above 'proportionality' and the protection of civilian objects is another significant obstacle to holding the guilty responsible

[174] See Freeland (2015), above n 108 at 274–75.

[175] See Z Wenqi, 'On Co-operation by States Not Party to the International Criminal Court' (2006) 88 *International Review of the Red Cross* 87, 92–93; U Palwankar, 'Measures Available to States for Fulfilling Their Obligation to Ensure Respect for International Humanitarian Law' (1994) 34 *International Review of the Red Cross* 9; JS Pictet, *Commentary on the Third Geneva Convention* (Geneva, ICRC Press, 1960) 18; Sandoz et al (1987), above n 45 at paras 45–46, p 36; Henckaerts and Doswald-Beck (2005), above n 10 at 509.

for the environmental impacts caused by the destruction of natural resources. Given that both principles deal with military objectives in relation to other values, rather than whether the environmental damage caused is widespread, long-term and severe, the ground has increasingly been prepared for hostiles to target and damage the natural environment during armed conflicts as one of the most prevalent methods of warfare.

More precisely, it should be borne in mind that necessity is a customary rule of *jus in bello* limiting the military actions of armed forces. Necessity only permits measures that are necessary to accomplish a legitimate military objective and are not otherwise prohibited by *jus in bello*, while the only legitimate military objective is to weaken the military capacity of the enemy by taking into consideration that civilians and civilian objects must be protected against attacks, as the primary aim of *jus in bello*, if they are not proportionate to the expected military advantage. In essence, necessity is inadmissible if the purpose for which the measure was taken (eg environmental destruction) was itself contrary to *jus in bello*.

As pointed out by the International Criminal Tribunal for the former Yugoslavia (ICTY):

> The protection of civilians in times of armed conflict, whether international or internal, is the bedrock of modern humanitarian law ... Indeed, it is now a universally recognised principle recently stated by the [ICJ] that deliberate attacks on civilians or civilian objects are absolutely prohibited by international humanitarian law.[176]

Viewed from this perspective, therefore, the claim for the necessity of the attacks on any objectives proportionate to the expected military advantage brings us to a major challenge to *jus in bello* that serves the US war-sustaining criteria in targeting the territorial states' natural resources occupied by the ANSAs. This also stems from the lack of a systematic mechanism to prevent states or corporations from causing environmental damage or for looting natural resources, particularly in non-international armed conflicts. Moreover, the customary rules related to environmental protection asserted by the ICRC that apply in non-international armed conflicts are inadequate, and the usefulness of these rules is limited to a high level of environmental damage (Rule 45 of the ICRC Customary International Humanitarian Law Study).[177]

Therefore, it seems that the sole way out of this inextricable knot in trying to hold the perpetrators responsible for environmental crimes during armed conflicts is that protection might be bestowed by other rules of *jus in bello* for that purpose. As noted earlier, the rules regarding the protection of 'state property' contained in Article 23(g) of the IV Hague Convention, Article 147

[176] International Tribunal for the Prosecution of Persons Responsible for Serious Violations of International Humanitarian Law Committed in the Territory of the Former Yugoslavia since 1991, Prosecutor v Kupreˇski'c et al (Trial Judgement), IT-95-16-T, ICTY (14 January 2000), para 521.

[177] Henckaerts and Doswald-Beck (2005), above n 10, Rule 45 at 151.

of the IV Geneva Convention must be considered as the basis for protecting the natural environment through the identification of states' natural resources as their property. This will prohibit the 'destruction or seizure of the property of an adversary unless required by imperative necessity' as a norm of customary international law and applicable in both international and non-international armed conflicts.

V. CONCLUDING REMARKS

Having identified military occupation by an ANSA as subject to *jus in bello*, Chapter 3 has demonstrated that granting an occupying power the right of usufruct gives it an incentive to respect *jus in bello*. It has also shown that the legal frameworks of occupation, including the Geneva Conventions and the IV Hague Convention, clarify the material factors which are needed for occupying powers to be held responsible for wasting and destroying the occupied state's natural resources. In that sense, it has been shown that the unlawful and wanton destruction by the occupying power of real or personal property belonging to the state is considered a war crime under the Rome Statute. However, the legal frameworks indicate that an occupier does not have any rights to take advantage of property for purposes other than the maintenance of public order and safety in the occupied territory. This chapter has found that the destruction of Iraqi and Syrian energy resources in order to weaken the military capabilities of Islamic State is a blatant violation of *jus in bello* and the law of occupation which entails its responsibility under international law.

The second section examined the legality of the destruction of Islamic State's energy resources by the US-led coalition forces. To that end, Chapter 3 has discussed the US's war-sustaining theory as part of the US domestic law and its jurisdiction, which characterises the destruction of the natural environment during hostilities as being related to the objectives that contribute to the 'war-sustaining capability' of the enemy, and that the US cannot be considered responsible for the environmental destruction caused during the conflict. This is an approach that has been reaffirmed by US official John Kirby, who emphasised that the environmental destruction in the war with Islamic State has been exercised under governmental authority. The chapter's purpose in inspecting the US statement is to determine how, when and to what extent the destruction of energy resources that are part of the natural environment may be acceptable under *jus in bello*. The main point that emerges from this chapter is that destroying or seizing the enemy's property without imperative necessity in international and non-international armed conflicts is a direct violation of *jus in bello*. Despite the disputed nature of the general prohibition of widespread, long-term and severe damage to the natural environment and the controversies on its customary legal nature in Additional Protocol I and the ENMOD Convention, the 1998 Rome Statute considers these acts to constitute serious violations of the laws and customs applicable both in international and non-international armed conflicts, and they can, therefore, be considered as war crimes.

Concerning the international criminal responsibility of the coalition states for the destruction of natural resources during the war with Islamic State, it was argued that the only way to counteract the lack of a systematic mechanism to prevent states from causing environmental damage or from looting natural resources is for the protection of natural resources to be drawn up under another set of rules of *jus in bello* for that purpose. This may be proved by the rules surrounding the protection of 'state property' contained in Article 23(g) of the IV Hague Convention and Article 147 of the IV Geneva Convention as the basis for the protection of state property, which prohibit the 'destruction or seizure of the property of an adversary unless required by imperative necessity' as a norm of customary international law and applicable in both international and non-international armed conflicts.

Conclusion

THE USE OF military force has always been resorted to by states in order to achieve their political objectives, and civilians and civilian objects have always been the primary victims of such force. Regardless of the legal basis for the justification of using armed force, the protection of non-combatants and refraining from targeting civilian objects, including the natural environment, comes into question during armed conflicts. The evidence indicates, in general, that states do not hesitate to resort to indiscriminate, disproportionate and unnecessary armed force in order to ensure their national security and political independence. The emergence of violent groups, including terrorist organisations and ANSAs, inter alia, has made states more eager than ever to use extraterritorial defensive armed force, either with or without consent of the territorial state. In this respect, the rise of Islamic State in Iraq and Syria, with the goal of establishing an Islamic Caliphate, has been a constant global threat for almost a decade. Taking control of a large number of oilfields through the occupation of significant parts of Iraqi and Syrian territory, they carried out violent terrorist attacks at both the national and international level. Compared with legitimate states, the exploiting of energy resources by terrorist organisations and ANSAs such as Islamic State have become a particular cause for global concern.

Given the significant improvements in the current legal framework regulating the use of force in international law, there is room for hostiles to seek justification for the use of force and extraterritorial military interventions against ANSAs, despite the certainty of civilian casualties. Alongside the profound humanitarian impacts of the extraterritorial use of armed force, military intervention in the absence of a territorial state's invitation or consent questions the assumptions and justifications legitimising violations of territorial integrity, political independence and national sovereignty of a territorial state when fighting violent ANSAs. In this particular context, the legal aspects of the use of force against Islamic State, which is a new challenge for the international community, is important and worthy of note from the perspectives of both *jus ad bellum* and *jus in bello*.

The war with Islamic State engages various areas of international law. Chapter 1 analysed the rise of Islamic State in both Iraq and Syria by tracing certain interrelated aspects: the rise and strengthening of Islamic State; identification of the status of Islamic State from a legal standpoint; the link between energy resources and armed conflict; and the potential role of energy resources in facilitating Islamic State's military operations. Having identified Islamic State as a violent ANSA, it was emphasised that the mismanagement and uneven distribution of resources or energy-related incomes in states that are home to different ethnic-religious groups have created the grounds for ethnic and religiously based armed conflicts.

With regard to the correlation between energy resources and armed conflict, Chapter 1 illustrated that energy resources, including oil and natural gas, have been a major source of revenue for violent ANSAs, as it presents them with a huge number of extortion opportunities. In this sense, Iraqi and Syrian oil, as one of Islamic State's sources of revenue, has extended the conflicts in both Iraq and Syria, since the group enhanced its military capabilities by exercising different forms of control over its captured oil resources as the key to its development. Even then, however, Chapter 1 concluded that losing access to its energy resources in Iraq and Syria as a result of the US-led coalition's airstrikes could not bring an end to Islamic State because the captured energy resources were not the group's only source of revenue. Therefore, it was able to continue generating considerable sums of revenue through ways that have already been identified by the UNSC.

Chapter 2 examined the legal basis for the extraterritorial use of armed force against Islamic State in both Iraq and Syria. Given the major motivating factors for using force against Islamic State, the chapter examined the war using two different aspects of military intervention: 'military intervention in the absence of the territorial state's consent or request' and 'military intervention by request of the territorial state'. In doing so, it has been remarked that military intervention against Islamic State in the absence of a territorial state's consent or request has been justified under the 'unwilling or unable theory'. However, it was argued that although UNSC Resolution 2249 (2015) calls on states to use all necessary measures to fight Islamic State, resorting to extraterritorial armed force under the 'unwilling or unable theory' is problematic because that theory does not have a basis in international law and is not supported in the ICJ's jurisprudence. Another military intervention without a territorial state's request evaluated in this part was Turkey's cross-border operations in Syria, which it justified under the 1998 Adana Security Agreement and the 2010 Joint Cooperation Agreement. Both treaties enable Turkey to remove terrorist and violent groups, including Kurdish fighters and Islamic State, from the border region so that they can no longer threaten Turkey's national security. It was argued that clearing terrorist groups from a 35-km area of Syrian territory adjacent to Turkey means that Turkey achieved its objectives under the Adana Security Agreement.

However, the chapter also showed that Turkey's continued military presence within Syrian territory might be considered a violation of Syria's territorial integrity as it ignored the legitimacy and authority of the Syrian government. In other words, seizing control of 35 km of Syrian territory could be characterised as an act of military occupation, which is considered to be an act of aggression and violates *jus ad bellum*. In the same way, although Turkey had been permitted to use force against the PKK in Iraqi Kurdistan without the prior consent of the Iraqi government, justifying military intervention against Islamic

State in Iraq under the 1926 Frontier Treaty is problematic from a legal perspective. While the Frontier Treaty was comprised of the principle of respect for sovereignty, and the respective rights and interests of the contracting parties, any form of intervention in the other's territory would nevertheless be characterised as a violation of territorial integrity and political independence.

The second motivating factor for using force against Islamic State that was examined in Chapter 2 was the matter of military assistance at the request of the territorial state. To articulate the legality and consequences of military assistance in the war with Islamic State, the US-led coalition's military intervention in Iraq, and Russia and Iran's military assistance to the Syrian government in the war with Islamic State, were discussed in the second part of Chapter 2. Having identified the legitimacy and effectiveness of a territorial state's government as a basis for legitimising military intervention by request, it was concluded that the impacts of such an intervention must be the primary concern of the international community of states. Given the humanitarian impacts of the US, Russia and Iran's military intervention against Islamic State in Iraq and Syria, it was remarked that the operations conducted under military assistance at the request of the partially effective governments of Iraq and Syria have exceeded their primary objective of defending the requesting state's borders from external attacks, internal disturbances and isolated guerrilla or terrorist activities. Even by taking the request of the Iraqi and Syrian governments into consideration, the major question that remains is whether military assistance aims to protect the requesting state's people from terrorist actions and to minimise civilian casualties, given that the increased number of civilian casualties and the targeting of civilian objects in the wake of the extraterritorial use of force by request has led to additional challenges with regard to violations of *jus in bello*.

Chapter 3 analysed the US doctrine of war-sustaining capabilities as a justification for environmental violence against natural resources. Starting with the US's doctrine indicating that the 'destruction of energy resources controlled by Islamic State has been exercised under governmental authority', this chapter questioned the lawfulness of the argument within the context of the general principles of *jus in bello*, including necessity, distinction and proportionality. Looking at the lawfulness of the US-led coalition's airstrikes on oilfields controlled by Islamic State in Iraq and Syria, and in light of Article 56 of the 1977 Additional Protocol I to the 1949 Geneva Conventions on works and installations containing dangerous forces and based on the provisions on property, Chapter 3 has referred to the threshold of extensive environmental damage subject to Article 55(1) of Additional Protocol I 'prohibiting attacks on the natural environment'. Having differentiated between the two provisions, the chapter clarified the extent to which the Articles 56 and 55(1) could protect energy resources, mainly oil wells. The major point made in this chapter was about the disputed nature of the general prohibition of widespread, long-term and severe damage to the natural environment and the controversies surrounding its customary legal nature under Additional Protocol I regarding the protection of the natural environment in times of armed conflict. The chapter pointed out that the ambiguity of the wording allowed the US to justify its destruction of natural resources during the war with Islamic State.

However, it was emphasised that destroying or seizing the 'enemy's property' without imperative necessity in international and non-international armed conflicts is a direct violation of *jus in bello*. In addition, the Rome Statute considers these acts to constitute serious violations of the laws and customs applicable in both international and non-international armed conflicts and classes them as war crimes. In other words, regardless of the lack of clarity in Additional Protocol I regarding widespread, long-term and severe damage and the exact threshold for damage contained in Article 55(1), a state's responsibility for the destruction of energy resources as part of the natural environment is contained under other provisions which protect civilian objects and state property, and their customary legal natures are not a subject of controversy.

Regarding the matter of criminal responsibility, Chapter 3 then discussed the ICC and Rome Statute as sets of secondary norms that criminalise the destruction of energy resources that are part of the natural environment during armed conflicts. As far as the US is not a party to either the ICC or the Rome Statute, the contradictory provisions regulated under Article 8 of the Rome Statute regarding the international and non-international armed conflicts in terms of the punishment of war crimes have been criticised as the basis of a step backwards for the international criminal justice. Despite this, Chapter 3 concluded that the nature of a conflict is irrelevant when humanitarian issues come into question, and the ICC is therefore expected to take the lead in stating that non-international armed conflicts are a common problem that needs to be tackled by the international community of states in the same way as international armed conflicts.

As research in general has mostly focused on the lawfulness of the war with Islamic State from a variety of legal aspects, this book is certainly not an exhaustive account of civilian protection and victimisation during wars with ANSAs. The book has nonetheless attempted to make inroads into the most controversial aspects of contradictions in the application of *jus ad bellum* and *jus in bello*, particularly when discussing the use of extraterritorial armed force against ANSAs, and the obligation to protect civilian objects, including the natural environment, in times of war against such ANSAs. The consequence is that legal theory and state practice are still problematic as to how and under what conditions states can justify resorting to military force in foreign territory, and to what extent they can target natural resources as being part of state property. This present work is an attempt to close the gaps in *jus in bello* by contextualising the questions of civilian protection, victimisation and state responsibility by evaluating the US's war-sustaining theory as justification for the destruction of a territorial state's natural resources that are occupied by ANSAs.

Bibliography

BOOKS, CHAPTERS AND ARTICLES

'Abdullah Gül: Irak Bölünürse, Hakkımız Doğar', *Yeni Akit* (10 June 2014).

Abi-Habib, Maria, 'For ISIS, Losing Territory Means Losing Revenue', *The Wall Street Journal* (18 October 2017).

Addison, Tony and Brück, Tilman, 'Economic Agendas in Civil Wars: What We Know, What We Need to Know' in Tony Addison and Tilman Brück (eds), *Making Peace Work: The Challenges of Social and Economic Reconstruction* (London, Palgrave Macmillan, 2009) 31–50.

Adede, Andronico O, 'Protection of the Environment in Times of Armed Conflict: Reflections on the Existing and Future Treaty Law' (1994) 1 *Annual Survey of International & Comparative Law* 161.

Adnan, Sinan and Reese, Aaron, *Beyond the Islamic State: Iraq's Sunni Insurgency* (Washington, DC, Institute for the Study of War, 2014).

Aini, Desy Churul and Banjarani, Desia Rakhma, 'Environmental Protection in Armed Conflict According to International Humanitarian Law' (2018) 3 *Tadulako Law Review* 12.

'Airstrikes Destroy ISIL Infrastructure in Syria, Iraq', *US Department of State* (11 August 2015).

'Airstrikes Destroy ISIL Oil Infrastructure, Tactical Vehicles', *US Department of Defence* (8 June 2015).

Ajjoub, Orwa and Williams, Matt HCK, 'Crushing Rojava: Turkey's War in Syria', *The Conflict Archives* (23 October 2019).

Akande, Dapo and Liefländer, Thomas, 'Clarifying Necessity, Imminence, and Proportionality in the Law of Self-Defense' (2013) 107 *American Journal of International Law* 563.

Akbar, Jay, 'Tentacles of Terror: Chilling Map Shows the 31,000 Mercenary 'Gun for Hire' Jihadis from 86 Countries Who Left Their Homes to Join ISIS … and a Third May Return to Carry Out Paris-Style Attacks', *Mail Online* (16 December 2015).

Al-Damkhi, Ali Mohamed, 'Kuwait's Oil Well Fires, 1991: Environmental Crime and War' (2007) 64 *International Journal of Environmental Studies* 31.

Alexandrov, Stanimir A, *Self-Defense against the Use of Force in International Law* (The Hague, Kluwer Law International, 1996).

Ali, Shaheen Sardar and Rehman, Javaid, 'The Concept of Jihad in Islamic International Law' (2005) 10 *Journal of Conflict & Security Law* 321.

Alkaff, Syed Huzaifah BO, 'Evolving Jihadist Landscape in the Middle East' (2019) 11 *Counter Terrorist Trends and Analyses* 1.

Almukhtar, Sarah et al, 'Wave of Terror Attacks in Turkey Continue at a Steady Pace', *New York Times* (5 January 2017).

Ameringer, Charles D, 'Philippe Bunau-Varilla: New Light on the Panama Canal Treaty' (1966) 46 *The Hispanic American Historical Review* 28.

'Annual Report on Civilian Casualties in Connection with United States Military Operations', *US Department of State* (2018).

Aoun, Marie C, 'Oil and Gas Resources of the Middle East and North Africa: A Curse or a Blessing?' in Jean-Marie Chevalier and Patrice Geoffron (eds), *The New Energy Crisis* (London, Palgrave Macmillan, 2013) 133–60.

Arend, Anthony Clark, 'International Law and the Preemptive Use of Military Force' (2003) 26 *The Washington Quarterly* 89.

Arevalo, Luis Barrionuevo, 'The Work of the International Law Commission in the Field of International Environmental Law' (2005) 32 *Boston College Environmental Affairs Law Review* 493.

Arimatsu, Louise and Schmitt, Michael N, 'Attacking "Islamic State" and the Khorasan Group: Surveying the International Law Landscape' (2014) 53 *Columbia Journal of Transnational Law Bulletin* 1.

Arimatsu, Louise and Schmitt, Michael, 'The Legal Basis for the War against ISIS Remains Contentious', *The Guardian* (6 October 2014).

Arrington Sliney, Samantha, 'Right to Act: United States Legal Basis Under the Law of Armed Conflict to Pursue the Islamic State in Syria' (2015) 6 *University of Miami National Security & Armed Conflict Law Review* 1.

'Background Briefing by Senior Administration Officials on Iraq', *The White House Office of the Press Secretary* (8 August 2014).

Baev, Pavel K and Kirişci, Kemal, 'An Ambiguous Partnership: The Serpentine Trajectory of Turkish-Russian Relations in the Era of Erdoğan and Putin' (2017) 13 *Brookings Policy Paper* 1.

Bahgat, Gawdat, *Energy Security: An Interdisciplinary Approach* (West Sussex, Wiley Publication, 2011).

Bahgat, Gawdat, 'The United States and the Middle East: Interdependence Not Independence' (2006) 30 *OPEC Review* 187.

Baker, Joseph R and Crocker, Henry G, *The Laws of Land Warfare: Concerning the Rights and Duties of Belligerents as Existing on August 1, 1914. US* (Washington, DC, Government Printing Office, 1919).

Baker, Peter and Schmitt, Eric, 'Many Missteps in Assessment of ISIS Threat', *New York Times* (29 September 2014).

Banai, Hussein, 'International and Regional Responses: An Appraisal' in Feisal al-Istrabadi and Sumit Ganguly (eds), *The Future of ISIS: Regional and International Implications* (Washington, DC, Brookings Institution Press, 2018) 151–72.

Bannelier-Christakis, Karine, 'Military Interventions against ISIL in Iraq, Syria and Libya, and the Legal Basis of Consent' (2016) 29 *Leiden Journal of International Law* 743.

Bannelier-Christakis, Karine, 'The Joint Committee's Drones Report: Far-Reaching Conclusions on Self-Defence Based on a Dubious Reading of Resolution 2249' (2016) 3 *Journal on the Use of Force and International Law* 217.

Bannelier, Karine and Christakis, Theodore, 'Under the UN Security Council's Watchful Eyes: Military Intervention by Invitation in the Malian Conflict' (2013) 26 *Leiden Journal of International Law* 855.

Basit, Abdul, 'Foreign Fighters in Iraq and Syria – Why So Many?' (2014) 6 *Counter Terrorist Trends and Analyses* 4.

Bassil, Youssef, 'Iraq War: Operations, Causes and Consequences' (2012) 4 *Journal of Humanities and Social Science* 29.

Bassiouni, M Cherif, 'The History of the Draft Code of Crimes against the Peace and Security of Mankind' (1993) 27 *Israel Law Review* 247.

Beaumont, Peter, 'Turkish MPs Pass Bill to Send Troops to Support Libyan Government', *The Guardian* (2 January 2020).

Beckerle, Kristine, 'Where Does the UN Security Council Stand on Yemen?', *Amnesty International* (8 November 2018).

Bell, Christine, 'Peace Settlements and International Law: From Lex Pacificatoria to Jus Post Bellum' in Nigel D White and Christian Henderson (eds), *Research Handbook on International Conflict and Security Law: Jus ad Bellum, Jus in Bello and Jus Post Bellum* (Cheltenham, Edward Elgar, 2013) 499–546.

Bellal, Annyssa, Giacca, Gilles and Casey-Maslen, Stuart, 'International Law and Armed Non-State Actors in Afghanistan' (2011) 93 *International Review of the Red Cross* 47.

Benvenisti, Eyal, *The International Law of Occupation* (Oxford, Oxford University Press, 2012).

Bethlehem, Daniel, 'Self-Defense against an Imminent or Actual Armed Attack by Nonstate Actors' (2012) 106 *American Journal of International Law* 770.

Bindner, Laurence and Poirot, Gabriel, *ISIS Financing in 2015* (Paris, CAT, 2016).

Black, Ian, 'ISIS Air Strikes: Obama's Plan Condemned by Syria, Russia and Iran', *The Guardian* (12 September 2014).
Black, Jeremy, *War and New Disorder in the 21st Century* (London, Continuum, 2004).
Blannin, Patrick, 'Islamic State's Financing: Sources, Methods and Utilisation' (2017) 9 *Counter Terrorist Trends and Analyses* 13.
Bodner, Matthew, 'Russia Begins Airstrikes in Syria', *The Moscow Times* (30 September 2015).
Bond, James E et al, 'Determining Customary International Law Relative to the Conduct of Hostilities in Non-International Armed Conflicts' (1987) 2 *American University Journal of International Law and Policy* 415.
Boothby, Bill, 'The Law of Weaponry – Is It Adequate?' in Michael N Schmitt and Jelena Pejic (eds), *International Law and Armed Conflict: Exploring the Faultlines* (Leiden, Martinus Nijhoff, 2007) 297–316.
Boothby, William H, *The Law of Targeting* (Oxford, Oxford University Press, 2012).
Borger, Julian, 'Russia Committed War Crimes in Syria, Finds UN Report', *The Guardian* (2 March 2020).
Bothe, Michael et al, 'International Law Protecting the Environment During Armed Conflict: Gaps and Opportunities' (2010) 92 *International Review of the Red Cross* 569.
Bowett, Derek W, *Self-Defense in International Law* (Manchester, Manchester University Press, 1958).
Brandis QC, George H, 'The Right of Self-Defence against Imminent Armed Attack in International Law', *EJIL: Talk!* (25 May 2017).
Brands, Hal and Feaver, Peter, 'Was the Rise of ISIS Inevitable?' (2017) 59 *Survival: Global Politics and Strategy* 7.
Brodie, Bernard, *War and Politics* (London, Cassel Ltd, 1973).
Bromley, Simon, 'The United States and the Control of World Oil' (2005) 40 *Government and Opposition* 225.
Brooke-Holland, Louisa, *Unmanned Aerial Vehicles (Drones): An Introduction* (London, House of Commons Library, 2012).
Brooks, Rosa Ehrenreich, 'Failed States, or the State as Failure?' (2005) 72 *The University of Chicago Law Review* 1159.
Brown, Graham, Langer, Arnim and Stewart, Frances, 'A Typology of Post-Conflict Environments' (2011) 1 *Centre for Research on Peace and Development Working Paper* 1.
Brownlie, Ian, *International Law and the Use of Force by States* (Oxford, Oxford University Press, 1963).
Bruch, Carl et al, 'Facilitating Peace or Fuelling Conflict? Lessons in Post-Conflict Governance and Natural Resource Management' in Carl Bruch, Carroll Muffett, Sandra S Nichols (eds), *Governance, Natural Resources and Post-Conflict Peacebuilding* (London, Routledge, 2016) 960–95.
Butchard, Patrick M, 'Digest of State Practice: 1 July – 31 December 2018' (2019) 6 *Journal on the Use of Force and International Law* 131.
Byman, Daniel, 'Six Bad Options for Syria' (2016) 38 *The Washington Quarterly* 171.
Byrne, Max, 'Consent and the Use of Force: An Examination of 'Intervention by Invitation' As a Basis for US Drone Strikes in Pakistan, Somalia and Yemen' (2016) 3 *Journal on the Use of Force and International Law* 97.
Byron, Christine, *War Crimes and Crimes against Humanity in the Rome Statute of the International Criminal Court* (Manchester, Manchester University Press, 2009).
Cambou, Dorothée and Smis, Stefaan, 'Permanent Sovereignty Over Natural Resources from a Human Rights Perspective: Natural Resources Exploitation and Indigenous Peoples' Rights in the Arctic' (2013) 22 *Michigan State International Law Review* 347.
Carlisle, Madeleine, 'Trump Keeps Talking About Syria's Oil Fields: Here's What's Going on with Them', *Time* (26 October 2016).
Carment, David, 'Assessing State Failure: Implications for Theory and Policy' (2003) 24 *Third World Quarterly* 407.
Cassese, Antonio, *International Law* (Oxford, Oxford University Press, 2005).

Cassese, Antonio, *Self-Determination of Peoples: A Legal Reappraisal* (Cambridge, Cambridge University Press, 1994).
Charountaki, Marianna, 'Turkish Foreign Policy and the Kurdistan Regional Government' (2012) 17 *Perceptions* 185.
Chaudhry, Kiren A, *The Price of Wealth: Economies and Institutions in the Middle East* (New York, Cornell University Press, 1997).
Chinkin, Christian, 'The Security Council and Statehood' in Christine Chinkin and Freya Baetens (eds), *Sovereignty, Statehood and State Responsibility: Essays in Honour of James Crawford* (Cambridge, Cambridge University Press, 2015) 155–71.
Christakis, Theodore, 'Challenging the 'Unwilling or Unable' Test' (2017) 77 *Heidelberg Journal of International Law* 19.
Christakis, Theodore, 'Symposium on the Fight against ISIL and International Law – Editor's Introduction' (2016) 29 *Leiden Journal of International Law* 737.
Chulov, Martin, 'Syria: Videos of Turkey-Backed Militias Show Potential War Crimes', *The Guardian* (26 October 2019).
'Civilian Deaths in the Anti-ISIS Bombing Campaigns 2014–2015', *Ceasefire Centre for Civilian Rights and Minority Rights Group International* (November 2015).
Claggett, Brice M and Johnson Jr, O Thomas, 'May Israel as a Belligerent Occupant Lawfully Exploit Previously Unexploited Oil Resources of the Gulf of Suez' (1978) 72 *American Journal of International Law* 558.
Cockburn, Patrick, 'ISIS is Proof of the Failed War on Terror', *Quartz* (24 February 2015).
Colgan, Jeff D, 'Fuelling the Fire: Pathways from Oil to War' (2013) 38 *International Security* 147.
Colgan, Jeff D, 'Oil, Domestic Conflict, and Opportunities for Democratization' (2005) 52 *Journal of Peace Research* 3.
Collier, Paul, 'Economic Causes of Civil Conflict and Their Implications for Policy', *World Bank* (April 2006).
Collier, Paul, 'Doing Well Out of War: An Economic Perspective' in David M Malone and Mats Berdal (eds), *Greed & Grievance: Economic Agendas in Civil Wars* (Boulder, Lynne Rienner Publishers, 2000) 91–111.
Collier, Paul and Hoeffler, Anke, *The Political Economy of Secession* (Washington, DC, Development Research Group, 2002).
Colonomos, Ariel, 'War in the Face of Doubt: Early Modern Classics and the Preventive Use of Force' in Stefano Recchia and Jennifer M Welsh (eds), *Just and Unjust Military Intervention: European Thinkers from Vitoria to Mill* (Cambridge, Cambridge University Press, 2013) 48–69.
Colville, Rupert, 'Press Briefing Note on Syria', OHCHR (11 October 2019).
'Combined Joint Task Force Continues Airstrikes against ISIL', *US Department of Defence* (5 January 2015).
Conde, Gilberto, 'Water and Counter-Hegemony: Kurdish Struggle in the Tigris and Euphrates in Turkey' (2016) 9 *Revista de Paz y Conflictos* 43.
Connable, Ben, Lander, Natasha and Jackson, Kimberly, *Beating the Islamic State: Selecting the New Strategy for Iraq and Syria* (California, RAND Publication, 2017).
Cordesman, Anthony H and Wagner, Abraham R, *The Lessons of Modern War – Vol 2: The Iran-Iraq War* (Boulder, Westview Press, 1990).
Corten, Oliver, 'The "Unwilling or Unable" Test: Has It Been, and Could It Be, Accepted?' (2016) 29 *Leiden Journal of International Law* 777.
Coşar, Nevin and Demirci, Sevtap, 'The Mosul Question and the Turkish Republic: Before and after the Frontier Treaty, 1926' (2006) 42 *Middle Eastern Studies* 123.
Cottee, Simon, 'What ISIS Really Wants Revisited: Religion Matters in Jihadist Violence, But How?' (2017) 40 *Studies in Conflict & Terrorism* 439.
'Country Brief: Syria', *Conflict and Environment Observatory* (26 March 2018).
Crawford, James R, *The Creation of States in International Law* (Oxford, Oxford University Press, 2006).

Cronin Audrey K, 'ISIS Is Not a Terrorist Group: Why Counterterrorism Won't Stop the Latest Jihadist Threat' (2015) 94 *Foreign Affairs* 87.

Crook, John R, 'United States Responds to ICRC Study on Customary International Law' (2007) 101 *American Journal of International Law* 639.

Cuddy, Brian, 'Was It Legal for the US to Bomb Cambodia?', *New York Times* (12 December 2017).

Cuddy, Brian, *Wider War: American Force in Vietnam, International Law, and the Transformation of Armed Conflict, 1961–1977* (PhD Dissertation, University of Cornell, 2016).

Czuperski, Mark et al, *Distract, Deceive, Destroy: Putin at War in Syria* (Washington, DC, Atlantic Council, 2016).

D'Aspremont, Jean, 'The Rise and Fall of Democracy Governance in International Law: A Reply to Susan Marks' (2011) 22 *European Journal of International Law* 549.

D'Aspremont, Jean, 'Legitimacy of Governments in the Age of Democracy' (2006) 38 *New York University Journal of International Law and Politics* 877.

Dam-de Jong, Daniella, 'Standard-Setting Practices for the Management of Natural Resources in Conflict-Torn States: Constitutive Elements of Jus Post Bellum' in Carsten Stahn, Jens Iverson and Jennifer S Easterday (eds), *Environmental Protection and Transitions from Conflict to Peace: Clarifying Norms, Principles, and Practices* (Oxford, Oxford University Press, 2017) 169–91.

Dam-de Jong, Daniella, *International Law and Governance of Natural Resources in Conflict and Post-Conflict Situations* (Cambridge, Cambridge University Press, 2015).

Dapkus, Simonas, 'Turkey's Security Dilemma on the Border with Syria: Situation Assessment and Perspectives of the Intervention' (2016) 33 *Lithuanian Foreign Policy Review* 48.

Darmstadter, Joel and Lansberg, Hans H, 'The Economic Background' in Raymond Vernon (ed), *The Oil Crisis: In Perspective* (Massachusetts, MIT Press, 1975) 15–37.

Das, Onita, *Environmental Protection, Security and Armed Conflict: A Sustainable Development Perspective* (Cheltenham, Edward Elgar Publishing, 2013).

David, Charles-Philippe and Gagné, Jean-François, 'Natural Resources: A Source of Conflict?' (2007) 62 *International Journal* 5.

'Death in the City: High Levels of Civilian Harm in Modern Urban Warfare Resulting from Significant Explosive Weapons Use', *Airwars* (May 2018).

De Hoogh, Andre, 'Jus Cogens and the Use of Armed Force' in Marc Weller (ed), *The Oxford Handbook of the Use of Force in International Law* (Oxford, Oxford University Press, 2015) 1161–86.

De Souza, IM Lobo, 'Revisiting the Right of Self-Defence against Non-State Armed Entities' (2016) 53 *Canadian Yearbook of International Law* 202.

De Wet, Erika, 'From Free Town to Cairo via Kiev: The Unpredictable Road of Democratic Legitimacy in Governmental Recognition' (2014) 108 *AJIL Unbound* 201.

Dederer, Hans-Georg, 'Enemy Property' in Frauke Lachenmann and Rüdiger Wolfrum (eds), *The Law of Armed Conflict and the Use of Force: The Max Planck Encyclopedia of Public International Law* (Oxford, Oxford University Press, 2016) 359–71.

Deeks, Ashley, 'US Airstrikes against ISIS in Syria? Possible International Legal Theories', *Lawfare Blog* (23 August 2014).

Deeks, Ashley S, 'Consent to the Use of Force and International Law Supremacy' (2013) 54 *Harvard International Law Journal* 1.

Deeks, Ashley S, 'Unwilling or Unable: Toward a Normative Framework for Extraterritorial Self-Defense' (2012) 52 *Virginia Journal of International Law* 483.

Denny, Elaine K and Walter, Barbara F, 'Ethnicity and Civil War' (2014) 51 *Journal of Peace Research* 199.

'Department of Defence Press Briefing by Rear Admiral Kirby in the Pentagon Briefing Room', *US Department of Defence* (25 September 2014).

Di John, Jonathan, 'Oil Abundance and Violent Political Conflict: A Critical Assessment' (2007) 43 *Journal of Development Studies* 961.

Dill, Janina, *Applying the Principle of Proportionality in Combat Operations* (Oxford, Oxford Institute for Ethics, Law and Armed Conflict, 2010).
Dinstein, Yoram, *The Conduct of Hostilities under the Law of International Armed Conflict* (Cambridge, Cambridge University Press, 2016).
Dinstein, Yoram, *War, Aggression and Self-Defence* (Cambridge, Cambridge University Press, 2012).
Dinstein, Yoram, *The International Law of Belligerent Occupation* (Cambridge, Cambridge University Press, 2009).
Dinstein, Yoram, 'Legitimate Military Objectives under the Current Jus in Bello' (2002) 78 *International Law Studies* 139.
Dinstein, Yoram, 'Protection of Environment in International Armed Conflicts' (2001) 5 *Max Planck Yearbook of United Nations Law* 523.
Dörmann, Knut, 'Preparatory Commission for the International Criminal Court: The Elements of War Crimes – Part II: Other Serious Violations of the Laws and Customs Applicable in International and Non-International Armed Conflicts' (2001) 83 *International Review of the Red Cross* 461.
Dörr, Oliver and Schmalenbach, Kirsten (eds), *Vienna Convention on the Law of Treaties: A Commentary* (Heidelberg, Springer, 2012).
Doswald-Beck, Louise, 'The San Remo Manual on International Law Applicable to Armed Conflicts at Sea' (1995) 89 *American Journal of International Law* 192.
Doswald-Beck, Louise (ed), *San Remo Manual on International Law Applicable to Armed Conflicts at Sea* (Cambridge, Cambridge University Press, 1995).
Doswald-Beck, Louise, 'The Legal Validity of Military Intervention by Invitation of the Government' (1985) 56 *British Yearbook of International Law* 189.
Droge, Cordula and Tougas, Marie-Louise, 'The Protection of the Natural Environment in Armed Conflict – Existing Rules and Need for Further Legal Protection' (2013) 82 *Nordic Journal of International Law* 21.
Dupuy, Pierre-Marie and Viñuales, Jorge E, *International Environmental Law* (Cambridge, Cambridge University Press, 2018).
Durac, Vincent, 'The Role of Non-State Actors in Arab Countries after the Arab Uprisings' (2015) *IEMed Mediterranean Yearbook* 37.
Dworkin, Anthony, 'Beyond Good and Evil: Why Europe Should Bring ISIS Foreign Fighters Home', *European Council on Foreign Relations* (25 October 2019).
Dyer, Charles and Crismier, Chuck, *The ISIS Crisis: What You Really Need to Know* (Chicago: Moody Publishers, 2015).
Eaton, Tim et al (eds), *Conflict Economies in the Middle East and North Africa. Chatham House Report* (London, Chatham House, 2019).
Eck, Kristine (2005), 'A Beginner's Guide to Conflict Data: Finding and Using the Right Dataset', *UCDP Paper No 1.*
Edward Collins and Martin A Rogoff, 'The Caroline Incident of 1837, the McLeod Affair of 1840–1841, and the Development of International Law' (1990) 20 *American Review of Canadian Studies* 81.
'Eight Years Since the Start of the Popular Uprising in Syria, Terrible Violations Continue: From Minority Rule, Repression and Dictatorship Towards Pluralism, Human Rights and Democracy', *The Syrian Network for Human Rights* (11 March 2019).
El-Katiri, Laura, 'Why Middle East Conflict Is a Bigger Threat to UK Energy Security Than Putin', *The Guardian* (4 September 2014).
Eleftheriadou, Marina, 'Elements of 'Armed Non-State Actors' Power: The Case of Al-Qaeda in Yemen' (2014) 25 *Small Wars & Insurgencies* 404.
Elias, Olufemi, 'The Nature of the Subjective Element in Customary International Law' (1995) 44 *International and Comparative Law Quarterly* 501.
Emery, James, 'The Convoluted Coalition against ISIS', *Small Wars Journal* (19 January 2016).

Engeland, Anicée Van, 'Statehood, Proto States and International Law: New Challenges, Looking at the Case of ISIS' in James Crawford, Abdul Koroma, Said Mahmoudi and Alain Pellet (eds), *The International Legal Order: Current Needs and Possible Responses* (Leiden, Brill Publications, 2017) 75–86.

Evans, Alex (2011), 'Resource Scarcity, Fair Shares and Development', *A WWF/Oxfam Discussion Paper*.

Fairman, Charles, 'The Interpretation of Treaties' (1934) 20 *Transactions of the Grotius Society* 123.

Fettweis, Christopher J, 'No Blood for Oil: Why Resource Wars Are Obsolete' in Gal Luft and Anne Korin (eds), *Energy Security Challenges for the 21st Century* (California, Greenwood Press, 2009) 66–77.

'Fire and Oil: The Collateral Environmental Damage from Airstrikes on ISIS Oil Facilities', *Conflict and Environment Observatory* (13 January 2016).

Flibbert, Andrew, 'The Consequences of Forced State Failure in Iraq' (2013) 128 *Political Science Quarterly* 67.

Fortin Katharine, *The Accountability of Armed Groups under Human Rights Law* (Oxford, Oxford University Press, 2017).

Fox, Gregory H, 'Intervention by Invitation' in Marc Weller (ed), *Oxford Handbook of the Use of Force in International Law* (Oxford, Oxford University Press, 2015) 816–40.

Franck, Thomas M, 'On Proportionality of Countermeasures in International Law' (2008) 102 *American Journal of International Law* 715.

Freeland, Steven R, *Addressing the Intentional Destruction of the Environment During Warfare Under the Rome Statute of the International Criminal Court* (Cambridge, Intersentia Publishers, 2015).

Frerks, Georg, Dietz, Ton and Van Der Zaag, Pieter, 'Conflict and Cooperation on Natural Resources: Justifying the CoCooN Programme' in Maarten Bavinck, Lorenzo Pellegrini and Erik Mostert (eds), *Conflicts Over Natural Resources in the Global South – Conceptual Approaches* (London, CRC Press, 2014) 13–34.

Gardiner, Richard K, *Treaty Interpretation* (Oxford, Oxford University Press, 2015).

Gasser, Hans-Peter, 'For Better Protection of the Natural Environment in Armed Conflict: A Proposal for Action' (1995) 89 *American Journal of International Law* 637.

Gerges, Fawaz A, *ISIS: A History* (Princeton, Princeton University Press, 2016).

Gess, Karol N, 'Permanent Sovereignty over Natural Resources: An Analytical Review of the United Nations Declaration and Its Genesis' (1964) 13 *International and Comparative Law Quarterly* 398.

Giladi, Rotem, 'The Jus Ad Bellum/Jus in Bello Distinction and the Law of Occupation' (2018) 41 *Israel Law Review* 246.

Gill, Terry D, 'Classifying the Conflict in Syria' (2016) 92 *International Law Studies* 355.

Gill, Terry D et al (eds), 'Final Report ILA Study Group on the Conduct of Hostilities' (2016) 19 *Yearbook of International Humanitarian Law* 287.

Gilman, Ryan, 'Expanding Environmental Justice after War: The Need for Universal Jurisdiction over Environmental War Crimes' (2011) 22 *Colorado Journal of International Environmental Law and Policy* 447.

Gisel, Laurent, 'Relevant Incidental Harm for the Proportionality Principle' (2015) *Proceedings of the 16th Bruges Colloquium: Urban Warfare* 118.

Gleditsch, Nils P et al, 'Armed Conflict 1946–2001: A New Dataset' (2002) 39 *Journal of Peace Research* 315.

Goodman, Ryan, 'The Obama Administration and Targeting "War-Sustaining" Objects in Non-International Armed Conflict' (2016) 110 *American Journal of International Law* 663.

Goodrich, Leland M, 'The Maintenance of International Peace and Security' (1965) 19 *International Organization* 429.

Grady, Broderick C, 'Article 5 of the North Atlantic Treaty: Past, Present, and Uncertain Future' (2002) 31 *Georgia Journal of International and Comparative Law* 167.

Graefrath, Bernhard, 'Complicity in the Law of International Responsibility' (1996) 29 *Belgian Review of International Law* 371.
Gray, Christine D., *International Law and the Use of Force* (Oxford, Oxford University Press, 2008).
Green, James A, 'The Article 51 Reporting Requirement for Self-Defense Actions' (2015) 55 *Virginia Journal of International Law* 563.
Green, James A, *The International Court of Justice and Self-Defence in International Law* (Oxford, Hart Publishing, 2009).
Green, James A, 'Docking the Caroline: Understanding the Relevance of the Formula in Contemporary Customary International Law Concerning Self-Defence' (2006) 14 *Cardozo Journal of International and Comparative Law* 429.
Green, James A, 'The Oil Platforms Case: An Error in Judgment?' (2004) 9 *Journal of Conflict and Security Law* 357.
Green, James A. and Waters, Christopher PM, 'Military Targeting in the Context of Self-Defence Actions' (2015) 84 *Nordic Journal of International Law* 3.
Greenwood, Christopher J, 'Current Issues in the Law of Armed Conflict: Weapons, Targets and International Criminal Liability' (1997) 1 *Singapore Journal of International & Comparative Law* 441.
Gumrukcu, Tuvan, 'Turkey says U.S. Support for Syrian Kurdish YPG a Big Mistake', *Reuters* (18 November 2018).
Gurmendi, Alonso, 'State Practice Regarding Self-Defence against Non-State Actors: An Incomplete Picture', *Opinio Juris* (17 October 2018).
Guzman, Andrew T, 'Saving Customary International Law' (2005) 27 *Michigan Journal of International Law* 115.
Haddad, Bassam and Wind, Ella, 'The Fragmented State of the Syrian Opposition' in Mehran Kamrava, *Beyond the Arab Spring: The Evolving Ruling Bargain in the Middle East* (Oxford, Oxford University Press, 2014) 397–436.
Haddad, Fanar, *Sectarianism in Iraq: Antagonistic Vision of Unity* (Oxford, Oxford University Press, 2016).
Hafner, M Gerhard, 'Present Problems of the Use of Force in International Law: A Report of Sub-Group C on Military Assistance on Request' (2011) 49 *Archiv des Völkerrechts* 469.
Hakimi, Monica, 'Defensive Force against Non-State Actors: The State of Play' (2015) 91 *International Law Studies* 1.
Hamasaeed, Sarhang and Garrett, Nada, 'Iraq Timeline: Since the 2003 War', *United States Institute of Peace* (9 July 2019).
Handl, Günther (2012), 'Declaration of the United Nations Conference on the Human Environment (Stockholm Declaration), 1972 and the Rio Declaration on Environment and Development, 1992' (2012) *UN Audiovisual Library of International Law* 1.
Hansen-Lewis, Jamie and Shapiro, Jacob N, 'Understanding the Daesh Economy' (2015) 9 *Perspectives on Terrorism* 142.
Harary, David C, 'Environmental Decisions in the Context of War: Bombing ISIL's Oil', *Centre for Development and Strategy* 2016 (2).
Hassan, Daud, 'Rise of the Territorial State and the Treaty of Westphalia' (2006) 9 *Yearbook of New Zealand Jurisprudence* 62.
Hathaway, Oona A, 'Between Power and Principle: A Political Theory of International Law' (2005) 72 *The University of Chicago Law Review* 469.
Hawramy, Fazel, 'ISIS Militants Kidnap Turkish Diplomats After Seizing Consulate in Mosul', *The Guardian* (11 June 2014).
Hayashi, Nobuo, 'Requirements of Military Necessity in International Humanitarian Law and International Criminal Law' (2010) 28 *Boston University International Law Journal* 39.
Heißner, Stefan et al, *Caliphate in Decline: An Estimate of Islamic State's Financial Fortunes* (London: The International Centre for the Study of Radicalisation and Political Violence, 2017).

Heller, Kevin Jon, 'Do Attacks on ISIS in Syria Justify the "Unwilling or Unable" Test?', *Opinio Juris* (13 December 2014).

Heller, Thomas C and Sofaer, Abraham D, 'Sovereignty: The Practitioner's Prospective' in Stephen D Krasner (ed), *Problematic Sovereignty: Contested Rules and Political Possibilities* (New York, Colombia University Press, 2001) 24–52.

Henckaerts, Jean-Marie, 'Study on Customary International Humanitarian Law: A Contribution to the Understanding and Respect for the Rule of Law in Armed Conflict' (2005) 87 *International Review of the Red Cross* 175.

Henckaerts, Jean-Marie and Doswald-Beck, Louise, *Customary International Humanitarian Law – Volume I: Rules* (Cambridge, Cambridge University Press, 2005).

Henckaerts, Jean-Marie and Doswald-Beck, Louise, *Customary International Humanitarian Law – Volume II: Practice* (Cambridge, Cambridge University Press, 2005).

Hossain, Kamrul, 'The Concept of Jus Cogens and the Obligation under the U.N. Charter' (2005) 3 *Santa Clara Journal of International Law* 72.

Hubbard, Ben, Savage, Charlie, Schmitt, Eric and Kingsley, Patrick, 'Abandoned by US in Syria, Kurds Find New Ally in American Foe', *New York Times* (13 October 2019).

Hulme, Karen, 'Natural Environment' in Elizabeth Wilmshurst and Susan Breau (eds), *Perspectives on the ICRC Study on Customary International Humanitarian Law* (Cambridge, Cambridge University Press, 2007) 204–37.

Hulme, Karen, *War Torn Environment: Interpreting the Legal Threshold* (Leiden, Martinus Nijhoff, 2004).

Humphreys, Macartan, 'Natural Resources, Conflict, and Conflict Resolution: Uncovering the Mechanisms' (2005) 49 *Journal of Conflict Resolution* 508.

Huston, Meredith DuBarry, 'Wartime Environmental Damages: Financing the Cleanup' (2002) 3 *University of Pennsylvania Journal of International Law* 899.

ICC/OTP, Policy Paper on Case Selection and Priotisation (15 September 2016).

ICRC, *The Law of Armed Conflict: Conduct of Operations – Part A* (Geneva, ICRC Press, 2002).

International Crisis Group, 'The PKK's Fateful Choice in Northern Syria' (2017) 176 *Middle East Report* 1.

International Crisis Group, 'Iraq's Jihadi Jack in the Box' (2014) 38 *Middle East Briefing* 1.

International Law and Policy Institute, *Protection of the Natural Environment in Armed Conflict: An Empirical Study* (Oslo, ILPI, 2014).

International Law Association, Final Report on Aggression and the Use of Force (Sydney Conference, 2018).

'Iran Says to Maintain Military Presence in Syria Despite US Pressure', *Routers* (28 August 2018).

'Iraq: Forced Marriage, Conversion for Yezidis Victims, Witnesses Describe Islamic State's Brutality to Captives', *Human Rights Watch* (11 October 2014).

'IRGC Official Hits Back at US's Pompeo over Anti-Iran Remarks', *Tasnim News Agency* (25 May 2018).

Issawi, Charles, 'Oil and Middle East Politics' (1973) 31 *Proceedings of the Academy of Political Science* 111.

Itani, Faysal and Stein, Aaron, 'Turkey's Syria Predicament', Atlantic Council Issue Brief (3 May 2016).

Iyi, John Mark, *Humanitarian Intervention and the AU-ECOWAS Intervention Treaties Under International Law: Towards a Theory of Regional Responsibility to Protect* (Heidelberg, Springer, 2016).

Jager, Jeff, 'Turkey's Operation Euphrates Shield: An Exemplar of Joint Combined Arms Maneuver', *Small Wars Journal* (17 October 2016).

Janse, Daniel, 'International Terrorism and Self-Defence' (2006) 36 *Israel Yearbook on Human Rights* 149.

Jayaraman, Shiva, 'International Terrorism and Statelessness: Revoking the Citizenship of ISIL Foreign Fighters' (2016) 17 *Chicago Journal of International Law* 178.

Jennings, Robert, 'The Caroline and McLeod Cases' (1983) 32 *American Journal of International Law* 82.
Jennings, Robert and Watts, Arthur (eds), *Oppenheim's International Law – Volume 1: Peace* (London, Longman, 1996).
Jones, Seth G, *Waging Insurgent Warfare: Lessons from the Vietcong to the Islamic State* (Oxford, Oxford University Press, 2017).
Jones, Toby Craig, 'America, Oil, and War in the Middle East' (2012) 99 *Journal of American History* 208.
Joyner, Christopher C and Kirkhope, James T, 'The Persian Gulf War Oil Spill: Reassessing the Law of Environmental Protection and the Law of Armed Conflict' (1992) 24 *Case Western Reserve Journal of International Law* 29.
Justitia et Pace Institut de Droit International, 'The Principle of Non-Intervention in Civil Wars, Session of Wiesbaden' (14 August 1975).
Kahgan, Carin, 'Jus Cogens and the Inherent Right to Self-Defence' (1997) 3 *ILSA Journal of International & Comparative Law* 767.
Kajtar, Gabor, 'The Use of Force against ISIL in Iraq and Syria – A Legal Battlefield' (2017) 34 *Wisconsin International Law Journal* 535.
Kaldor, Mary, Karl, T Lynn and Said, Yahia (eds), *Oil Wars* (London, Pluto Press, 2007).
Kammerhofer, Jörg, 'Uncertainty in the Formal Sources of International Law: Customary International Law and Some of Its Problems' (2004) 15 *European Journal of International Law* 523.
Kaye, Josie Lianna, *Renewable Resources and Conflict* (New York, United Nations Interagency Framework Team for Preventive Action, 2012).
Keen, David, *Syria: Playing into their Hands* (London, Safeworld, 2017).
Kelly, Patrick, 'Preemptive Self-Defense, Customary International Law, and the Congolese Wars', *E-International Relations* (3 September 2016).
'Keynote Address by General John Allen, Special Presidential Envoy for the Global Coalition to Counter-ISIL', *Brooking Institution* (3 June 2015).
Khadduri, Majid, *War and Peace in the Law of Islam* (New Jersey, Lawbook Exchange Publishers, 2010).
Kirk, Ashly, 'Iraq and Syria: How Many Foreign Fighters Are Fighting for ISIL?', *The Telegraph* (24 Mart 2016).
Klare, Michael, *Rising Powers, Shrinking Planet: The New Geopolitics of Energy* (Oxford, Oneworld Publications, 2008).
Koçak, Nalan, 'Russia Open to Turkish Ops in Syria under Adana Agreement', *Daily News* (18 February 2019).
Koivurova, Timo, 'Due Diligence' (2013) *Max Planck Encyclopaedia of Public International Law* 1.
Kolb, Robert and Hyde, Richard, *An Introduction to the International Law of Armed Conflicts* (Oxford, Hart Publishing, 2008).
Koutroulis, Vaios, 'Of Occupation, Jus ad Bellum and Jus in Bello: A Reply to Solon Solomon's "The Great Oxymoron: Jus in Bello Violations as Legitimate Non-Forcible Measures of Self-Defense: The Post-Disengagement Israeli Measures towards Gaza as a Case Study"' (2011) 10 *Chinese Journal of International Law* 897.
Koutroulis, Vaios, 'The Fight against the Islamic State and Jus in Bello' (2016) 29 *Leiden Journal of International Law* 827.
Kreß, Claus, 'A Collective Failure to Prevent Turkey's Operation "Peace Spring" and NATO's Silence on International Law', *EJIL: Talk!* (14 October 2019).
Kress, Claus, 'The Fine Line Between Collective Self-Defense and Intervention by Invitation: Reflections on the Use of Force against "IS" in Syria', *Just Security* (17 February 2015).
Kretzmer, David, 'The Inherent Right to Self-Defence and Proportionality in Jus Ad Bellum' (2013) 24 *European Journal of International Law* 235.
Kretzmer, David, 'Use of Lethal Force against Suspected Terrorists' in Ana Maria SD Frias, Katja L Samuel and Nigel D White (eds), *Counter-Terrorism: International Law and Practice* (Oxford, Oxford University Press, 2012) 618–55.

Krisch, Nico, 'International Law in Times of Hegemony: Unequal Power and the Shaping of the International Legal Order' (2005) 16 *European Journal of International Law* 369.

Lang, Arabella, 'Legal Basis for UK Military Action in Syria' (2015) 7404 *House of Commons Library Briefing Paper* 7.

Langenkamp R Dobie and Zedalis, Rex J, 'What Happens to the Iraqi Oil? Thoughts on Some Significant, Unexamined International Legal Questions Regarding Occupation of Oil Fields' (2003) 14 *European Journal of International Law* 417.

Lanovoy, Vladyslav, 'The Use of Force by Non-State Actors and the Limits of Attribution of Conduct' (2017) 28 *European Journal of International Law* 563.

Lauterpacht, Hersch, 'Recognition of States in International Law' (1944) 53 *Yale Law Journal* 385.

Le Billon, Philippe, 'Oil Prices, Scarcity, and Geographies of War' (2009) 99 *Annals of the Association of American Geographers* 836.

Le Billon, Philippe, *Fuelling War: Natural Resources and Armed Conflicts* (London, Routledge, 2005).

Le Billon, Philippe, 'Corruption, Reconstruction and Oil Governance in Iraq' (2005) 26 *Third World Quarterly* 685.

Le Billon, Philippe, 'The Political Economy of War: Natural Resources and Armed Conflict' (2001) 20 *Political Geography* 561.

Le Mon, Christopher J, 'Unilateral Intervention by Invitation in Civil Wars: The Effective Control Tested' (2003) 35 *New York University Journal of International Law and Politics* 741.

Lecuona, Rafael A, 'International Law, Cuba, and the United States of America' (1997) 14 *International Journal on World Peace* 37.

Lesser, Ian O, Nardulli, Bruce R and Arghavan, Lory A, 'Sources of Conflict in the Greater Middle East' in Zalmay Khalilzad and Ian O Lesser (eds), *Sources of Conflict in the 21st Century: Regional Futures and US Strategy* (Santa Monica: Rand Publications, 1998) 171–229.

Letter from Secretary of State Daniel Webster to British Minister to the United States, Lord Alexander Baring Ashburton (6 August 1842).

Levallois, Agnès, 'The Financing of the 'Islamic State' in Iraq and Syria (ISIS)' (2017) *Directorate-General for External Policies of the European Union* 1.

Levitt, Matthew (ed), *The Rise of ISIL* (Washington, DC, The Washington Institute for Near East Policy, 2015).

Levy, Walter J, 'Issues in International Oil Policy' (1957) 35 *Foreign Affairs* 454.

Lieblich, Eliav, 'Intervention and Consent: Consensual Forcible Interventions in Internal Armed Conflicts as International Agreements' (2011) 29 *Boston University International Law Journal* 337.

Lijnzaad, Liesbeth and Tanja, Gerard J, 'Protection of the Environment in Times of Armed Conflict: The Iraq-Kuwait War' (1993) 40 *Netherlands International Law Review* 169.

Lohr, Michael Franklin, 'Legal Analysis of US Military Responses to State-Sponsored International Terrorism' (1985) 34 *Naval Law Review* 1.

Longobardo, Marco, *The Use of Armed Force in Occupied Territory* (Cambridge, Cambridge University Press, 2018).

Longrigg, Stephen H, *Oil in the Middle East: Its Discovery and Development* (Oxford, Oxford University Press, 1968).

Lowe, Vaughan (eds), *The United Nations Security Council and War: The Evolution of Thought and Practice since 1945* (Oxford, Oxford University Press, 2010).

Lubell, Noam, *Extraterritorial Use of Force against Non-State Actors* (Oxford, Oxford University Press, 2010).

Lubell, Noam and Wood, Michael, 'The ILA's 2018 Report on Aggression and the Use of Force' (2019) 6 *Journal on the Use of Force and International Law* 4.

Lujal, Päivi, 'The Spoils of Nature: Armed Civil Conflict and Rebel Access to Natural Resources' (2010) 47 *Journal of Peace Research* 15.

Lumsden, Eleanor, 'An Uneasy Peace: Multilateral Military Intervention in Civil Wars' (2003) 35 *New York University Journal of International Law and Politics* 795.

Macak, Kubo, *Internationalized Armed Conflicts in International Law* (Oxford, Oxford University Press, 2018).
Mandsager, Dennis, Dorosin, Joshua L and Lavoyer, Jean-Philippe, 'Jus in Bello: Occupation Law and the War in Iraq' (2004) 98 *Proceedings of the Annual Meeting (American Society of International Law)* 117.
Mann, Michael, 'The Autonomous Power of the State: Its Origins, Mechanisms, and Results' (1984) 25 *European Journal of Sociology* 185.
Marinelli, Stefano, 'The Use of Force of Turkey in Rojava after the Capture of Afrin: Consequences for International Law and for the Syrian Conflict', *International Law Blog: Fresh Perspectives on International Law* (26 March 2018),
Martin, Craig, 'Challenging and Refining the "Unwilling or Unable" Doctrine' (2019) 52 *Vanderbilt Journal of Transnational Law* 387.
Martin, Michaela and Solomon, Hussein, 'Islamic State: Understanding the Nature of the Beast and Its Funding' (2017) 4 *Contemporary Review of the Middle East* 18.
Marxsen, Christian, 'Territorial Integrity in International Law – Its Concept and Implications for Crimea' (2015) 75 *Heidelberg Journal of International Law* 7.
McCoy, Terrence, 'ISIS Just Stole $425 Million and Became the World's Richest Terrorist Group', Washington Post (12 June 2014).
McKernan, Bethan, 'Turkey Unleashes Airstrikes against Kurds in North-East Syria', *The Guardian* (9 October 2019).
Melling, Graham and Dennett, Anne, 'The Security Council Veto and Syria: Responding to Mass Atrocities Through the 'Uniting for Peace' Resolution' (2017) 57 *Indian Journal of International Law* 285.
Mendelson, Maurice, 'The Subjective Element in Customary International Law' (1995) 66 *British Yearbook of International Law* 177.
Michael, Brent, 'Responding to Attacks by Non-State Actors: The Attribution Requirement of Self-Defence' (2009) 16 *Australian International Law Journal* 133.
Milanovic, Marko, 'The Soleimani Strike and Self-Defence against an Imminent Armed Attack', *EJIL: Talk!* (7 January 2020).
Miller, Chris, 'Putin and Erdogan's Deal for Syria Can't Last', *Foreign Policy* (28 October 2019).
Mohdin, Aamna, 'ISIL's Foreign Fighters Are Surprisingly Well-Educated, According to the World Bank', *Quartz* (6 October 2016).
Moir, Lindsay, *Reappraising the Resort to Force: International Law, Jus ad Bellum and the War on Terror* (Oxford, Hart Publishing, 2010).
Moynihan, Harriet, 'Assessing the Legal Basis for UK Military Action in Syria', *Chatham House* (26 November 2015).
Murphy, Sean D, 'Democratic Legitimacy and the Recognition of States and Governments' (1999) 48 *International and Comparative Law Quarterly* 545.
Nachman, Amikam, *Turkey: Facing a New Millennium: Coping with Intertwined Conflicts* (Manchester, Manchester University Press, 2003).
Newman, Edward, 'Weak States, State Failure, and Terrorism' (2007) 19 *Terrorism and Political Violence* 463.
Ng'ambi, Sangwani Patrick, 'Permanent Sovereignty Over Natural Resources and the Sanctity of Contracts, from the Angle of Lucrum Cessans' (2015) 12 *Loyola University Chicago International Law Review* 153.
Ní Aoláin, Fionnuala, 'Authorizing Force: A Review of Turkish, Dutch and French Action', *Just Security* (16 October 2014).
Nolte George, 'Intervention by Invitation' (2010) *Max Planck Encyclopaedias of International Law*.
Noreng, Øystein, *Crude Power: Politics and the Oil Market* (London, IB Tauris, 2002).
Nowak, Christina, 'The Changing Law of Non-Intervention in Civil Wars – Assessing the Production of Legality in State Practice after 2011' (2018) 5 *Journal on the Use of Force and International Law* 40.

O'Bagy, Elizabeth, *Middle East Security Report: Jihad in Syria. Report No: 6* (Washington, DC, Institute for the Study of War, 2012).

O'Connor, Laurie, 'Legality of the Use of Force in Syria against Islamic State and the Khorasan Group' (2016) 3 *Journal on the Use of Force and International Law* 70.

'Occupation and International Humanitarian Law: Questions and Answers', *ICRC* (4 April 2004).

Odell, Peter R, 'World Oil Resources, Reserves and Production' (1994) 15 *The Energy Journal (Special Issue on the Changing World Petroleum Market)* 89.

Odell, Peter R, 'The Significance of Oil' (1968) 3 *Journal of Contemporary History* 93.

Oeter, Stefan, 'Methods and Means of Combat' in Dieter Fleck and Michael Bothe (eds), *The Handbook of International Humanitarian Law* (Oxford, Oxford University Press, 2013) 119–236.

Ohanyan, Anna, *NGOs, IGOs, and the Network Mechanisms of Post-Conflict Global Governance in Microfinance* (New York, Palgrave Macmillan Press, 2008).

Okimoto, Keiichro, 'The Cumulative Requirements of Jus ad Bellum and Jus in Bello in the Context of Self-Defense' (2012) 11 *Chinese Journal of International Law* 45.

'Operation Inherent Resolve Targeted Operations to Defeat ISIS', *US Department of Defence* (31 December 2016).

'Operation Inherent Resolve: Targeted Operations against ISIL Terrorists', *US Department of Defence* (1 January 2017).

Orakhelashvili, Alexander, *The Interpretation of Acts and Rules in Public International Law* (Oxford, Oxford University Press, 2008).

Palwankar, Umesh, 'Measures Available to States for Fulfilling Their Obligation to Ensure Respect for International Humanitarian Law' (1994) 34 *International Review of the Red Cross* 9.

Pertile, Marco, 'The Changing Environment and Emerging Resource Conflicts' in Marc Weller (ed), *The Oxford Handbook of the Use of Force in International Law* (Oxford, Oxford University Press, 2014) 1077–94.

Peters, Anne, 'The Turkish Operation in Afrin (Syria) and the Silence of the Lambs', *EJIL: Talk!* (30 January 2018).

Peters, Pauline E, 'Inequality and Social Conflict Over Land in Africa' (2004) 4 *Journal of Agrarian Change* 269.

Pettersson, Therese and Wallensteen, Peter, 'Armed Conflicts, 1946–2014' (2015) 52 *Journal of Peace Research* 536.

Pictet, Jean S (ed), *Commentary on the Third Geneva Convention* (Geneva, ICRC Press, 1960).

Pitts, Jennifer, 'Intervention and Sovereign Equality: Legacies of Vattel' in Stefano Recchia and Jennifer M Welsh (eds), *Just and Unjust Military Intervention: European Thinkers from Vitoria to Mill* (Cambridge, Cambridge University Press, 2013) 132–53.

'PM Statement Responding to FAC Report on Military Operations in Syria', *UK Prime Minister's Office* (26 November 2015).

Proninska, Kamila, 'Energy and Security: Regional and Global Dimensions' in Stockholm International Peace Research Institute (SIPRI), *SIPRI Yearbook 2007: Armaments, Disarmament and International Security* (Oxford, Oxford University Press, 2006) 215–40.

Proninska, Kamila, 'Resource Wars in Contemporary International Relations' (2005) 14 *The Polish Quarterly of International Affairs* 29.

'Proposed Russian Control of Syria Border Unlikely to Appeal to Turkey', *The New Arab* (25 January 2019).

Quigley, John, 'The Afghanistan War and Self-Defense' (2003) 37 *Valparaiso University Law Review* 541.

Ramazani, Rouhollah K, 'The Changing United States Policy in the Middle East' (1964) 40 *Virginia Quarterly Review* 369.

Rayfuse, Rosemary, 'Rethinking International Law and the Protection of the Environment' in Rosemary Rayfuse (ed), *War and the Environment: New Approaches to Protecting the Environment in Relation to Armed Conflict* (Leiden, Brill Nijhoff, 2014) 1–10.

Rayfuse, Rosemary, 'The Draft Code of Crimes against the Peace and Security of Mankind: Eating Disorders at the International Law Commission' (1997) 8 *Criminal Law Forum* 43.

Reisman, W Michael, 'Termination of the USSR's Treaty Right of Intervention in Iran' (1980) 74 *American Journal of International Law* 144.

Reisman, W Michael and Armstrong, Andrea, 'The Past and Future of the Claim of Preemptive Self-Defense' (2006) 100 *American Journal of International Law* 525.

'Report Highlights Health and Environmental Impact of Makeshift Oil Refineries in Syria', *Conflict and Environment Observatory* (5 September 2016).

Republic of Turkey Ministry of Foreign Affairs, Press Release Regarding Certain Comments in the International Community on Operation Peace Spring, No 297 (11 October 2019).

Richards, Peter J and Schmitt, Michael N, 'Mars Meets Mother Nature: Protecting the Environment during Armed Conflict' (1999) 28 *Stetson Law Review* 1047.

Roberts, Adam, 'Environmental Issues in International Armed Conflict: The Experience of the 1991 Gulf War' (1996) 69 *International Law Studies* 222.

Roberts, Adam, 'Humanitarian War: Military Intervention and Human Rights' (1993) 69 *International Affairs* 429.

Roberts, Anthea and Sivakumaran, Sandesh, 'Lawmaking by Nonstate Actors: Engaging Armed Groups in the Creation of International Humanitarian Law' (2012) 37 *Yale Journal of International Law* 107.

Rodley, Nigel S, 'Collective Intervention to Protect Human Rights and Civilian Populations: The Legal Framework' in Nigel Rodley (ed), *To Loose the Bands of Wickedness: International Intervention in Defence of Human Rights* (London, Brassey's, 1992) 14–42.

Rogers, APV, *Law on the Battlefield* (Manchester, Manchester University Press, 2004).

Rogers, APV, 'Zero-Casualty Warfare' (2000) 82 *International Review of the Red Cross* 165.

Rose-Ackerman, Susan, 'Corruption and Post-Conflict Peace-Building' (2008) 34 *Ohio Northern University Law Review* 405.

Rosen, David M, *Child Soldiers in the Western Imagination: From Patriots to Victims* (New Jersey, Rutgers University Press, 2015).

Ross, Michael L, 'Blood Barrels: Why Oil Wealth Fuels Conflict' (2008) 78 *Foreign Affairs* 2.

Ross, Michael L, 'How Do Natural Resources Influence Civil War? Evidence from Thirteen Cases' (2004) 58 *International Organization* 35.

Ross, Michael L, 'What Do We Know about Natural Resources and Civil War' (2004) 41 *Journal of Peace Research* 337.

Ross, Michael L, 'Oil, Drugs, and Diamonds: The Varying Roles of Natural Resources in Civil War' in Karen Ballentine and Jake Sherman, *The Political Economy of Armed Conflict: Beyond Greed and Grievance* (London, Lynne Rienner, 2003) 47–70.

'Russia Positive on Turkey's Plans to Secure Its Borders: FM Çavuşoğlu', *Daily News* (24 January 2019).

Ruys, Tom, *'Armed Attack' and Article 51 of the UN Charter: Evolutions in Customary Law and Practice* (Cambridge: Cambridge University Press, 2010).

Ruys, Tom, 'Quo Vadit Jus ad Bellum? A Legal Analysis of Turkey's Military Operations against the PKK in Northern Iraq' (2008) 9 *Melbourne Journal of International Law* 334.

Ruys, Tom and Verhoeven, Sten, 'DRC v Uganda: The Applicability of International Humanitarian Law and Human Rights Law in Occupied Territory' in Roberta Arnold and Noelle Quenivet (eds), *International Humanitarian Law and Human Rights Law: Towards a New Merger in International Law* (Leiden, Martinus Nijhoff, 2008) 155–97.

Ruys, Tom and Verlinden, Nele, 'Digest of State Practice 1 January–30 June 2014' (2014) 1 *Journal on the Use of Force and International Law* 323.

Salameh, Mamdouh G, 'Oil Wars' (2014) 14-163 *USAEE Working Paper* 1.

Sandal, Nukhet, 'Apocalypse Soon Revolutionary Revanchism of ISIS' in Feisal al-Istrabadi and Sumit Ganguly (eds), *The Future of ISIS* (Washington, DC, Brookings Institution Press, 2018) 17–38.

Sandoz, Yves, Christophe Swinarski and Bruno Zimmermann, *Commentary on the Additional Protocols to the Geneva Conventions* (Geneva, Martinus Nijhoff, 1987).

Sands, Philippe, *Principles of International Environmental Law* (Cambridge, Cambridge University Press, 2003).

Schabas, William A, *The International Criminal Court: A Commentary on the Rome Statute* (Oxford, Oxford University Press, 2016).

Schachter, Oscar, 'The Role of Power in International Law' (1999) 93 *Proceedings of the Annual Meeting (American Society of International Law)* 200.

Schachter, Oscar, 'In Defence of International Rules on the Use of Force' (1986) 53 *The University of Chicago Law Review* 113.

Schachter, Oscar, 'The Right of States to Use Armed Force' (1984) 82 *Michigan Law Review* 1620.

Scharf, Michael P, 'How the War against ISIS Changed International Law' (2016) 48 *Case Western Reserve Journal of International Law* 1.

Scharf, Michael P, 'Application of Treaty-Based Universal Jurisdiction to Nationals of Non-Party States' (2001) 35 *New England Law Review* 363.

Schindler, Dietrich and Toman, Jiří (eds), *The Laws of Armed Conflicts: A Collection of Conventions, Resolutions, and Other Documents* (Dordrecht, Martin Nijhoff, 1998).

Schmidt, Dennis, 'Turkey's Syria Invasion: German Research Report Says Illegal on All Counts', *Just Security* (15 November 2019).

Seacor, Jesica E, 'Environmental Terrorism: Lessons from the Oil Fires of Kuwait' (1996) 10 *American University International Law Review* 481.

Sekulow, Jay et al (eds), *The Rise of ISIS: A Threat We Can't Ignore* (Brentwood, Howard Books, 2014).

Sengupta, Somini, 'US Invokes Iraq's Defense in Legal Justification of Syria Strikes', *New York Times* (23 September 2014).

Shaheen, Kareem, 'US Decision to Arm Kurds in Syria Poses Threat to Turkey, Says Ankara', *The Guardian* (10 May 2017).

Shaheen, Kareem, 'Turkey Nightclub Shooting: Istanbul on Alert after Aunman Kills Dozens', *The Guardian* (1 January 2017).

Shaun Walker, 'Russian Ambassador to Turkey Shot Dead by Police Officer in Ankara Gallery', *The Guardian* (20 December 2016).

Shaw, Malcolm N, *International Law* (Cambridge, Cambridge University Press, 2014).

Shaw, Malcolm N, *Title to Territory* (Oxford, Oxford University Press, 1986).

Shue, Henry and Wippman, David, 'Limiting Attacks on Dual-Use Facilities Performing Indispensable Civilian Functions' (2002) 35 *Cornell International Law Journal* 559.

Simma, Bruno, 'NATO, the UN and the Use of Force: Legal Aspects' (1999) 10 *European Journal of International Law* 1.

Simons, Anna and Tucker, David, 'The Misleading Problem of Failed States: A Socio-Geography of Terrorism in the Post-9/11 Era' (2007) 28 *Third World Quarterly* 387.

Sivakumaran, Sandesh, *The Law of Non-International Armed Conflict* (Oxford, Oxford University Press, 2012).

Slama, Jo Lynn, 'Opinio Juris in Customary International Law' (1990) 15 *Oklahoma City University Law Review* 603.

Sluglett, Peter, 'Deadly Implications: The Rise of Sectarianism in Syria' in Martin Beck, Dietrich Jung and Peter Seeberg, *The Levant in Turmoil: Syria, Palestine, and the Transformation of Middle Eastern Politics* (New York, Palgrave Macmillan, 2016) 39–55.

Smith, Benjamin, 'Oil Wealth and Regime Survival in the Developing World, 1960–1999' (2004) 48 *American Journal of Political Science* 232.

Smith, Tara, 'Critical Perspectives on Environmental Protection in Non-International Armed Conflict: Developing the Principles of Distinction, Proportionality and Necessity' (2019) 32 *Leiden Journal of International Law* 759.

Solf, Waldemar A, 'Protection of Civilians against the Effects of Hostilities Under Customary International Law and Under Protocol I' (1986) 1 *American University International Law Review* 117.

Soliev, Nodirbek, 'The Terrorist Threat in Turkey: A Dangerous New Phase' (2017) 9 *Counter Terrorist Trends and Analyses* 24.
Somer, Jonathan, 'Jungle Justice: Passing Sentence on the Equality of Belligerents in Non-International Armed Conflict' (2007) 89 *International Review of Red Cross* 655.
Spero, Joan Edelman, 'Energy Self-Sufficiency and National Security' (1973) 31 *Proceedings of the Academy of Political Science* 123.
'Statement by Ambassador Matthew Rycroft of the UK Mission to the UN at the Security Council adoption of Resolution 2249 on ISIL', *Foreign & Commonwealth Office* (23 November 2015).
'Statement of the UK Attorney-General, Lord Goldsmith, Speaking in the House of Lords' (21 April 2004).
Stec, Stephen and Baraj, Besnik (eds), *Energy and Environmental Challenges to Security* (Dordrecht, Springer, 2007).
Stern, Jessica and Berger, JM, *ISIS: The State of Terror* (New York, Harper Collins, 2015).
Stewart, Patrick, 'Failed States and Global Security: Empirical Questions and Policy Dilemmas' (2007) 9 *International Studies Review* 644.
Stirk, Peter MR, 'The Westphalian Model and Sovereign Equality' (2012) 38 *Review of International Studies* 641.
Stupples, David, 'To Defeat Islamic State We Must Sever Its Oil Lifeline – Here's How', *The Conversation* (3 December 2015).
'Syria and Iraq: ICRC Calls for Better Compliance with Humanitarian Law', *ICRC News* (26 September 2014).
'Syria: Unprecedented Investigation Reveals US-led Coalition Killed More Than 1,600 Civilians in Raqqa "Death Trap"'.
'Syria: US Ally's Razing of Villages Amounts to War Crimes', *Amnesty International* (13 October 2015).
Szasz, Paul C, 'Role of the United Nations in Internal Conflicts' (1983) 13 *Georgia Journal of International and Comparative Law* 345.
Taher, Abdulhady H, 'The Middle East Oil and Gas Policy' (1978) 3 *Journal of Energy and Development* 260.
Takeyh, Ray and Gvosdev, Nikolas, 'Do Terrorist Networks Need a Home?' (2002) 25 *Washington Quarterly* 97.
Talmon, Stefan, 'Determining Customary International Law: The ICJ's Methodology between Induction, Deduction and Assertion' (2015) 26 *European Journal of International Law* 417.
Tams, Christian J and Devaney, James G, 'Applying Necessity and Proportionality to Anti-Terrorist Self-Defence' (2012) 45 *Israel Law Review* 91.
Terry, Patrick CR, 'The War in Afghanistan – Was the Use of Force Legal and/or Wise?' (2011) 9 *New Zealand Yearbook of International Law* 69.
Tertrais, Bruno (2016), 'Article 5 of the Washington Treaty: Its Origins, Meaning and Future' (2016) 130 *NATO Defense College Research Paper* 1.
Thakurta, Paranjoy Guha, 'Conflicts to Control Oil: Economic Implications of the Wars in Afghanistan and Iraq' (2003) 30 *India International Centre Quarterly* 142.
'Thank You for Demanding Justice for Syrians Killed by US-led Coalition', *Amnesty International* (24 September 2019).
'The Legal Framework for the United States' Use of Military Force Since 9/11', A Speech Delivered by Stephen W Preston in Annual Meeting of the American Society of International Law (Washington, DC, 10 April 2015).
The Rt Hon Jeremy Wright QC MP, 'The Modern Law of Self-Defense', *EJIL: Talk!* (11 January 2017).
The Soufan Group, *Foreign Fighters: An Updated Assessment of the Flow of Foreign Fighters into Syria and Iraq* (New York, 2015).
'The War in Iraq and International Humanitarian Law: Frequently Asked Questions on Occupation (FAQ)', *Human Rights Watch* (16 May 2003).

'The War in Iraq and International Humanitarian Law: Frequently Asked Questions (FAQ)', *Human Rights Watch* (7 April 2003).

Theodor, Meron, *The Humanization of International Law* (Leiden, Martinus Nijhoff, 2006).

Tibori-Szabó, Kinga, 'The 'Unwilling or Unable' Test and the Law of Self-Defence' in Christophe Paulussen et al, *Fundamental Rights in International and European Law: Public and Private Perspectives* (The Hague, TMC Asser Press, 2016) 73–97.

Tichý1, Lukáš, 'The Islamic State Oil and Gas Strategy in North Africa' (2019) 24 *Energy Strategy Reviews* 254.

Tladi, Dire and Shaqra, Maryam, 'Assessing the Legality of Coalition Air Strikes Targeting the Islamic State in Iraq and the Levant (ISIS) in Syria under International Law' (2015) *South African Yearbook on International Law* 281.

Todeschini, Vito, 'Turkey's Operation "Peace Spring" and International Law', *Opinio Juris* (21 October 2019).

Townsend, Mark, 'The Core ISIS Manual That Twisted Islam to Legitimise Barbarity', *The Guardian* (13 May 2018).

Trapp, Kimberley N, 'The Turkish Intervention against the PKK in Northern Iraq – 2007–08' in Tom Ruys, Olivier Corten and Alexandra Hofer (eds), *The Use of Force in International Law: A Case-Based Approach* (Oxford, Oxford University Press, 2018) 689–701.

Trapp, Kimberley N, 'Back to Basics: Necessity, Proportionality, and the Right of Self-Defence against Non-State Terrorist Actors' (2007) 56 *International and Comparative Law Quarterly* 141.

Travalio, Greg and Altenburg, John, 'Terrorism, State Responsibility, and the Use of Military Force' (2003) 4 *Chicago Journal of International Law* 97.

Tsagourias, Nicholas, 'Self-Defence against Non-State Actors: The Interaction between Self-Defence as a Primary Rule and Self-Defence as a Secondary Rule' (2016) 29 *Leiden Journal of International Law* 801.

Turns, David, 'Military Objectives' in Rain Liivoja and Tim McCormack (eds), *Routledge Handbook of the Law of Armed Conflict* (London, Routledge, 2016) 139–56.

UK Ministry of Defence, *The Manual of the Law of Armed Conflict* (Oxford, Oxford University Press, 2005).

'Under Kurdish Rule: Abuses in PYD-run Enclaves of Syria', *Human Rights Watch* (19 June 2014).

UNEP, *Desk Study on the Environment in Iraq* (Nairobi, UNEP Publications, 2003).

UNEP, *From Conflict to Peacebuilding: The Role of Natural Resources and the Environment* (Nairobi, UNEP Publications, 2009).

UNEP, *Protecting the Environment During Armed Conflict: An Inventory and Analysis of International Law* (Nairobi, UNEP Publications, 2009).

'US-led Coalition in Iraq and Syria', *Airwars* (November 2019).

US War Department, *Rules of Land Warfare 1914* (Washington, DC, Government Printing Office, 1914).

Valensi, Carmit, 'Non-State Actors: A Theoretical Limitation in a Changing Middle East' (2015) 7 *Military & Strategic Affaires* 59.

Van der Steenhoven, Nick, 'Conduct and Subsequent Practice by States in the Application of the Requirement to Report Under UN Charter Article 51' (2019) 6 *Journal on the Use of Force and International Law* 242.

Van Steenberghe, Raphaël, 'Proportionality under Jus Ad Bellum and Jus in Bello: Clarifying Their Relationship' (2012) 45 *Israel Law Review* 107.

Venard, Brtrand, 'How ISIS Terrorists Neutralise Guilt to Justify Their Atrocities', *The Conversation* (6 October 2016).

Verwey, Wil D, 'Protection of the Environment in Times of Armed Conflict: In Search of a New Legal Perspective' (1995) 8 *Leiden Journal of International Law* 7, 7–40.

Visser, Laura, 'Intervention by Invitation and Collective Self-Defence: Two Sides of the Same Coin?' (2020) 7 *Journal on the Use of Force and International Law* 292.

Visser, Laura, 'May the Force Be with You: The Legal Classification of Intervention by Invitation' (2019) 66 *Netherlands International Law Review* 21.
Visser, Reidar, 'Historical Myths of a Divided Iraq' (2008) 50 *Survival: Global Politics and Strategy* 95.
Walzer, Michael, *Just and Unjust Wars: A Moral Argument with Historical Illustrations* (New York, Harper Collins, 1977).
Watkin, Kenneth, 'Military Advantage: A Matter of "Value", Strategy, and Tactics' (2014) 17 *Yearbook of International Humanitarian Law* 277.
Watkin, Kenneth, 'Targeting "Islamic State" Oil Facilities' (2014) 90 *International Law Studies* 499.
Weber, Max (1964) *The Theory of Social and Economic Organization* (New York, Free Press, 1964).
'We Had Nowhere Else to Go: Forced Displacement and Demolitions in Northern Syria', *Amnesty International* (12 October 2015).
Weir, Doug and Minor, Elizabeth, 'Environmental Harm' in Ray Acheson et al (eds), *The Humanitarian Impact of Drones* (New York, Pace University, 2017) 29–34.
Weiss, Michael and Hassan, Hassan, *ISIS: Inside the Army of Terror* (New York, Regan Arts, 2015).
Wenqi, Zhu, 'On Co-operation by States Not Party to the International Criminal Court' (2006) 88 *International Review of the Red Cross* 87.
Wheeler, Skye, 'UN Panel Reports on ISIS Crimes on Yezidis: "Unimaginable Horrors"', *Human Rights Watch* (26 June 2016).
White, Nigel D, *Democracy Goes to War: British Military Deployments under International Law* (Oxford, Oxford University Press, 2009).
Whyte, Dave, 'Hire an American! Economic Tyranny and Corruption in Iraq' (2007) 34 *Social Justice* 153.
Wilmshurst, Elizabeth, 'The Chatham House Principles of International Law on the Use of Force in Self-Defence' (2006) 55 *International and Comparative Law Quarterly* 963.
Wimmen, Heiko, *Syria's Path from Civic Uprising to Civil War* (Washington, DC, Carnegie Endowment for International Peace, 2016).
Wimmer, Andreas, 'Democracy and Ethno-religious Conflict in Iraq' (2017) 45 *Survival: Global Politics and Strategy* 111.
Winter, Harlie and Al-Saud, Abdullah K, 'The Obscure Theologian Who Shaped ISIS', *The Atlantic* (4 December 2016).
Wippman, David, 'Prodemocratic Intervention by Invitation' in Gregory H Fox and Brad R Roth (eds), *Democratic Governance and International Law* (Cambridge, Cambridge University Press, 2000) 293–327.
Wippman, David, 'Military Intervention, Regional Organizations, and Host-State Consent' (1996) 7 *Duke Journal of Comparative and International Law* 209.
Wippman, David, 'Treaty-Based Intervention: Who Can Say No?' (1995) 62 *The University of Chicago Law Review* 607.
Wolfrum, Rudiger and Philipp, Christiane, *United Nations: Law and Policies and Practice – Volume II* (Verlag, CH Beck Munchen, 1995).
Wood, Michael, 'The Caroline Incident – 1837' in Tom Ruys, Olivier Corten and Alexandra Hofer (eds), *The Use of Force in International Law: A Case-Based Approach* (Oxford, Oxford University Press, 2018) 5–16.
Wright, Quincy, 'The Legality of Intervention Under the United Nations Charter' (1957) 51 *Proceedings of the American Society of International Law at Its Annual Meeting (1921–1969)* 79.
Yayla, Ahmet S and Clarke, Colin P, 'Turkey's Double ISIS Standard', *Foreign Policy* (12 April 2018).
Yosufi, Abdul Basir, 'The Rise and Consolidation of Islamic State: External Intervention and Sectarian Conflict' (2016) 15 *Connections: The Quarterly Journal* 91.
Zamir, Noam, 'The Armed Conflict(s) against the Islamic State' (2015) 18 *Yearbook of International Humanitarian Law* 91.
Zwijnenburg, Wim and Te Pas, Kristine, *Amidst the Debris: A Desktop Study on the Environmental and Public Health Impact of Syria's Conflict* (Utrecht, Pax for Peace Organization, 2015).

Zwijnenburg, Wim and Waleij, Annica, 'Fire and Oil: The Collateral Environmental Damage of Airstrikes on ISIS Oil Facilities', *New Security Beat* (13 January 2016).

UN Documents

'Attacks on Syrian Civilians and Aid Workers in Aleppo Were War Crimes', *OHCHR* (3 March 2017).
'Human Rights Council Holds Urgent Debate on the Situation in Syria's Eastern Ghouta', *UN Human Rights Council – Commission Press Releases* (28 February 2012).
'Humanitarian Chief Concludes Visit to Ankara and Turkey/Syria Border', *OCHA* (11 October 2019).
Identical Letters dated 20 January 2018 from the Chargé d'affaires a.i. of the Permanent Mission of Turkey to the United Nations addressed to the Secretary-General and the President of the Security Council, UN Doc S/2018/53 (22 January 2018).
Identical Letters dated 24 December 2019 from the Chargé d'affaires a.i. of the Permanent Mission of the Syrian Arab Republic to the United Nations addressed to the Secretary-General and the President of the Security Council, UN Doc S/2019/987 (24 December 2019).
Identical Letters dated 31 October 2019 from Permanent Representative of the Syrian Arab Republic to the United Nations addressed to the Secretary-General and the President of the Security Council, UN Doc S/2019/856 (31 October 2019).
Identical Letters dated September 16, 2015 from the Permanent Representative of the Syrian Arab Republic to the United Nations addressed to the Secretary-General and the President of the Security Council, UN Doc S/2015/718 (17 September 2015).
'ISIL's 'Scorched Earth Policy' Creating Environmental and Health Havoc in Mosul, Warns UN', *UN News Centre* (27 October 2016).
'Israel's Exploitation of Palestinian Resources is Human Rights Violation, Says UN Special Rapporteur for the Situation of Human Rights in the OPT', *UN Press Release* (18 March 2019).
Letter date 17 July 1981 from the Chargé d'affairs a.i. Mission of Lebanon to the United Nations addressed to the President of the Security Council (S/14596), UN SCOR, 36th session, 2292d meeting at 5, UN Doc S/PV.2292 (17 July 1981).
Letter dated 1 September 2015 from the Permanent Representative of the Russian Federation to the United Nations addressed to the Secretary-General (S/2015/678), UN Doc S/2014/695 (30 September 2015).
Letter dated 20 September 2014 from the Permanent Representative of Iraq to the United Nations addressed to the President of the Security Council, UN Doc S/2014/691 (22 September 2014).
Letter dated 23 September 2014 from the Permanent Representative of the United States of America to the United Nations addressed to the Secretary-General, UN Doc S/2014/695 (23 September 2014).
Letter dated 24 July 2015 from the Chargé d'affaires a.i. of the Permanent Mission of Turkey to the United Nations addressed to the President of the Security Council, UN Doc S/2015/563 (24 July 2015).
Letter dated 25 June 2014 from the Permanent Representative of Iraq to the United Nations addressed to the Secretary-General, UN Doc S/2014/440 (25 June 2014).
Letter dated 9 October 2019 from the Permanent Representative of Turkey to the United Nations addressed to the President of the Security Council, UN Doc S/2019/804 (9 October 2019).
Letter of Permanent Representative of the Russian Federation to the UN addressed to the UN Secretary-General, Annex, UN Doc S/2002/1012/Annex (12 September 2002).
Letter of Turkish Ministry of Foreign Affairs addressed to the UN Secretary-General and to the President of the UN Security Council, UN Doc S/1996/479 (2 July 1996).
'On International Day, UN Urges Protection of Environment from Ravages of War: The UN Secretary General Message for the International Day for Preventing the Exploitation of the Environment in War and Armed Conflict', *UN News* (6 November 2014).
Preliminary Report on the Protection of the Environment in Relation to Armed Conflicts, submitted by Special Rapporteur Marie G. Jacobsson to the International Law Commission, UN Doc A/CN.4/674 (Geneva, 5 May-6 June and 7 July-8 August 2014).
'Refugees and Asylum Seekers in Turkey: 2019 Planning Summary', *UNHCR* (15 February 2019).

'Save Idlib from 'Transforming into a Blood Bath', UN Chief Guterres Urges Fighters and Their Allies', *UN News* (11 September 2018).
'Security Council: Two Draft Resolutions, Zero Consensus on Ceasefire in Syria's Idlib', *UN New* (19 September 2019).
'UN Commission of Inquiry on Syria: The Siege and Recapture of Eastern Ghouta Marked by War Crimes, Crimes against Humanity', *UN Human Rights Council* (20 June 2018).
UN Human Rights Council, 'Report of the Independent International Commission of Inquiry on the Syrian Arab Republic', UN Doc A/HRC/25/65 (12 February 2014).
UN Human Rights Council, 'Report of the Independent International Commission of Inquiry on the Syrian Arab Republic', UN Doc A/HRC/44/61 (2 July 2020).
UN Secretary General, 'Sharing Benefits of Natural Resources Helps Conflict Prevention, Sustainable Development, Secretary-General Tells Security Council', Press Release, UN Doc SG/SM/19303-SC/13541-ENV/DEV/1896 (16 October 2018).
UNAG, 'Permanent Sovereignty Over Natural Resources', UN Doc A/RES/1803 (XVII) (14 December 1962).
UNGA, 'Implications, Under International Law, of the United Nations Resolutions on Permanent Sovereignty Over Natural Resources, on the Occupied Palestinian and Other Arab Territories and on the Obligations of Israel Concerning Its Conduct in These Territories – Report of the Secretary-General', UN Doc A/38/265- E/1983/85 (21 June 1983), Annex.
UNGA, 'In Larger Freedom: Towards Development, Security and Human Rights for All', Report of the Secretary-General, UN Doc A/59/2005 (21 March 2005).
UNGA, 'Permanent Sovereignty of the Palestinian People in the Occupied Palestinian Territory, Including East Jerusalem, and of the Arab Population in the Occupied Syrian Golan Over Their Natural Resources', UN Doc A/C.2/74/L.45 (24 October 2019).
UNGA, 'Permanent Sovereignty of the Palestinian People in the Occupied Palestinian Territory, Including East Jerusalem, and of the Arab Population in the Occupied Syrian Golan Over Their Natural Resources', UN Doc A/RES/66/225 (13 January 2012).
UNGA, 'Report of the High-Level Panel on Threats, Challenges and Change on a More Secure World: Our Shared Responsibility', UN Doc A/59/565 (2 December 2004).
UNGA, 'Report of the High-Level Panel on Threats, Challenges and Change: Note by the Secretary-General Follow-up to the Outcome of the Millennium Summit', UN Doc A/59/565 (2 December 2004).
UNGA, 'Report of the Independent International Commission of Inquiry on the Syrian Arab Republic submitted to the Human Rights Council', UN Doc A/HRC/28/69 (5 February 2015).
UNGA, 'Situation of human rights in the Syrian Arab Republic', Resolution A/HRC/21/L.32 (24 September 2012).
UNGA, 'Speakers Disagree Over Suitable Level of Intervention for Stopping Atrocity Crimes, as General Assembly Concludes Debate on Responsibility to Protect', UN Doc GA/12038 (2 July 2018).
UNGA, Resolution 3175, UN Doc A/RES/3175 (17 December 1973).
UNGA, Resolution 3314, Definition of Aggression, UN Doc 3314 (XXIX) (14 December 1974).
UNGA, Resolution 377 [V], Uniting for Peace Resolution, UN Doc A/1456 (3 November 1950).
UNGA, Resolution 47/37, UN Doc A/RES/47/37 (25 November 1992).
UNHCR, 'Operational Portal: Turkey' (last updated on 9 December 2020).
UNSC, 'Islamic State/Da'esh Using Social Media, Extortion to Retain Might after Military Setbacks, Territory Loss, Top Counter-Terrorism Official Tells Security Council', UN Doc SC/13202, 8178th meeting (AM) (8 February 2008).
UNSC, 'Note by the President of the UN Security Council', UN Doc S/23500 (31 January 1992).
UNSC, 'Turkey's Military Operation Has Displaced Thousands of Civilians, Worsened Syria's Dire Humanitarian Crisis, Top Official Warns Security Council', 8645th meeting (PM), UN Doc SC/13994 (24 October 2019).
UNSC, Resolution 1261, UN Doc S/RES/1261 (30 August 1999).
UNSC, Resolution 1368, UN Doc S/RES/1368 (12 September 2001).

UNSC, Resolution 1373, UN Doc S/RES/1368 (28 September 2001).
UNSC, Resolution 1607, UN Doc S/RES/1607 (21 June 2005).
UNSC, Resolution 1647, UN Doc S/RES/1647 (20 December 2005).
UNSC, Resolution 2170, UN Doc S/RES/2170 (15 August 2014).
UNSC, Resolution 2178, UN Doc S/RES/2178 (24 September 2014).
UNSC, Resolution 2191, UN Doc S/RES/2191 (17 December 2014).
UNSC, Resolution 2199, UN Doc S/RES/2199 (12 February 2015).
UNSC, Resolution 2201, UN Doc S/RES/2201 (15 February 2015).
UNSC, Resolution 2249, UN Doc S/RES/2249 (20 November 2015).
UNSC, Resolution 2253, UN Doc S/RES/2253 (17 December 2015).
UNSC, Resolution 387, UN Doc S/RES/387 (31 March 1976).
UNSC, Resolution 540, UN Doc S/RES/540 (31 October 1983).
UNSC, Resolution 661, UN Doc S/RES/661 (6 August 1990).
UNSC, Resolution 687, UN Doc S/RES/687 (3 April 1991).
UNSC, Resolution 84, UN Doc S/RES/84 (7 July 1950).
UNSC, Statement by the President, UN Doc S/PRST/2007/22 (25 June 2007).
UNSC, Statement by the President, UN Doc S/PV.2730 (22 December 1986).
UNSDN, Indigenous Peoples: Conflict, Peace and Resolution (15th session of UNPFII, 17 May 2016).
'Why Legal Principles on War and Environment Matter', *UNEP* (20 August 2019).

Index

www.ingramcontent.com/pod-product-compliance
Ingram Content Group UK Ltd.
Pitfield, Milton Keynes, MK11 3LW, UK
UKHW020817290926
15470UKWH00003B/1216

9 781509 950515